Carl Engel

Musical Myths and Facts

Vol. 2

Carl Engel

Musical Myths and Facts
Vol. 2

ISBN/EAN: 9783337084851

Printed in Europe, USA, Canada, Australia, Japan

Cover: Foto ©Thomas Meinert / pixelio.de

More available books at **www.hansebooks.com**

MUSICAL

MYTHS AND FACTS

BY

CARL ENGEL.

IN TWO VOLUMES.—VOL. II.

LONDON:
NOVELLO, EWER & CO.,
1, BERNERS STREET (W.), AND 80 & 81, QUEEN STREET, CHEAPSIDE (E.C.)
NEW YORK: J. L. PETERS, 843, BROADWAY.

MDCCCLXXVI.

NOVELLO, EWER AND CO.,
TYPOGRAPHICAL MUSIC AND GENERAL PRINTERS,
1, BERNERS STREET, LONDON.

CONTENTS OF VOLUME II.

MATTHESON ON HANDEL.

THE biographical notices of Handel's youth transmitted to us are but scanty and unsatisfactory. The same might, however, be said of most of our celebrated musicians, and the cause of the meagreness is, as we have seen in another place, easily explicable.* Of Handel's musical pursuits before his arrival in Hamburg, at the age of eighteen, we know scarcely more than that he was a pupil of Zachau, an organist at Halle, where Handel was born; that, as a boy, he paid a short visit to Berlin, where his talent attracted some attention; and that subsequently he studied Law, at the University of Halle. The latter fact indicates that the choice of music as a profession was not hastily determined in his childhood; and this surmise accords with the stated reluctance of his father, a medical practitioner in Halle, to have his son brought up as a musician.

Arrived in Hamburg, in the year 1703, Handel soon made the acquaintance of Mattheson, an intelligent and industrious young musician, who was competent to appreciate the genius of Handel, and faithfully to record the progress of the promising youth during his sojourn in Hamburg, which lasted about three years. Mattheson was four years older than Handel,—a difference which, between two lads of twenty-two and eighteen, is not without some weight in their mutual intercourse, especially if the elder is already enjoying a certain success, while the younger is a new comer, intent upon gaining a footing. Mattheson's observations about Handel, although occasionally tinged

---

* Vol. I., p. 94.

with jealousy of his talented brother artist, are therefore particularly noteworthy in the biography of the great composer.

Johann Mattheson, born in Hamburg, in the year 1681, was at the time of Handel's arrival tenor singer and musical composer at the theatre of the town, and teacher of singing, the harpsichord, and thorough-bass. When, in the year 1705, an increasing deafness compelled him to relinquish his engagement as singer and actor in operas at the theatre, his accomplishments, combined with commendable habits of industry and punctuality, induced the British Ambassador at Hamburg to engage him as tutor for his son, and afterwards to appoint him his secretary. During an active life of unusual duration,—he died in the year 1764, at the age of 83,—Mattheson published a great number of treatises on musical subjects, some of which still possess value as books of reference. His vanity, not unfrequently exhibited in his writings, may in some measure have been nourished by his many flatterers among his musical contemporaries, who evidently feared his sarcastic pen all the more because they did not possess the literary ability to engage successfully in a controversy with him when they disagreed with his opinion.

As regards the musical compositions of Mattheson, we know from his own statement, in his autobiography, that his operas were greatly admired by the public; but this favourable opinion is hardly supported by such of his compositions as have appeared in print. A collection of twelve Suites for the harpsichord, the manuscript of which he sent to England, where it was published in two volumes, in the year 1714, bears the title:—'Pièces de Clavecin, en deux Volumes, consistant des Ouvertures, Preludes, Fugues, Allemandes, Courentes, Sarabandes, Giques et Aires, composées par J. Mattheson, Secr.—London, printed for J. D. Fletcher.' The work is prefaced by an address to the musical public, written by the editor, J. D. Fletcher, in which he says:—"Britain may now hope to return those arts with interest, which she borrowed from other nations; and foreigners in time may learn of those whom their forefathers taught . . . . As the harpsichord is an instrument yet capable of greater improvement, so the following pieces claim a precedence of all others of this nature; not only that they are composed by one of the greatest masters of the age, in a taste altogether pleasing and sublime; but, as they are peculiarly adapted to that instrument, and engraven with an exactness that cannot be equall'd by any of their nature yet extant." Sir John Hawkins, who probably had not seen these Suites, relates: "Mattheson had sent over to England, in order to their being published here, two collections of lessons for the harpsichord, and they were accordingly engraved on copper, and printed for Richard Meares in St. Paul's Church-yard, and published in the year 1714. Handel was at that time in London, and in the afternoon was used to frequent St. Paul's Church for the sake of hearing the service, and of playing on the organ after it was over; from whence he and some gentlemen of the choir would frequently adjourn to the Queen's Arms tavern in St. Paul's Church-yard, where was a harpsichord. It happened one afternoon, when they were thus met together, Mr. Weely, a gentleman of the choir, came in and informed them that Mr. Mattheson's lessons were then to be had at Mr. Meares' shop; upon which Mr. Handel ordered them immediately to be sent for, and upon their being brought, played them all over without rising from the instrument." Still more odd appears Hawkins' statement that Handel "approved so highly of the compositions of Mattheson, particularly his lessons, that he was used to play them for his private amusement."*

If Handel really could amuse himself by playing these lessons, which are in no respect superior to the usual productions of the mediocre musicians of his time, it probably was only from feelings of curiosity and kindness towards a former friend. Mattheson composed a great deal, and made at last even his own Funeral Anthem, which after his death was performed to his honour, and which, if report speaks correctly, sounded truly miserable; and this

* Hawkins's 'History of Music,' Vol. V., p. 253.

may well be believed, considering that when he composed the music Mattheson had been deaf for nearly thirty years. Still, though he was but a poor composer, he possessed ample musical knowledge and practical skill to enable him to judge the works of his superior contemporaries. His jealous disposition, however, sometimes prevented him from forming a just opinion. His disparaging critique of an early work of Handel, in his 'Critica Musica,' Hamburg, 1725, at a time when Handel had become a resident in London, was evidently influenced by jealousy, and the same is more or less observable in his other writings. Nevertheless, he took every opportunity to keep up a correspondence with Handel, and to boast of his former familiarity with the celebrated man. Mattheson, having solicited Handel's opinion upon a certain theoretical question on which he was in dispute with some German musicians, and having also expressed the hope that Handel might favour him with some biographical notices, Handel, at the conclusion of his letter in reply, excuses himself for not complying with the second point in question:—

"Pour ce qui est du second point, vous pouvez juger vous même qu'il demande beaucoup de recueillement, dont je ne suis pas le maître parmi les occupations pressantes, que j'ai par devers moi. Dès que j'en ferai un peu debarassé, je repasserai les Epoques principales que j'ai eues dans le cours de ma Profession, pour vous faire voir l'estime et la consideration particulière avec laquelle j'ai l'honneur d'être,

Monsieur,

Votre très humble et très

Obeissant Serviteur,

G. F. HANDEL.

A Londres, Fevr. 24, 1719."

In the year 1740, Mattheson published his *Grundlage einer Ehrenpforte* ('Foundation of a Triumphal Arch'), which contains a series of biographies of the celebrated musicians of his time,—Mattheson's included. During the preparation of this work, he addressed another request to Handel to supply him with materials for a correct biography.

He also dedicated twelve fugues of his own composition to Handel, of which he sent him a copy to ensure prompt attention. Handel's reply was again evasive:—

"A Londres ce 29 de Juillet, 1735.

Monsieur,

Il y a quelque tems que j'ai reçu une de vos obligeantes lettres; mais à présent je vien de recevoir votre dernière avec votre ouvrage. Je vous en remercie, Monsieur, et je vous assure que j'ai toute l'estime pour votre mérite, je souhaiterois seulement que mes circonstances m'étaient plus favorables pour vous donner des marques de mon inclination à vous servir. L'ouvrage est digne de l'attention des connoisseurs, et quand à moi, je vous rends justice.

Au reste, pour rammasser quelque époque, il m'est impossible puisqu'une continuelle application au service de cette cour et noblesse me détourne de toute autre affaire.

Je suis, avec une considération très parfaite, etc."

Handel was at this period in circumstances by no means flourishing, his operatic enterprises having failed. Mattheson's request came therefore at a very inopportune time, since it would have been only painful to Handel to occupy his mind with recollections of events of his earlier life, and with the record of expectations which he now found were not to be realized.

It is singular that almost all Handel's letters to Germans which have been preserved, including those to his brother-in-law in Halle, are written in French. Besides, they are so extremely formal and ceremonious, even those to his nearest relations! This may be in great measure accounted for by the usages of his time, and by the circumstance of his coming frequently into contact with persons of a higher position in society than himself. But, however reserved he may appear in his letters, evidences are not wanting testifying to his kindheartedness and generosity.

When Mattheson found that it was useless to endeavour to elicit information direct from Handel for his 'Ehrenpforte,' he compiled a biography interspersed with recollections of their mutual experiences during the years of their intercourse in Hamburg. The following extracts from Mattheson's gossip are translated as literally as possible:—

"In the summer of the year 1703 he came to Hamburg, rich in abilities and good intentions. I was almost the first acquaintance he made, and I took him to the organs and choirs of the town, and to operas and concerts. I also introduced him to a certain family where all were extremely devoted to music."

In another place Mattheson records that he made Handel's acquaintance accidentally at the organ of the church of St. Mary Magdalen, and that he took him at once with him to his father's house, and paid him every possible attention. Mattheson further relates:—

"At first he played the second violin in the orchestra of the opera, and seemed as if he could not count above five; in fact, he was naturally much inclined to dry humour. But, one day, when a harpsichord player was wanted, he allowed himself to be persuaded to take his place, and showed himself a man, when no one but I expected it. I I am sure if he reads this he will laugh in his sleeve, for outwardly he seldom laughs. Especially will he laugh if he recollects the pigeon-dealer who once travelled post with us to Lübeck; likewise, the son of the pastry-cook who had to blow the bellows while we were playing the organ in the church of St. Mary Magdalen of this place. This was on the thirtieth of July, 1703, after our having been out on the water on the fifteenth."

"He composed at that time very long, long airs, and almost endless cantatas, which, although the harmonious treatment was perfect, nevertheless had not the requisite fitness; nor did they exhibit the proper taste. However, the high school of the opera soon put him on the right track."

"He was great upon the organ, greater than Kuhnau in fugues and counterpoint, especially in extemporizing. However, he knew but very little of melody before he had to do with the operas in Hamburg. On the other hand, Kuhnau's pieces were all exceedingly melodious, and suited for the voice, even those arranged for playing. In the preceding century scarcely any one thought of melody; all aimed merely at harmony."

"At that time he dined almost daily by invitation with my father, and in return opened to me some particular manœuvres in counter point. On the other hand, in dramatic style I have been of no little service to him; so that one hand washed the other."

"On the seventeenth of August, in the year 1703, we travelled together to Lübeck, and in the carriage composed many double-fugues, *da mente non da penna*. I had been invited there by the President of the Privy Council, Magnus von Wedderkopp, in order to choose a successor for the excellent organist, Dieterich Buxtehude. I took Handel there with me. We tried almost all the organs and harpsichords in Lübeck; and, with regard to our playing, we arranged between ourselves that he should play exclusively on the organ, and I on the harpsichord. We also heard with due attention the above-mentioned artist in his St. Mary's Church. But when we found that a certain marriage, for which neither of us had the slightest inclination, was a stipulated condition with the appointment, [the successful candidate had to marry the daughter of Buxtehude] we departed thence, after having received much honour, and having enjoyed many entertainments. Johann Christian Schieferdecker subsequently accommodated himself to the requirements, conducted the bride home, and obtained the fine appointment."

"In the year 1704, when I was in Holland, intending to proceed to England, I received in Amsterdam, on the twenty-first of March, a letter from Handel in Hamburg, so obliging and pressing, that it at once induced me to return home. The letter, which is dated March 18th, 1704, contains, among others, these expressions :—

'I much desire your highly agreeable conversation, the privation of which will soon be repaired, as the time approaches in which it will be impossible to undertake anything in the way of operas without your presence. I therefore pray you obediently to inform me of your departure, that I may have the opportunity of showing my obligation by meeting you with Miss Sbülens,' etc., etc."

These extracts from Mattheson's 'Ehrenpforte' are quoted here because they throw light upon some occurrences alluded to in the remarks with which Mattheson has interspersed his German translation of Mainwaring's 'Memoirs of the Life of the late George Frederick Handel; to which is added a Catalogue of his works, and observations upon them; London, 1760.'

Mainwaring was a young clergyman, whose admiration of Handel induced him to collect as much material for the compilation of a biography as he was able to obtain. His work, published anonymously a year after Handel's death, much as it has been disparaged on account of its chronological inaccuracies and its want of musical erudition, is certainly valuable as containing the fullest account of Handel's life in England written by a contemporary of the great musician. Mattheson's German translation, with annotations, is entitled *Georg Friderich Händel's Lebensbeschreibung, nebst einem Verzeichnisse seiner Ausübungswerke und deren Beurtheilung; übersetzt, auch mit einigen Anmerkungen, absonderlich über den hamburgischen Artikel, versehen von Legations-Rath Mattheson. Hamburg. Auf Kosten des Uebersetzers*, 1761. ('George Frederick Handel's Biography, with a list of his Compositions, and a critical examination of them; translated, and annotated with some remarks, especially upon the part relating to Hamburg, by Mattheson, Councillor of Legation. Hamburg. Published at the expense of the translator, 1761.') The book is now scarce. Victor Schœlcher, in his 'Life of Handel,' London, 1857, notices it only with the remark: "My endeavours have hitherto been in vain to obtain a copy of this in Germany, and it is not to be found in the British Museum." At any rate, it is not likely to be known to many English musicians. A translation of Mattheson's annotations is therefore offered here.

As regards the Introduction with which Mattheson has prefaced his translation, it is so diffuse, and contains so little about Handel, that few musicians now would care to read it entirely. It is headed by a quotation in English, from the *Tatler* (No. 92):—"*Panegyricks are frequently ridiculous, let them be addressed where they will.*"

Mattheson aims more at impressing the reader with his own merits than with those of Handel. He says, for instance: "In describing an artist's life, it is not sufficient to represent the man only as an artist; the artist must rather be considered also as a man; for thus only can his merits be properly understood. However, no one is able to know or to do everything in his vocation. Thus, in music, one performer excels on the organ-pedals, while another surpasses him on the harpsichord. The first may be called coarse; the second, delicate. The first may be only appreciated by connoisseurs; the second, by everyone. A company of artists—if any such exists—is like a bunch of different keys. No one of these is to be extolled before the other but only in so far as it opens an important lock which encloses a treasure. One musician is not only a player, but also a singer; another never opens his mouth to sing—nay, not even to laugh. The former, besides being able to compose, to sing, to play, and to dance, acts a principal character on the stage; the latter, with his quantity of musical scores, has taken care not to appear upon the boards of the theatre. Indeed, he would have cut a funny figure had he done so. Here, some one who occupies himself with music, and also with various sciences, in a superior manner, works at the same time for kings and princes; there some one employs his gifts principally in the service and for the amusement of the subjects. From this it is clear that each in his particular line may deserve honour and laudation; not properly on account of his person, but on account of his achievements. . . . . . No mere *Musicus practicus ecclesiastico-dramaticus*, who took a high rank as a director of the orchestra, and a still higher rank as an organist, but who was neither a singer nor an actor, and least of all a mathematician—has ever, before Handel, attained to this, that without his help a special book of a considerable size on his life has been written, and supplied with instructive observations—still more, that his biography has been translated into another language by a brother-artist by no means of the common class. Competing successors do not feel hurt by these stimulating spurs!"

In order to render the following annotations by Mattheson properly intelligible, the statements of Mainwaring to which they refer are inserted with them. The latter are copied exactly as they were originally written; while Mattheson's annotations are translated from the German.

Mainwaring (P. 1). "George Frederick Handel was born at Hall,* a city in the circle of Upper-Saxony, the 24th February, 1684,† by a second wife of his father, who was an eminent surgeon and physician of the same place, and above sixty when his son was born."

Mattheson. "The author is wrong in calling Halle a town of Upper-Saxony. It lies in the Dukedom of Magdeburg, which belongs to Lower-Saxony. Handel was, therefore, no Upper-Saxon, but rather a Lower-Saxon."

Mainwaring (P. 6). "It may not be unpleasant to the reader just now to remind him of the minute and surprising resemblance between the early periods of Handel's life and some which are recorded in that of the celebrated M. Pascal, written by his sister. Nothing could equal the bias of the one to Mathematics but the bias of the other to Music; both in their very childhood out-did the efforts of maturer age; they pursued their respective studies not only without any assistance, but against the consent of their parents, and in spite of all the opposition they contrived to give them."

Mattheson. "Almost the same was the case with Tycho Brahe, and with the translator of this biography, each in his vocation."

Mainwaring (P. 15). "Zackaw [Zachau] was proud of a pupil who already began to attract the attention of all persons who lived near Hall [Halle], or resorted thither from distant quarters. And he was glad of an assistant who, by his uncommon talents, was capable of supplying his place whenever he had an inclination to be absent, as he often was, from his love of company and a cheerful glass."

Mattheson. "Could not the life of Handel have been written without aspersing the brave tone-artist Zachau forty years after his death on account of a glass of wine?"

---

* Halle. † Should be 1685.

Mainwaring (P. 15). "It may seem strange to talk of an assistant of seven years of age, for he could not be more, if indeed he was quite so much, when first he was committed to the care of this person."

Mattheson. "The author appears to have not the least scruple in committing the most palpable anachronism by making his hero the younger the taller he grows. This will presently appear evident."

Mainwaring (P. 16). "We have already hinted at some striking coincidences of life and character which are found in him and the famous Pascal. In this place we may just observe that the latter at the age of twelve compos'd a treatise on the propagation of sounds, and at sixteen another upon conic sections."

Mattheson. "But it must be remembered that afterwards he entirely gave up mathematics. *See* Bayle."

Mainwaring (P. 18). "It was in the year 1698 that he went to Berlin. The opera there was in a flourishing condition under the direction of the King of Prussia (grandfather of the present), who, by the encouragement which he gave to singers and composers, drew thither some of the most eminent from Italy and other parts."

Mattheson. "Anno 1698 there was no King in Prussia; the first dated from 1701. Handel has, therefore, seen no king in Berlin. That the author is as bad a genealogist and politician as he is a chronologist, is proved by his mistaking the grandfather of the present king for the father, and by his always mentioning the then reigning Elector as the King."

Mainwaring (P. 20). "Attilio's fondness for Handel commenced at his first coming to Berlin, and continued to the time of his leaving it. He would often take him on his knee, and make him play on his harpsichord for an hour together, equally pleased and surprised with the extraordinary proficiency of so young a person; for at this time he could not exceed thirteen, as may easily be seen by comparing dates."

Mattheson. "He was born anno 1684.* He arrived in

---

* That Handel was born on the 23rd of February, 1685, and not on the 24th of February, 1684, is correctly stated in J. J. Walther's 'Musicalisches Lexicon,' Leipzig, 1732. To settle the uncertainty about the

Berlin anno 1698. Even if the various occurrences with Buononcini and Attilio, with the Elector and his court, took only a few hours—nay, even if they are not taken into account at all, there are still at least fourteen years. One should think that he was much above seven years when Ariosti (Attilio) took him on his lap."*

Mainwaring (P. 31). "Before we advance any farther in his history, it is necessary some account should be given of the opera at Hamburg, as well as some character of the composer and singers. The principal singers were Conratini and Mathyson. The latter was secretary to Sir Cyril Wych, who was resident for the English court, had Handel for his music-master, and was himself a fine player on the harpsichord. Mathyson was no great singer, for which reason he sung only occasionally; but he was a good actor, a good composer of lessons, and a good player on the harpsichord. He wrote and translated several treatises. One that he wrote was on composition. He had thoughts of writing the life of Handel many years before his death. Had he pursued this design, he would have had advantages beyond what we can pretend to, *i.e.*, ampler and fresher materials; at least, for so much of the life as had then elapsed. All that is here intended, is to give a plain, artless account of such particulars as we have been able to learn, and such only as we have reason to believe authentic."

Mattheson. "This whole story, with everything subsequently recorded about the operas in Hamburg, is so full of

---

date, which appears to have arisen chiefly through Mainwaring's misstatement, J. J. Eschenburg consulted the Baptismal Register of the Frauenkirche in Halle, where he found the year 1685 given. (*See* 'Dr. Karl Burney's Nachricht von Georg Friedrich Händel's Lebens umständen, und der ihm zu London im May und Juny, 1784, angestellten Gedächtnissfeyer, aus den Englischen übersetzt von J. J. Eschenburg; Berlin, 1785).—Förstemann ('Händel's Stammbaum,' Leipzig, 1844), and others, have subsequently convinced themselves that Eschenburg's date is correct. The year 1684, given on Handel's Monument in Westminster Abbey, therefore, requires rectifying.

* Chrysander ('G. F. Handel,' Leipzig, 1858, vol. I., p. 52) surmises that Handel was not in Berlin in 1698, but in 1696, when he was eleven years old.

errors that one can scarcely rectify them. The Conradin (not Conratini) possessed almost perfect beauty, and had withal an extraordinary splendid voice, which extended in equal power from  to  . This gave her claim to be the principal singer. Mattheson (not Mathyson) instructed her for several years; *i.e.*, he sung everything to her daily until she could retain it in her memory. At that time no gentleman was called a great singer unless he had a soprano voice, and such a gentleman we did not possess. An inferior teacher would certainly have been of no use to the Conradin. It is ridiculous to say of Mattheson that he sang only occasionally, considering that he was fifteen years at the theatre, that he acted almost always the principal character, exciting his audience by means of his unaffected singing as well as by his mimic art, which is of the utmost importance in opera, sometimes fear and terror, sometimes tears, sometimes merriment and delight. On the 9th of June, 1703, he made Handel's acquaintance at an organ, when Handel was $19\frac{1}{4}$ years old, and Mattheson $21\frac{3}{4}$, so that the difference in age amounted only to two years and a half.* On the 17th of August, in the same year, they travelled together to Lübeck, and played in that town, as well as in Hamburg, on the organ and harpsichord, so to say in emulation, in which Handel proved himself the most successful on the former instrument, but acknowledged himself obliged to yield the palm to his rival on the latter instrument; so that they made a compact together never to encroach upon each other's ground. This they have also faithfully kept during five or six years. On the 20th of October, Mattheson brought out his fifth, or sixth opera, called Cleopatra, on which occasion Handel played the harpsichord under the direction of the former. Soon afterwards, on the 7th of November in the same year, Sir John Wich,† Knight, Royal Ambassador of Great

---

* This is a mis-statement. Handel, born in 1685, was 18 years old; and Mattheson, born in 1681, was 22 years old.

† Wych?

Britain, engaged Mattheson as teacher and tutor for his son Cyril Wich, nine years old; and soon afterwards he made him his Secretary, with a salary of three hundred Reichsthaler, and two hundred *ditto* perquisites *per annum*. This gave occasion for jealous looks, especially as he now bid farewell to the theatre. Thus, after a secure foundation had been laid, the progress was very perceptible. True, the young master Wich had already had a few very unimportant lessons from Handel; they did not give satisfaction; the tutor was therefore appealed to, and under his guidance the young gentleman attained, in the course of time, a high degree of perfection. He succeeded his father, after the death of the latter, and obtained in 1729 the hereditary dignity of a Baronet. Mattheson always remained in royal service, was twelve or thirteen times 'Chargé des Affaires,' was employed on important missions, etc.,—as has already been circumstantially recorded in the 'Ehrenpforte,' published in 1740. At last, after the lapse of fifty years, the highly-meritorious Baronet departed to a better world on the 18th of August, when he had just returned from an embassy to Russia. If the author of the present biography had consulted Mattheson's books, especially the above-mentioned 'Ehrenpforte,' and the 'Critica Musica,' which are *publici juris*, he would not have been devoid of authentic materials. Under those favourable conditions the though not *great* yet formerly *principal* singer and actor composed, notwithstanding all diplomatic and pressing dispatches in the whole district of Lower-Saxony, not only a great number of sacred pieces for the Church, but oratorios, operas, and music for the harpsichord and other instruments, which cannot be unknown in England. Besides he was occupied as Kapellmeister of the Duke of Holstein, as Canonicus et Cantor Cathedralis Hamburgensis, and as director of several grand concerts; he wrote not *one*, but *eighty-six* books, most of which treat profoundly of the theory of music and the art of singing. Furthermore, when the St. Michael's Church was burnt down, he contributed some forty thousand marks for a new organ, paid the money in advance, and intends to do more *per codicillum* in different ways. His life, led in the fear of God, extends now to the eightieth year, in cheerfulness and useful works. For the sake of truth this is here inserted."

Mainwaring (P. 32). "Conratini excelled greatly, both as an actress and as a singer. Keysar * did the same as a composer; but, being a man of gaiety and expence, involved himself in debts, which forced him to abscond. His operas for some time continued to be performed during his absence. On his disappearing, the person who before had played the second harpsichord demanded the first. This occasioned a dispute between him and Handel, the particulars of which, partly for the sake of their singularity, and partly on account of their importance, may deserve to be mentioned. On what reasons Handel grounded his claim to the first harpsichord I do not understand. He had played a violin in the orchestra, he had a good command on this instrument, and was known to have a better on the other. But the older candidate † was not unfit for the office, and insisted on the right of succession. Handel seemed to have no plea but that of natural superiority, of which he was conscious, and from which he would not recede. This dispute occasioned parties in the Opera-house. On the one side it was said, with great appearance of reason, that to set such a boy as Handel over a person so much his senior, was both unjust and unprecedented. On the other, it was urged with some plausibility, that the opera was not to be ruined for punctilios; that it was easy to foresee, from the difficulties Keysar was under, that a composer would soon be wanted, but not so easy to find a person capable of succeeding him, unless it were Handel. In short, matters, they said, were now at that pass that the question, if fairly stated, was not who should conduct the opera, but whether there should be any opera at all. These arguments prevailed; and he to whom the first place seemed of course to be due, was constrained to yield it to his stripling competitor. But, how much he felt the indignity may be guessed from the nature and degree of his resentment, more suited to the glowing

---

* Keiser. † Mattheson.

temper of an Italian, than to the phlegmatic constitution of a German."

Mattheson. "He calls the Germans phlegmatic, and a *querelle allemande* does not occur to him."

Mainwaring (P. 35). "For, determined to make Handel pay dear for his priority, he stifled his rage for the present, only to wait an opportunity to give it full vent. As they were coming out of the orchestra, he made a push at him with a sword, which, being aimed full at his heart, would for ever have removed him from the office he had usurped, but for the friendly *Score* which he accidentally carried in his bosom; and through which to have forced it, would have demanded all the might of Ajax himself. Had this happened in the early ages, not a mortal but would have been persuaded that Apollo himself had interposed to preserve him, in the form of a music-book. From the circumstances which are related of this affair, it has more the appearance of an assassination than of a rencounter; if the latter, one of Handel's years might well be wanting the courage, or the skill, to defend himself; if the former, supposing him capable of making a defence, he could not be prepared for it. How many great men, in the very dawning of their glory have been planted, like him, on the very verge of destruction! as if Fortune, jealous of Nature, made a show of sacrificing her noblest productions only to remind her of that supremacy to which she aspires. Whatever might be the merits of the quarrel at first,"——

Mattheson. "Here I must again interrupt the subtle reasoner, in order to show him his confusion, which is even greater and ruder than the preceding one, since that contained only above a dozen falsehoods, while we have here double the number. The cause of the quarrel was, indeed, quite different from what is here related. It was already mentioned long since, with all possible modesty, in the 'Ehrenpforte,' p. 94 and 193; but there was then no occasion, as there is now, to remind the reader that a cool box on the ear is no assassination, but rather a necessary warning to prepare for defence. This settles the first statement. The incorrectly-informed author relates a fable rather than a true event. Never, so long as can be remembered, have two harpsichords been played together in the orchestra of the opera in Hamburg at the same time; and as there has always been but one, a dispute about it, as narrated, could not possibly have occurred. Now, as to this dispute is attributed the origin of the fight, the remainder of the invention falls with it to the ground. There we have the second blunder. Subsequently erroneous statements are so frequent that it is scarcely possible to count them. Handel, in the beginning, played only the second violin in the orchestra; and he was, as may easily be conceived, not a more accomplished performer on that instrument than any other member of the orchestra. There we have the third falsehood, which is besides a boasting untruth. The fray occurred on the 5th of December, 1704. Handel, whom the biographer insists, as much as is in his power, on making younger the older he grows, was nearly twenty-one years of age,* tall, strong, broad, and vigorous in body; he was, consequently, man enough to defend himself, and to make use of the sword which he had hanging at his side. That is the fourth point, and a strong one too, which a writer very sensitive of his reputation should especially bear in mind when he, instead of recording real facts, indulges in high-flown laudations, and occasions the translator much unnecessary trouble."

Mainwaring (P. 37). "Whatever might be the merits of the quarrel at first, Handel seemed now to have purchased his title to precedence by the dangers he had incurred to support it. What he and his friends expected, soon happened. From conducting the performance, he became composer of the opera. Keiser, from his unhappy situation, could no longer supply the manager, who therefore applied to Handel, and furnished him with a drama to set. The name of it was Almira, and this was the first opera which he made. The success of it was so great that it ran for thirty nights without interruption. He was at this time not much above fourteen; before he was fifteen he made a second, entitled Florinda; and soon after, a third, called Nerone; which were heard with the same applause."

---

* He was not quite twenty years old.

Mattheson. "The fifth brag, as to a certain opera having been performed in Hamburg, with every advantage and good result, thirty times without intermission, is surely not worth mentioning. The sixth, however, is even still finer. Let us just analyze it a little. 'Almira' was performed the first time on the 8th of January, anno 1705. Now, our chronologist counts from the 24th of February, 1684, when Handel was born, until the 8th of January, 1705, as a little more than fourteen years, while the period really is nearly twenty-one years.* But he is not particular about seven years. A fine arithmetician, to be sure! Mistake No. 7. 'Nero' was not the third of Handel's operas, as our author erroneously states (mistake No. 8), but the second; and it was performed for the first time on the 25th of February, in 1705. Thus, there were only forty-eight days between the two performances; at the utmost, seven weeks. In the seven weeks there were seven Sundays, seven Saturdays, fourteen post-days, not to count the St. Mary-days and the holydays. How is it then possible that the 'Almira' could have been represented thirty times without interruption? Whoever believes only half of what this historicus here writes, believes too much. That was mistake No. 9. The tenth concerns the Florindo as a man, not the Florinda as a female. Handel's opera called 'Florindo' was not his second, but his third; and it was performed in 1708, three years after 'Nero.' Meanwhile, Keiser had not only composed a new 'Almira,' as well as the operas 'Octavia,' 'Lucretia,' 'Fedelta coronata,' 'Masagnello furioso,' 'Sueno,' 'Genio di Holsatia,' Carnival of Venice;' but also Schieferdecker had brought out his 'Justin'; Grünwald, his 'Germanicum;' and Graupner his 'Dido.' In the year 1708, Handel produced another opera, called 'Daphne,' which was the fourth of those he wrote for Hamburg, and which appears to be unknown to his biographer, as he omits it entirely. Has the man not had trustworthy sources for information?† Howbeit, the dozen mistakes is complete,

* See the note above, page 11.

† Mainwaring had probably obtained some of his information from Handel himself; but he may have forgotten the dates, or Handel may not have remembered them exactly.

and we merely remark in addition, that in 1708 Handel was not 15 years of age, but quite 24. This *error calculi* may be regarded as a master stroke. Did we not know with certainty that George Frederick Handel died anno 1759, on the fourteenth of April, at the age of 76, * and we had to rely upon this blundering prosaic Homer for information respecting our musical Achilles, he would have remained constantly fifteen years, perhaps even *imberbis* until he came to the grave, and our barber in Hamburg, who every alternate day attended him, during five or six years, would have gained his money wrongfully. If an Englishman thinks that he can entertain us with his dreams in his mixture-language, he must be prepared for an answer from us in our heroic language. We understand him well, and have learnt his tongue; if he does not understand us, he may still learn this too. . . . . Having observed Handel during his sojourn in Hamburg, we leave the celebrated man to the Italians and the English; but we do not believe that the moon is made of green cheese."

Mainwaring (P. 42). "Four or five years had elapsed from the time of his coming to Hamburg to that of his leaving it."

Mattheson. "Should say five or six."

Mainwaring (P. 42). "Instead of being chargeable to his mother he began to be serviceable to her before he was well settled in his new situation. Though he had continued to send her remittances from time to time, yet, clear of his own expenses, he had made up a purse of 200 ducats. On the strength of this fund he resolved to set out for Italy."

Mattheson. "Anno 1709 he was still in Hamburg, but did nothing.† Then there occurred the opportunity of his travelling with Herr von Binitz to Italy, free of expense; and in 1710 he had his 'Agrippina' performed at Venice."

---

* Handel was 74 years old when he died.

† Mattheson is mistaken here. It has been satisfactorily ascertained that Handel left Hamburg for Italy in the year 1706. (See G. F. Händel, von F. Crysander, Leipzig, 1858, vol. I., p. 139.)

Mainwaring (P. 44). "The very first answer of the fugue in the overture for 'Mucius Scævola' [an opera by Handel] affords an instance of this kind [viz., a musical licence]. Geminiani, the strictest observer of rule, was so charmed with this direct transgression of it that, on hearing its effect, he cried out *Quel semitono* (meaning the F-sharp) *vale un mondo!*"

Mattheson. "What does that prove? Nothing!"

Mainwaring (P. 50). "At the age of eighteen he made [at Florence] the opera of Rodrigo, for which he was presented with 100 sequins and a service of plate."

Mattheson. "Actually an intentional miscalculation of eight years!"

Mainwaring (P. 52). "In three weeks he finished [at Venice] his 'Agrippina,' which was performed twenty-seven nights successively."

Mattheson. "In the year 1709, at his departure from Hamburg, Handel was 25 years old. He resided a year in Florence before he went to Venice, where he had his 'Agrippina' performed at the theatre of St. Gio Crisostomo, during the Carnival in 1710. Now, let him calculate who can, and convince himself whether this makes, from February 24th, 1684, eighteen years, as our biographer says, or whether it amounts to twenty-six."

Mainwaring (P. 74). "It was in the winter of the year 1710 when he arrived at London."

Mattheson. "In this year he performed his 'Agrippina' at Venice, and in 1709 he was still in Hamburg." *

Mainwaring (P. 74). "During this period scarce a mail arrived from Holland which did not bring some fresh accounts of victories or advantages gained by the English hero [Marlborough] over the armies of a monarch but lately the terror of Europe, though now the scorn of every Dutch burgomaster."

---

* The following well-authenticated data may serve to correct the "corrections" of Mattheson:—Handel was born in 1685; went to Hamburg in 1703; thence to Italy in 1706; from Italy to Hanover in 1710; thence to London in 1710; back to Hanover in 1711; returned to England in 1712, where he died in 1759.

Mattheson. "What a Frenchman may say to this is his own concern. In Handel's biography it is lugged in; and such scurrilities reveal an ignoble heart."

Mainwaring (P. 88). "Our business is not to play the panegyrist but the historian."

Mattheson. "If you know that, blessed are you if you act upon it."

Mainwaring (P. 110). "Having one day some words with Cuzzoni on her refusing to sing *Falsa imagine* in 'Ottone': 'Oh! Madame,' Handel said, 'je scais bien que vous êtes une véritable diablesse; mais je vous ferai scavoir, moi, que je suis Beelzebub, le *chef* des diables!' With this he took her up by the waist, and swore that if she made any more words he would fling her out of the window. It is to be noted that this was formerly one of the methods of executing criminals in some parts of Germany, a process not unlike that of the Tarpeian rock, and probably derived from it."

Mattheson. "This heroic deed was undoubtedly accomplished unawares. Who could face such a woman with her claws? The Quixotic story with its ingenious reference to the Tarpeian rock, and to criminal processes, testify to the author's extensive reading in law and history. Whoever can read it without a smile is commendable, especially if he is a German, better informed and phlegmatic."

Mainwaring (P. 115). "The little taste he [Handel] had already had of adversity lessened that self-confidence which success is apt to inspire. He found that it was not the necessary consequence of great abilities, and that without prudence the greatest may be almost annihilated in the opinions of men."

Mattheson. "To this the British proverb applies: 'Give a man luck and throw him into the Thames.'"

Mainwaring (P. 116). "He now removed to Covent-garden, and entered into partnership with Rich, the master of that house. Hasse and Porpora were the composers at the Haymarket. When the former was invited over, it is remarkable that the first question he asked was whether Handel was dead. Being answered in the negative he refused to come, from a persuasion that where his countryman was—for they were both Saxons by birth—no other person of the same profession was likely to make any figure."

Mattheson. "This agrees with a remark of mine before made. Hasse was born in Bergedorf, a small town belonging to Hamburg and Lübeck in common; he is, therefore, a Lower-Saxon of the highest type. . . . . However, the reason why these two Saxons did not wish to encroach upon each other's precincts was a very different one from that indicated by our biographer."

Mainwaring (P. 132). "Dublin has always been famous for the gaiety and splendour of its court, the opulence and spirit of its principal inhabitants, the valour of its military, and the genius of its learned men. Where such things were held in esteem he [Handel] rightly reckoned that he could not better pave the way to his success than by setting out with a striking instance and public act of generosity and benevolence. The first step that he made was to perform his Messiah for the benefit of the city-prison."

Mattheson. "On a beau être généreux et liberal, quand il n'en coute que des chansons, et que d'autres payent les violons; c'est en bon allemand: *Mit der Wurst nach dem Schinken werfen* ('To throw the sausage at the ham')."

Mainwaring (P. 135). "The Foundling Hospital [in London] originally rested on the slender foundation of private benefactions. At a time when this institution was yet in its infancy; when all men seemed to be convinced of its utility; when nothing was at all problematical but the possibility of supporting it;—Handel formed the noble resolution to lend his assistance, and perform his Messiah annually for its benefit. The sums raised by each performance were very considerable, and certainly of great consequence in such a crisis of affairs. But, what was of much greater, was the magic of his name and the universal character of his sacred drama."

Mattheson. "Notes were his magic, or his black-art."

Mainwaring (P. 137). "So that it may truly be affirmed that one of the noblest and most extensive charities that ever was planned by the wisdom, or projected by the piety of men, in some degree owes its continuance as well as prosperity to the patronage of Handel."

Mattheson. "By this he was not out of pocket; it rather brought him credit, which is better than money."

Mainwaring (P. 138). "In the year 1751 a gutta serena deprived him of his sight. This misfortune sunk him for a time into the deepest despondency. He could not rest until he had undergone some operations as fruitless as they were painful. Finding it no longer possible for him to manage alone, he sent to Mr. Smith to desire that he should play for him, and assist him in conducting the oratorios."

Mattheson. "He remained blind until his death,—a period of eight years. Nothing is said here of a so-called monumental column, and of an amazingly large property left by Handel, although it has been a subject of much gossip."

Mainwaring (P. 141). "His incessant and intense application to the studies of his profession, rendered constant and large supplies of nourishment the more necessary to recruit his exhausted spirits."

Mattheson. "J. Sirach, chap. xxxviii., v. 34; Phil., chap. iii., v. 19."

Mainwaring (P. 142). "The design of the foregoing sheets is only to give the reader those parts of his character as a Man, that any way tend to open and explain his character as an Artist."

Mattheson. "If this were done, the arts and the manners would exhibit not unfrequently striking contrasts."

"*Mainwaring* (P. 143). "The author has nothing to add but his sincere wishes that every artist who is truly deserving in his profession may meet with a person equally desirous of doing justice to his memory."

Mattheson. "This wish is as kind as it is reasonable. It proves the belief of the author that there must be other people, unknown to him, who, on account of their arts, deserve quite as much honour as Handel. Alas! how much pains has the 'Great-Thorough-Bass School' taken to show this, not to mention the 'Triumphal Arch.* . . . Bach,

---

* Two works by Mattheson.

Fux, Graun, Graupner, Grünewald, Heinichen, Keiser, etc., have died without experiencing it; perhaps the same will happen with Hasse, and with several others."

Mainwaring (P. 149). "A great quantity of music, not mentioned in the Catalogue, was made [by Handel] in Italy and Germany. How much of it is yet in being, is not known. Two chests-full were left at Hamburg, besides some at Hanover, and some at Halle."

Mattheson. "We Hamburgians have hitherto heard nothing of those two chests. In Wich's music-book of the year 1704 are two minuets and half an air, that is all."

Mainwaring (P. 164). "The generality of mankind have not enough of delicacy to be much affected with minute instances of beauty, but yet are so formed as to be transported with every the least mark of grandeur and sublimity."

Mattheson. "That is true."

Mainwaring (P. 165). "The taste in music, both of the Germans and Italians, is suited to the different characters of the two nations. That of the first is rough and martial; and their music consists of strong effects produced, without much delicacy, by the rattle of a number of instruments."

Mattheson. "Surely this is not phlegmatic, as before said."

Mainwaring (P. 174). "However well some of the Italians may have succeeded in the management of the instrumental parts in their song-music, there is one point in which Handel stands alone, and in which he may possibly never be equalled; I mean in the instrumental parts of his choruses and full church-music."

Mattheson. "This is true enough; but it was all derived from Zachau and his organ-playing. Germany is the fatherland of all powerful harmony, elaborate compositions for the organ, fugues and chorales, used in Divine Service. Italy has melody for her daughter, with songstresses, singers, and very delicate solo-players on violin-instruments to touch the heart. France produces its magnificent choruses, instrumental pieces, dance-music, to cheer the heart; and to England we leave the honour of admiring and recompensing these rarities."

Mainwaring (P. 179). "But how shall we excuse for those instances of coarseness and indelicacy which occur so frequently in the airs of his oratorios? For, as the melody is a fundamental and essential part in vocal music, it should seem that nothing can atone for the neglect of it. The best painter would be blamed should he draw off the attention too much from the principal figure in his piece, however perfect, by the very high and exquisite finishing of some inferior object; but, much more would he deserve to be blamed if he left that figure the least finished which all the rules of his art required to be the most so. Now, in music, though there may sometimes be occasion for giving the instruments the ascendancy over the voices, yet never should the song-parts be unmeaning or inexpressive, much less coarse or ordinary."

Mattheson. "Golden words! All this, however, is owing to the circumstance that Handel was neither a singer nor an actor. During a period of five or six years, when we had daily intercourse with each other, I never heard a singing tone from his mouth. When Earl Granville (at that time Lord Carteret) was here in Hamburg, and heard me sing and also play, he said: 'Handel plays also thus, but he does not sing thus.' In my opinion singing and acting are of great assistance to a composer of dramatic music. Hasse knows this well, and has cultivated both earnestly, *me teste.* Keiser, likewise, sang very admirably. Both have, therefore, extraordinarily charming melodies."

Mainwaring (P. 202). "In his fugues and overtures, Handel is quite original. The style of them is peculiar to himself, and in no way like that of any master before him. In the formation of these pieces, knowledge and invention seem to have contended for the mastery."

Mattheson. "A certain philosopher recently made himself conspicuous by maintaining that the Fine Arts ought not to be regarded as Sciences, because their systems are sensuous. Nevertheless, the old adage always stands firm: *Nihil esse in intellectu quod non prius fuerit in sensu.* Our biographer belongs perhaps to that sect, for he scarcely uses the word *science*, even when he refers to the science of music, as on the present occasion. He always uses only the word *knowledge* or *skill*. Perhaps this is unintentional. Thus much, however, is certain: musicians are in need of literary works, and he who can only write notes, his honour and reputation are only *vox, pracleraque nihil*. On the second of March, this year [1761,] we had here, in Hamburg, a sale of a large number of scarce and valuable books on all sciences; but the science of music was not represented by a single work in the comprehensive catalogue. That is surely neglect of a science! If any one can show me that I am mistaken, I shall be happy."

Mainwaring (P. 208). "Little, indeed, are the hopes of ever equalling, much less of excelling, so vast a proficient in his own way; however, as there are so many avenues to excellence still open, so many paths to glory still untrod, it is hoped that the example of this illustrious foreigner will rather prove an incentive than a discouragement to the industry and genius of our own countrymen."

Mattheson. "Whoever intends to describe accurately the life of Handel, can hardly do it without a reference to the following books: 'Musica Critica,' Hamburg, 1722; 'The Musical Patriot,' Hamburg, 1728; 'Ehrenpforte,' Hamburg, 1740."

Mattheson now quotes an extract from a letter of Handel's, dated February 24th, 1719, which has already been given above;* and he remarks: "To promise, and to fulfil a promise, are two things." He quotes once more Handel's complimentary letter, also given above,† which evidently afforded him great satisfaction; and he adds: "Even the most insignificant letters in some degree depict the writer, in reference to the time and place in which they were written. Horace is quite right: *Coelum non animum mutant qui trans mare currunt.*"

Some writers have blamed Mattheson very much on account of his vanity and his jealousy of Handel. Still, it remains a debatable question whether the conceit of his detractors does not perhaps surpass his own. It is a common practice with inferior musical authors to assume

---

* Page 4. † Page 7.

an air of superiority, and to endeavour to make themselves important by finding fault with others who have distinguished themselves in the same field in which they are labouring, and to whom they ought to be grateful.

Mattheson had not only a better scientific education than most musicians of his time, but his literary productions are also more readable than those of his modern commentators who censure him.

DIABOLIC MUSIC.

It is a suggestive fact that those spirits of the mountains, rivers, and of lonely places, which delight in music and dancing, are, according to popular tradition, generally well-intentioned and harmless creatures. Sometimes, however, a very evil-disposed spirit resorts to these arts for the purpose of accomplishing some wicked design. A few stories from different countries which illustrate the superstitious notions on the subject will be given here. Although the stories are still in the mouth of the people, it can hardly be said that they are still really believed, at least not in European countries. But there are always ignorant persons who half believe whatever appeals forcibly to their imagination.

THE AWFUL DECEPTION.

At Arfeld, a small village in Germany, a number of young lads and lasses were assembled one winter evening in a warm and comfortable room, the girls spinning and singing, as they usually do on these occasions.

One of the lads, in silly playfulness, said to the girls he should like them to try whether they could hang him on a single thread of their spinning. The novel idea found ready approval. They made him stand on a chair, and bound a thin thread around his neck, fastening it on a nail under the ceiling.

At this moment all were greatly surprised by hearing strains of exquisitely fine music penetrating into the house. They directly hastened outside the door to ascertain whence it came; but there they neither heard nor saw anything.

On returning to the room, they found, to their great astonishment and dismay, that the chair had been drawn from under the lad, and that the poor fellow was hanging on the thread and was dead.*

THE INDEFATIGABLE FIDDLER.

The following strange event happened in the parish of Börne, two miles south of Ripen, in Denmark, and is still known to the people in all its details.

One Sunday evening, a company of young men and girls of the village had assembled in a farm-house, and were indulging in all kinds of frolic and flirting. After they had enjoyed their nonsense for some time they thought they should like to have a little dancing. In the midst of much noisy and useless debating how to procure a musician to play to them, one of the youths—the wildest of the party—cut the matter short by saying boastingly: "Now, my lads, leave that to me! I will bring you a musician, even if it should be the devil himself!" With these words the wicked youth placed his cap knowingly on one side of his head, and marched out of the room.

He had not advanced many steps along the road when he met with an old beggarly-looking man, who carried a fiddle under his arm. The lad lost no time in striking a bargain with the man, and triumphantly introduced him into the house. In a few minutes all the young folks were wildly dancing up and down the room to the old crowder's fascinating music; and soon the perspiration actually streamed down their faces. They now desired to stop for a moment to rest themselves a little. But this they found impossible so long as the old crowder continued playing; and they could not induce him to leave off, however earnestly they implored him. It was really an awful affair!

Soon they would have been all dead from sheer exhaustion, had it not so happened, fortunately for them, that there

---

* 'Sagen, Gebräuche, und Märchen aus Westfahlen, gesammelt von A. Kuhn. Leipzig, 1859.' Vol. I., p. 175.

resided in the lower part of the house an old deaf woman, the housekeeper of the farmer, who accidentally becoming aware of the desperate condition of the dancers, ran as fast as she could to fetch the parish priest. The holy man was already in bed, and it took some time to arouse him; and then he had to dress himself. But at last he was quite prepared; and when he arrived at the farm-house and saw the fearful scene, he at once took out of his pocket a little book, from which he read something in Latin or Hebrew. Scarcely had he read a verse, when the indefatigable fiddler let his arm sink, and drawing himself gradually up until he stood merely on the tips of his toes, he suddenly vanished through the ceiling, leaving no traces behind. Some people say, however, that there was a sulphurous odour about the house shortly after this miraculous event.

THE EFFECTUAL EXPEDIENT.

The next story, told by the Manx people, is almost literally transcribed from Waldron's 'History and Description of the Isle of Man,' London, 1744.

"A fiddler having agreed with a person, who was a stranger, for so much money, to play to some company he should bring him to, all the twelve days of Christmas, and having received an earnest for it, saw his new master vanish into the earth the moment he had made the bargain. Nothing could exceed the terror of the poor fiddler. He found he had engaged himself in the devil's service, and he looked on himself as already doomed; but, having recourse to a clergyman he received some hope. The clergyman desired him, as he had taken an earnest, to go when he should be summoned; but, whatever tunes should be called for, to play none but psalm-tunes.

"On the day appointed the same person appeared, with whom he went, but with what inward reluctance it is easy to guess. He punctually obeying the minister's directions, the company to whom he played were so angry that they all vanished at once, leaving him at the top of a high hill, and so bruised and hurt, though he was not sensible when or from what hand he received the blows, that it was with the utmost difficulty he got home."

THE OLD CHORALE.

The following is recorded from Oldenburg, North Germany.

The sexton at Esenshammer, one day on entering the church alone, heard the organ playing most charmingly. He looked up and saw to his great surprise that there was no player; it played by itself. He lost no time in running to the Pastor, to tell him what was going on in the church.

The Pastor quickly put on his gown and hastened with his sexton to witness the phenomenon. Sure enough; the organ was playing wonderfully all kinds of profane airs; they both heard it distinctly. But, look where they would, they could not see any performer.

After having recovered a little from his astonishment, the Pastor in a solemn tone of voice called out towards the organ:—

"If thou up there canst play everything, just play to me our old Chorale *Wer nur den lieben Gott lässt walten.*"

In a moment the organ was silent.

THE HAUNTED MANSION.

Diabolic musical performances have often been heard at midnight in a certain mansion in Schleswig-Holstein. Years ago, the young and gay daughter of the then lord of the manor, at a family festivity and grand ball, proved herself so insatiable in dancing, that, after having danced all the evening, she flippantly exclaimed: "And if the devil himself appeared and invited me to dance, I should not decline!"

Scarcely had she said these words, when the door of the ball-room flew open, and an unknown cavalier entered, went up to her, and led her to dance. Round and round they whirled, unceasingly, incessantly faster and faster, until—O, horror! suddenly she fell down dead.

A long time has elapsed since this occurred; but the lady still haunts the mansion. Every year on the day when the frightful event took place, precisely at midnight, the mansion resounds with the most diabolic music. The lady arises from her grave and repairs to the ball-room, where she anxiously waits for a partner; for, if any good Christian should come and dance with her, she afterwards will have rest. Hitherto no one has had the courage to stay in the house during the awful hour. A daring young adventurer once had nearly succeeded. In that case, the mansion would have come into his possession, according to an old deed found in the house. But as soon as the diabolic music began, his courage forsook him, and he made off as fast as he could. It terrified him so much, that even now when he hears violins he trembles all over, and imagines the diabolic noise is recommencing.

THE MODE ASBEIN.

A modern writer on Arabic music, as it is practised in Algiers and Tunis, mentions among the various Modes used at the present day a peculiarly impressive one, called Asbein, which the Mohammedans believe to have been especially appropriated by Satan for the purpose of tempting man. They have a long story respecting its origin and demoniac effects. The writer alluded to, a Frenchman, had the gratification of hearing a piece or two played in this Mode by a musician, who had the reputation of being one of the best performers in Tunis, and who used to entertain the frequenters of a certain coffee-house in a suburb. To this place the Frenchman repaired, and induced the musician to play in the Mode Asbein. To surmise from his description of the performance, there must have been something really frightful in the degree of ecstacy which the player exhibited. But there is something funny in the Frenchman's mode of reasoning, which deserves to be noticed, because it shows how opinions like the above are sometimes adopted readily enough even by professed sceptics. The Frenchman was a sceptic, and had made up his mind before he proceeded to examine the matter, that the impression of the Arabs respecting the Mode Asbein was due entirely to their religious enthusiasm. They are, of course, Mohammedans. Now, after the performance, the Frenchman accidentally learnt that the musician was a Jew. Then he no longer doubted the demoniac power of the Mode Asbein.

WITCHES.

Respecting the music of witches, a few short remarks may suffice. Every one knows that witches, at their meetings, amuse themselves especially with music and dancing. In Germany, the largest assemblages of these objectionable beings take place in the night of the first of May (Walpurgis), and the most favourite resort for their festivities is the summit of the Harz mountain, called Brocken, or Blocksberg. The musicians sit on old stumps of trees, or on projecting rocks, and fiddle upon skulls of horses.

Whoever desires to witness these ghastly scenes must provide himself with the upper board of an old coffin in which a knot has been forced out, and must peep through the hole.

THE CHANGELING.

According to an old superstition, which was widely spread during the Middle Ages, the elves sometimes steal a handsome, new-born child from its cradle, and substitute an ill-formed, ugly child of their own. The little Irish prodigy who is the hero of an event which happened in the county of Tipperary, was such a Changeling. The story told of him, it will be seen, is stamped with the peculiar wildness of fancy which generally characterizes Irish fairy-tales.

Mick Flanigan and his wife, Judy, were a poor couple, blessed with nothing but four little boys. Three of the children were as healthy and rosy-cheeked as any thriving

Irish boy you can meet with; but the fourth was a little urchin, more ugly than it is possible to imagine; and, even worse, he was as mischievous as he was ugly. Innumerable were the tricks which he played upon his brothers, and even upon his parents. Although before he was a twelve-month old he had already grown a formidable set of teeth, and ate like a glutton, he would nevertheless lie constantly in his cradle near the fire, even after he had reached the age of five years. Resting on his back, and half closing his little eyes, he would observe everything which was going on in the room, watching for opportunities to annoy the people.

Now, one afternoon it came to pass that Tim Carrol, the blind bagpiper, an old friend of the family, called in and sat down near the fire to have a bit of chat. As he had brought his bagpipe with him, they soon asked him to treat them with a tune. So blind Tim Carrol buckled on his bagpipe, and began to play.

Presently the little urchin raised himself in the cradle, moved his ugly head to and fro, and evidently manifested excessive delight at the nasal sounds. When the affectionate mother saw how eagerly the child stretched out both its hands for the bagpipe, she begged old blind Tim Carrol just to humour her little darling for a moment; and as blind Tim was not the man to say "No," he mildly laid the bagpipe upon the cradle. But how great was their astonishment when the urchin took up the instrument, and, handling it like a practised bagpiper, played without the least effort a lively jig, then another, even more lively, and several others, in rapid succession.

The first thing the father did was to sell his pig and to buy a bagpipe for his prodigy. It soon turned out that the rogue had a peculiar tune of his own, which made people dance however little they might feel disposed for dancing. Even his poor mother happening to come into the room one day with a pailfull of milk, and hearing that bewitching tune, must needs let the pail drop, spill all the milk, and spin round like a very top.

About the time when the boy was six years old, the farmer of the village, by whom Mick Flanigan was employed as day labourer, had various mischances with his cattle. Two of his cows lost their appetite, and gave little or no milk. A very promising calf stumbled, and broke both its hind legs. And shortly afterwards one of his best horses suddenly got the colic and died in no time. The people in the village had long since settled among themselves that there was something not right in Mick Flanigan's family; so it naturally occurred to the farmer that the imp with the bagpipe must be the cause of all his misfortunes. He therefore thought it wise to give warning at once to Mick Flanigan, and to advise him to look out for work elsewhere. Fortunately, poor Mick Flanigan soon succeeded in getting employment at a farmer's, a few miles off, who was in want of a ploughman.

On the appointed day the new master sent a cart to fetch the few articles of furniture which Mick Flanigan could call his own. Having placed the cradle with the boy and his bagpipe at the top, the whole family drove off to their new home. When they had got about half the way, they had to cross a river. Slowly they drove upon the rickety bridge, little anticipating the exciting scene which now occurred. The boy had hitherto remained very quiet in the cradle, apparently half asleep as usual. But, just when the cart had reached the middle of the bridge, he raised his head, looked wistfully at the water, and then suddenly grasping his bagpipe he jumped down into the river.

His terrified parents set up a cry of distress, and made some efforts to save him, when, to their unspeakable astonishment, they saw him swimming, diving and gamboling about in the water like a very otter. Nay, he actually began to play on his bagpipe, shouting lustily all the while and exhibiting other signs which clearly showed that he was now in his right element. Soon he disappeared entirely. Then the poor people became fully convinced that the boy was a Changeling, and had now gone home to his own kinsfolk.*

---

* 'Fairy Legends and Traditions of the South of Ireland, by T. Crofton Croker; London, 1862,' p. 22.—Compare also 'Hans mein Igel,' in Grimm's Kinder und Hausmärchen.

THE VENDISH SORCERER.

The Vends are a Slavonic race inhabiting some districts in Lusatia, Germany. Although living amidst Germans, they still preserve their own language, as well as a considerable number of national songs and legends of their own, some of which are very beautiful.

The Vendish Sorcerer, whose name was Draho, lived in a mountain, near the town of Teichnitz, at the time when the Christian religion was just beginning to take root in Lusatia. He was, of course, a pagan; and every scheme he could devise to hurt the defenceless Christians living scattered about the neighbourhood, he did not fail remorselessly to put into action. Moreover, his great power he derived from a magic whistle, by means of which he made certain mischievous spirits subservient to his will.

This sorcerer had a disciple, who, becoming acquainted with the blessings of Christianity, forsook his wicked master, and seizing a favourable opportunity when the old rogue was taking a nap, possessed himself of the magic whistle, and flew from the mountain into the valley to his friends the Christians.

Now, when the people learnt that the sorcerer had been deprived of his whistle, they knew that his power was gone, and that they might venture to approach him without incurring much danger. So they went up to the top of the mountain, provided with all kinds of arms, and soon succeeded in capturing the old pagan. Having securely bound him, they made a large fire of wood, upon which they placed him, and solemnly burnt him to death. Meanwhile, the disciple, who had already received Holy Baptism, stepped forward and threw the magic whistle into the flame, that it might be consumed without leaving a trace.

Nevertheless, every year in the spring, on the eve of Oculi Sunday, the old sorcerer appears on the top of the mountain, and in the night blows a most frightful shriek upon his magic whistle. The people who go out at midnight to listen for it have not long to wait before they hear the awful sound. For, what people are bent upon hearing, they are sure to hear, especially if it is something objectionable.

THE RAT-CATCHER OF HAMELN.

In the year 1284, the town of Hameln, situated on the river Weser, in Germany, became awfully infested with rats and mice. All kinds of traps, poisons, and other means employed to destroy the vermin proved of no avail, and the harassed citizens were actually at their wits' end what to do. The plague grew daily more formidable until the people had every reason to fear that before long not only their victuals but they themselves would all be devoured.

When the misery had reached a height positively frightful, there appeared in Hameln a strange man with a queer-shaped hat, who offered to deliver the town from the scourge for a stipulated reward. Some say the reward he demanded was a round sum of money; others maintain that he wanted to marry the burgomaster's pretty daughter. Whatever it may have been, there is certainly no doubt that it was readily promised him.

As soon as the bargain had been struck, the strange man drew from his pocket a small pipe, began to play and walked through the streets of the town. Presently, all the rats and mice came running out of their holes and followed him. Lustily playing he marched with his odd army out of the town and into the river Weser, where every rat and mouse was drowned.

Then the inhabitants of Hameln rejoiced greatly, as after a victory over a powerful enemy. But, when the strange man came to claim the promised reward, they withheld it from him, and treated him with derision.

However, a few days afterwards, how sorely were they punished for their ingratitude!

The enraged rat-catcher unexpectedly appeared, this time dressed entirely in red. Strange to say, even his face and hands seemed to be quite red. He took his pipe and walked through the streets, playing as before. Presently, all the little children of Hameln came running out of the houses and followed him. He marched with them out of the town into the mountains, where he vanished with them into a deep hole in a rock.

Some persons believe that the children afterwards came to light again, very far off in Transylvania. At all events, there are villages in that country in which the people speak the same language as in Hameln.

The gate through which the strange man took the children is still extant, and there are other evidences of similar importance to be found in Hameln, which prove to the satisfaction of certain respectable citizens that the story is quite true in all its details.

The earliest record of the Rat-catcher of Hameln written in English is probably the quaint one contained in 'A Restitution of decayed Intelligence in Antiquities by the studie and travaile of Richard Verstegan,' Antwerp, 1605. Verstegan concludes his relation with the statement: "And this great wonder hapned on the 22 day of July, in the yeare of our Lord one thowsand three hundreth seauentie and six." The brothers Grimm, however, than whom a better authority could not be adduced, say that according to the old records preserved in the town-hall of Hameln the memorable event occurred on the 22nd of June, Anno Domini 1284, and that there was formerly on the wall of the town-hall the following old and oddly-spelt inscription:

> Im Jahr 1284 na Christi gebort
> Tho Hamel worden uthgewort
> Hundert und dreiszig Kinder dasülwest geborn
> Dorch einen Piper under den Köppen verlorn.*

Which means in plain English—

> In the year 1284, after the birth of Christ,
> There were led out of Hameln
> One hundred and thirty children, natives of that place,
> By a Piper, and were lost under the mountain.

The reader will perhaps be surprised at the smallness of

* 'Deutsche Sagen, herausgegeben von den Brüdern Grimm; Berlin, 1816;' vol. I., p. 330.

the number recorded of the children lost. But, Hameln is not a large town, and was most likely even less populous six hundred years ago than it is at the present day.

THE EXQUISITE ORGAN.

The following story is told by the villagers in the Netherlands.

Once upon a time a countryman of the province of Hainault went on some business matters to the village of Flobeck, which lies not far from Krekelberg. When he was crossing the flat and lonely tract of land, some miles south-east of Flobeck, he heard some distant music, which came so sweetly through the air that he thought he would just take a few steps in the direction whence it proceeded to ascertain its origin.

He had not gone far when he saw a beautiful palace, from which the fascinating music evidently issued. This astonished him greatly; but he was not one of those faint-hearted men who would have crossed themselves and taken to their heels. Quite the contrary; he at once determined to investigate the matter a little nearer. And so he entered the palace.

Having ascended the broad staircase leading to the principal rooms, he opened the large door and paced from one hall to another. All were splendidly decorated, and most richly furnished. But, nowhere did he meet with any living being. Soon it became evident to him that the inmates were feasting and dancing in an interior court of the palace. Thither he bent his steps.

To be sure, there they were!—a large assemblage of odd-looking people in high glee dancing to the performance of a musician, who had on his lap an instrument in appearance not unlike a barrel-organ; for it had a long handle which the player turned with all his energy.

Now, when these strange people saw the countryman peeping in, they beckoned him to come forward. He availed himself gladly of the invitation, and took his seat by the side of the musician; for, no music he had ever heard in his life appeared to him comparable to that which the man produced on the admirable instrument with the long handle. Sometimes it was very soft and deep-toned;—suddenly it rose up to a high pitch, like an Æolian harp when a gust of wind passes over its strings;—now it gradually diminished in power, and its sweetness actually moved our countryman to tears;—now, again, it grew suddenly so loud, as if a whole military band was playing, only that it was much more beautiful.

The countryman expressed his admiration in the highest terms, adding that nothing in the world could delight him more than to be permitted to turn the handle of the exquisite organ for a little while. The musician showed himself quite willing to afford him this pleasure, and placed the instrument on his lap.

The delighted countryman turned the handle a few times round:—No sound was forthcoming.—He turned again, more vigorously:—The delicious music began.

"Oh! Ever-blessed Mother Mary! how exquisite!" exclaimed the enraptured countryman.

Scarcely had he said the words when everything vanished, and he found himself sitting in a fallow field, having on his lap a large cat whose tail he had been wrenching so vehemently that poor puss was still mewing from its very heart in most ear-piercing modulations. On the spot where the palace had stood he saw a large dust heap, and that was all.*

* 'Niederländische Sagen, herausgegeben von J. W. Wolf; Leipzig, 1843;' p. 464.

ROYAL MUSICIANS.

A ROYAL personage being a lover of music possesses many advantages for attaining proficiency in this art, which are rarely at the command of a poor musician, however talented he may be. The young prince has from the beginning the best instruction, excellent instruments, and every possible assistance in making progress. The most distinguished musicians consider it an honour to play to him whenever he is disposed to listen to them. If it affords him pleasure to be a composer, whatever he produces, even if it is a large orchestral work, he can directly have performed; and he is thus enabled to ascertain at once whether it sounds exactly as he contemplated in composing it, and whether the peculiar instrumental effects in certain bars, which he had aimed at producing, really answer his expectation. Repeated rehearsals, and revisions of the score, with the ready assistance of the most experienced professional musicians in his service, enable him to improve his composition as long as he likes. And should he be inclined to join the musicians with his instrument in a performance,—to become for a little while, so to say, one of them,—he may be sure that they will do everything to help him through by covering his mistakes and giving him, if possible, the opportunity of displaying his skill.

What can be more delightful for an influential amateur than to join with first-rate professional players in practising the classical Quartets of Haydn, Mozart, and Beethoven! All this, and more, is at the command of the royal musician; and the poor striving disciple of the art may have some excuse for envying him on this account.

However, if the poor disciple is a true artist, he will also duly appreciate the disadvantage under which the royal musician labours for attaining proficiency in the art. He will see how necessary it is for the sake of progress to know exactly the truth about one's own powers and requirements, and that in this respect even a musical beggar enjoys an advantage above the King,—or rather, he has it, whether he enjoys it or not; a candid opinion as to his musical accomplishments is gratuitously offered him, and it is often a just one. If his music is bad, he, instead of being deceived with fine words of flattery, will simply be told: "Leave off! Begone!" If it pleases, he will be rewarded. But the royal musician gets praise, however his music may be; there is no distinction made between good and bad.

No wonder, therefore, that history records but few good royal musicians, although many are known to have occupied themselves with music almost like professional musicians. As an example of an estimable one may be mentioned King David "the sweet singer of Israel," who, as a youth, soothed the evil spirit of Saul by playing upon his *kinnor;* and who later, as King, admonished his people in the psalms: "Praise ye the Lord! Praise him with the sound of the trumpet; praise him with the psaltery and harp. Praise him with the timbrel and dance: praise him with stringed instruments and organs. Praise him upon the loud cymbals. Praise him upon the high-sounding cymbals."

And in his religious fervour he joined his royal band in a procession conveying the ark. On this occasion "David danced before the Lord with all his might." The band consisted of vocal and instrumental performers. "And David was clothed with a robe of fine linen, and all the Levites that bare the ark, and the singers, and Chenaniah, the master of the song with the singers: David also had upon him an ephod of linen. Thus all Israel brought up the ark of the covenant of the Lord with shouting and with sound of the cornet, and with trumpets, and with cymbals, making a noise with psalteries and harps. And it came to pass, as the ark of the covenant of the Lord came to the city of David, that Michal, the daughter of Saul, looking out at a window, saw King David dancing and playing: and she despised him in her heart." (II. Sam. chap. vi., I. Chron. chap. xv.) Michal, Saul's daughter, was David's wife; nevertheless, after the ceremony she upbraided him: "How glorious was the King of Israel to-day, who uncovered himself in the eyes of the handmaids, as one of the vain fellows who shamelessly uncovereth himself!" If the musicians exhibited some vanity, they might, at any rate, be more easily excused than many of the present day; for it was an extraordinary honour for them to perform with a King who was certainly a noble musician, and of whose companionship they could have been proud even if he had not been a King. Moreover, he was, as is recorded in the Bible, not only "cunning in playing," but also "a mighty and valiant man, and a man of war, and prudent in matters, and a comely person, and the Lord was with him." There are not many royal musicians of whom thus much could be said without flattery.

The German common saying—

> Wo man singt da lass dich ruhig nieder,
> Böse Menschen haben keine Lieder;

is as untenable as Shakespeare's assertion—

> The man that has no music in himself,
> Nor is not mov'd with concord of sweet sounds,
> Is fit for treasons, stratagems and spoils;

considering that the Italian banditti sing hymns to the Virgin Mary, and that there are kind-hearted Englishmen who cannot distinguish between the airs of 'God save the Queen' and the 'Old Hundredth.' Anyhow, it may be doubted whether certain distinguished royal musicians had really music in their soul. Take, for instance, the Emperor Nero, who lived about the middle of the first century of our era. Some statements transmitted to us, respecting the depravity of this cruel monarch may be unfounded,—such as that the large conflagration of Rome, which occurred in his reign, was the work of incendiaries secretly hired by him, and that he amused himself with looking at the fire from the top of a high tower, and singing to the accompaniment of the lyre the destruction of Troy, of which he had read, and which he desired to see represented in the spectacle before him. Some say that he played on the bagpipe. His principal instruments, on which he practised assiduously, were the lyre and the harp. His voice was weak and hoarse; nevertheless, in contesting with the best singers of his time, he always, of course, gained the prize. Foreign musicians streamed to Rome to hear him, and to flatter him. About five thousand of them were successful in so far as they obtained appointments in his service with high salaries. He undertook a professional tour through Greece, to perform in public; and as those of his audience who did not applaud him ran the risk of losing their life, a brilliant success could not fail to be constantly the result of his appearance as a musician. The surest means of obtaining his favour was to praise his voice, to be enraptured by his singing, and distressed when he took the whim that he could not sing. It gratified him to be pressingly implored to sing. In short, he did not appreciate music for the sake of its beauties, but because it appeared to him a suitable means for flattering his excessive vanity.

Such miserable royal musicians would at the present day, fortunately, not be tolerated. But a rather harmless vanity like that shown in the following example is still not uncommon, and may easily be excused, as it is not incompatible with a good heart.

Joseph Clemens Cajetan, Elector and Archbishop of Cologne, sent in the year 1720, the following letter to the Jesuit Seminary in Munich. It is here translated from the German.

"Bonn, July 28th, 1720.

Dear Privy Councillor Rauch!

It may perhaps appear presumptuous that an Ignoramus, who knows nothing at all about music, ventures to compose. This applies to me, as I send you herewith eleven Motetts and other pieces, which I have composed myself. I have achieved this in a strange way, since I am not acquainted with the notes; nor have I the slightest understanding respecting the art of music. I am, therefore, compelled, when anything musical enters my head, to sing it to a musical composer, and he commits it to paper. However, I must have a good ear and good taste, because the public, when they hear my music, always applaud it. The method which I have prescribed to myself in composing is that of the bees, which extract the honey from the most beautiful flowers, and mix it together. Thus also I. Everything I have composed I have taken from only good masters whose works pleased me. I candidly confess my theft, while others deny theirs, as they want to appropriate whatever they have taken from others. No one, therefore, dares to be vexed if he hears old airs in my compositions; for, as they are beautiful, their antiquity cannot detract from their value. I have determined to present this work to the church Sti. Michaelis Archangeli, with the P. P. Societatis Jesu, wherein my grandparents founded a Seminarium Musicale; and I desire that this memorial of myself shall be preserved there for eternity, especially for the reason that I have composed most of this music in the time of my persecution. The causes which induced me to compose the several pieces I herewith add, thus:—

No. 1. Adjutorium nostrum in nomine Domini;—I made when I had to suffer the greatest persecution, anno 1706.

No. 2. Ne nobis Domine;—on account of obtained victories.

No. 3. Tempus est;—on leaving the two towns, Rüssel and Valencien, in gratitude for the many kindnesses which I and my kindred received from the inhabitants of those towns.

No. 4. Victoria;—after the battle of Belgrade against the Turks, in 1717.

No. 5. Per hoc vitæ spatium;—when I was debating with myself what pursuit I should follow, whether I should become spiritual or remain secular.

No. 6. Quare fremuerunt gentes;—for my own consolation at a time when I was unjustly persecuted to the utmost.

No. 7. Quem vidistis Pastores;—for Christmas.

No. 8. Parce Domine!—at Lent.

No. 9. Maria Mater gratiæ;—to the honour of the ever-blessed Mother of God.

No. 10. When my brother-in-law, the Dauphin, died, anno 1711.

No. 11. On the death of the nephew of the Dauphin and his consort, in 1712; which composition I request the Seminary to have sung also for me after my death.

I therefore desire you herewith to deliver the compositions, with this letter by my own hand, in my name, to the P. Magister Chori, and at the same time to assure him and the whole Seminary of my clemency. I attribute all this to Divine Grace which has enlightened me to accomplish thus much. I also assure you of my clemency.

JOSEPH CLEMENS."

For this present from the Elector, the Inspector of the Seminary in Munich, the Jesuit Gregorius Schilger, thanked him in a letter written in Latin, of which the following is a literal translation:—

"Most Exalted and Serene Prince and Elector! Most Gracious Lord and Master!

With most humble reverence, I kiss your gracious hand and your most valuable gift of your musical compositions, which to the great joy and with feelings of gratitude of us all, were handed to me, with your gracious letter, by your Serene Highness' Privy Councillor, Joannes Rauch. For, is it not a great blessing, not only to the Gregorian Institution of the Munich Seminary, but also to those on whom devolves the direction and management of it, that you so graciously remember them, and present them with a musical treasure so precious!

We, therefore, throw ourselves at the feet of your Serene Highness, and before the Archipiscopal Pastoral Staff, and express as well as it is in our power our most dutiful thanks, with every devotion and reverence, as we are in duty bound to your sovereign clemency for ever.

This memorial of your highest favour shall be permanently preserved in the archives of the Elector's church at Munich, to the everlasting glory of God, to the honour of the Holy Virgin and of the Holy Archangel Michael, and in memory of your gracious condescension.

Moreover, we admire the very great merit of the music of your Serene Highness not only on account of the high position of its composer, but also on account of its very pleasing artistic effect, which has astonished every one, when the music had been carefully examined by all the Gregorian musicians we summoned to try it. We all—not only I, who consider myself the most insignificant, but also the Gregorian disciples—we all pray in deep humility that the kindly blessings of Heaven may for many years support your Serene Highness in your beneficent functions, for the advantage of the Church, and for the consolation of all good people, especially also for the benefit of your dependants, of whom the Gregorian disciples delight in being the most humble. Permit me to recommend especially these, together with myself, your most humble servant, in our deepest reverence, to your most gracious favour and benevolence. We thus continually pray with bended knees, venturing to hope with the most implicit confidence that Heaven's blessing will result to us from the Archipiscopal Mitre and Pastoral Staff, which we humbly reverence with our kisses.

Your Serene Highness'
Most humble Servant,
GREGORIUS SCHILGER, Soc. Jesu,
Inspector of the St. Gregorian House.

Munich, August 7th, 1720."

There are some touching instances on record of royal personages in affliction finding relief and consolation in studying music. The last King of Hanover had the misfortune of being nearly deprived of his eyesight some time before he came to the throne. As Crown Prince he published a pamphlet entitled 'Ideas and Reflections on the Properties of Music,' from which a few short extracts may find a place here, as they show how soothing a balm this art was to him:—

"From early youth I have striven to make music my own. It has become to me a companion and comforter through life; it has become more and more valuable to me the more I learnt to comprehend and appreciate its boundless exuberance of ideas, its inexhaustible fulness, the more intimately its whole poetry was interwoven with my whole being. . . . . By means of music, ideas, feelings, and historical events, natural phenomena, pictures, scenes of life of all sorts, are as clearly and intelligibly expressed as by any language in words; and we are ourselves enabled to express ourselves in such a manner and to make ourselves understood by others. . . . . Of all the senses of man, sight and hearing are those by which most effect is produced upon mind and heart, and which are consequently the most powerful springs for the moral and rational feelings, actions, and opinions of men. But Hearing appears to be the most influential and operative of the two organs; for this reason, that by inharmonious discordant tones our feelings may be so shocked, even to their deepest recesses, and so painfully wounded as to drive us almost beside ourselves; which impression cannot possibly be produced in us by a bad picture, a dreary landscape, or a very faulty poem. . . . . I have known persons whose spirits were broken, and their hearts rent by care, grief, and affliction. They wandered about, murmuring at their fate, absorbed in meditation, in vain seeking hope, in vain looking for a way to escape. But, the excess of their inward pangs needed alleviation; the heart discovered the means of procuring it: the deep-drawn sighs of the oppressed bosom were involuntarily converted into tones of lamentation, and this unconscious effusion was productive of relief, composure, and courageously-calm resignation. Yes, indeed, it is above all in the gloomy hours of affliction that Music is a soothing comforter, a sympathizing friend to the sufferer; it gives expression to the gnawing anguish which rends the soul, and which it thereby mitigates and softens: it lends a tear to the stupefaction of grief; it drops mollifying healing balsam into every wounded heart. Whoever has experienced this effect himself, or witnessed it in others, will admit with me that for this fairest service rendered by the art we cannot sufficiently thank and revere it."

How sad and suggestive are these lines, penned by a royal musician!

Blind people delight in descriptive music depicting scenes which painters might use as subjects for pictures. By the help of a lively imagination, the ear to some extent serves also the purpose of the eye. Thus may be explained the preference given by the Crown Prince to certain compositions which are by no means of the highest class. Speaking of Bellini's opera 'Norma,' he remarks: "In the Introduction there is a most ingenious representation of a country. Commencing with low tones, it unfolds itself in sombre harmony, and faithfully reproduces the same impression that the darkness of the thick wood makes upon the wanderer. Single, sliding, and abrupt notes seem to denote lighter spots in the dark wood, and thus the first decoration of the opera, the grove of sacrifice, is appropriately represented. The reader will certainly be still more struck by the appositeness of this musical picture, when I assure him that I know a blind person who, when he first heard this introduction, immediately guessed that it was intended to represent a scene in a wood."

Beethoven's Pastoral Symphony is, as might be expected, an especial favourite with him, and he gives a detailed description of its several movements, prefaced by the exclamation: "How clearly are the daily occurrences and the individual scenes of rural life presented to the hearer!"

Neither is it surprising that Haydn's 'Creation,' with its many descriptive passages, should forcibly and very agreeably appeal to his imagination. In commenting upon certain beauties in this oratorio, which he especially admires, he remarks: "Above all, how strikingly has the composer represented with all the powers of music the moment called forth by the creative words 'Let there be light!' *and there was light.* At these words the orchestra discharges itself in a truly electric manner, so as absolutely to dazzle you. The hearer feels perfectly the impression which the real occurrence of this adorable miracle of Almighty power would make upon him; and in this delineation by tones is exhibited to the sense of mortal man the only possible representation of that sublime wonder in the most striking and convincing manner."

It not unfrequently happens to a musical composer that when a new idea occurs to him while he is extemporizing, it appears to him at the first moment more beautiful than he finds it to be on reconsideration. The Prince, who enjoyed extemporizing on the pianoforte, kept in his service a pianist, whose business it was to write down his inventions, which he played repeatedly to the pianist to enable him to sketch at once as faithfully as possible the chief ideas and modulations. These sketches the pianist, who was a talented musician, had to take home in order to work them out carefully according to the rules of musical composition. Having accomplished his task, he attended at the palace with the manuscript; and now it was his turn to play the new piece to his royal master. But, however anxious he had been to preserve intact the original ideas, he generally learnt to his concern that the music possessed no longer those beauties which had been dictated to him.

Royal musicians who have studied Thorough Bass are sometimes formidable critics. At any rate, it would appear so from some musical criticisms of Frederick II., and of his sister the Princess Amalia. Frederick II. (Frederick the Great) King of Prussia (born 1712, died 1786) was a composer as well as a virtuoso on the flute. He regularly practised his instrument daily. In earlier life it was his habit to play the scales every morning as soon as he had risen from his bed; and he often performed in the evening five concertos on the flute, which his royal orchestra had to accompany. In composing he wrote down only the melody, and he indicated with it in words how the bass and the other parts should be contrived; for instance,—"Here the bass shall be in Quavers;"—"Here the violins shall play alone," etc. These directions he gave to his Kapellmeister Agricola, who then completed the score.

The musical pursuits of Frederick II. are interesting, but are too well known to be here circumstantially recorded. Suffice it to mention his singular behaviour on the occasion of the performance of Graun's 'Te Deum,' after the termination of the Seven Years' War, in 1763. The orchestra and singers who had assembled in the royal palace at Charlottenburg punctually at the time at which they had been ordered to appear, found to their surprise that there was no audience assembling. After having waited for about half an hour in suspense, wondering whether the performance of the 'Te Deum' was to take place, or whether they had been summoned by inadvertence, they observed a side door being opened at the end of the hall opposite to them, through which the King entered quite alone, without any attendance. He sat down on a chair in a corner, and made a sign to them to commence. At some of the full choruses, when all the voices united, he held his hands before his eyes to hide his tears. Several of the musicians who saw him became so much affected that the tears rolled down their cheeks while they played. At the end of the performance the King thanked them by a slight inclination of his head, and retired through the side door through which he had entered.

This noble royal musician was, however, so prepossessed by the compositions of Graun, that hardly any composer, but such as wrote in Graun's style, had a chance of finding favour with him. Kirnberger, the celebrated theorist, in vain endeavoured to insinuate himself with the King by submitting to "His Majesty's approval" a new treatise of his on Thorough Bass. The treatise was soon returned to him with the following letter:—

"His Royal Majesty of Prussia, etc., our most gracious Lord, cannot persuade himself that the announced work of the Princely Chamber-musician Kirnberger, in Berlin, contains anything new, or particularly useful for the art of music, or for musical composition, considering that Thorough Bass was already brought to a certain perfection many years ago. This is, therefore, not to be withheld from the said Kirnberger, in reply to his solicitation of the day before yesterday.

FRIEDERICH.

Potsdam, February 25th, 1781."

The Princess Amalia, a pupil of Kirnberger, was a great upholder of the rules of Thorough Bass, and a sharp critic. As Gluck did not care much about many of those dry rules, it is perhaps not surprising that the Princess Amalia did not care much about Gluck. What she thought of him she has expressed forcibly enough in the following extract from a letter to Kirnberger, who had sent her the opera 'Iphigenia in Tauris:'—

"Mr. Gluck will, in my opinion, never pass for a clever man in musical composition. He has, firstly, not the least invention; secondly, a bad, miserable melody; and thirdly, no accent, no expression,—it is all alike. He is very different from Graun and Hasse, but very similar to . . . The introductory piece ought to be a kind of overture; but the good man does not like Imitations, and he is right, for they require labour. However, he is more fond of Transposition. This is not altogether objectionable; for, if a bar is often repeated, the hearer will all the more easily remember it; but Gluck appears to transpose the same idea from want of a new one. Finally, regarded in its entirety, the opera is very miserable. Now, this is in the new taste which has a great many adherents. However, I thank you for having sent it me. Through the faults of others one learns to know one's own. Be so kind as to procure for me the words of the whole opera; but, as regards the musical notation, I am not yet wise enough to find it beautiful."

If the letters of musicians to princes are often sadly devoid of sincerity, those of princes to musicians possess generally at least the negative merit of not containing intentional misrepresentations, since a prince has seldom a motive for disguising his likes and dislikes in music. Whether the estimable Kapellmeister Schulz had committed the indiscretion of suggesting to Princess Amalia that she was still capable of some improvement as a musical composer is uncertain, but appears probable, to judge from the following letter which she wrote to him after he had sent her the manuscript of his choruses to 'Athalia,' with the humble request for permission to dedicate them to her,—or, as he expressed himself, "to preface the work with the adorable name of so illustrious a connoisseur."

The reply he received from her is here translated from the German as literally as possible.

"To the Kapellmeister Schulz in Rheimsberg.

I surmise, Mr. Schulz, that by an oversight you have sent me, instead of your own work, the musical bungling of a child, since I cannot discover in it the least scientific art; on the contrary, it is throughout faulty from beginning to end, in the expression, sentiment, and meaning of the language as well as in the rhythm. The *motus contrarius* has been entirely neglected; there is no proper harmony; no impressive melody; the interval of the Third is often entirely omitted; the key is never clearly indicated, so that one has to guess in what key the music is meant to move. There are no canonic imitations, not the least trace of counterpoint, but plenty of consecutive fifths and octaves! And this is to be called music! May heaven open the eyes of those who possess such a high conceit of themselves, and enlighten their understanding to make them comprehend that they are but bunglers and fumblers. I have heard it said that the work ought to praise the master; now-a-day everything is reversed and confused, the masters are the only ones who praise themselves, even if their works are offensive. Enough of this.

AMALIA.

Berlin, January 31st, 1785."

The amiable and respected Kapellmeister Schulz, in mentioning to an old friend the contents of this letter, merely added: "All this may be true; but why tell it me so rudely?" *

No doubt the most praiseworthy royal musicians are those who make it less their object to be accomplished players, composers, or theorists, than to discover and to assist really talented professional musicians, and thus to promote the advancement of the art. Prince Louis Ferdinand of Prussia, who lost his life in the battle of Saalfeld in 1806, at the age of 34 years, may be noticed as a remarkable exception. He was a distinguished pianist; a fine composer,—perhaps the best of all the royal musicians whose compositions have been published or are otherwise known; and a true patron of the art,—which he showed by his cultivation of classical music as well as by his kindness to Beethoven, Dussek, Spohr, and other eminent composers. This is the prince of whom it is told that Beethoven, on hearing him play, exclaimed with surprise: "Your Royal Highness does not play like a Prince; you play like a musician!"

As a true patron of music, who in this capacity has been more useful to the art than if he had composed operas and symphonies, must be mentioned Rudolph, Archduke of Austria, the pupil of Beethoven. The subjoined letter by him, translated from the German, speaks for itself:—

"Dear Beethoven,

I shall return to Vienna as early as Tuesday, August 5th, and I shall then remain in town for several days. I only wish that your health may permit you to come then to town. In the afternoon, from four to seven o'clock, I am generally at home.

My brother-in-law, Prince Anton, has written to me already that the King of Saxony expects your beautiful Mass.

---

* 'Tonkünstler-Lexicon Berlin's, von C. Freiherrn von Ledebur;' Berlin, 1861; p. 6.

Respecting D——r, I have spoken with our gracious Monarch, and likewise with Count Dietrichstein. I do not know whether this recommendation will be of use, as there is to be a competition for the appointment in question, in which any one wishing to obtain it, has to prove his fitness. It would be a gratification to me if I could be useful to that clever man, whom I heard with pleasure playing the organ last Monday in Baden,—especially as I am convinced that you would not recommend an unworthy person.

I hope you have written down your Canon, and I pray you, in case it might be injurious to your health to come to town, not to exert yourself too soon out of attachment to me.

Your well-wishing

RUDOLPH. *

Vienna, July 31st, 1823."

No doubt, there have been in olden time kings who, as history records, possessed as much skill in music as their best bards or minstrels. If Alfred the Great could enter and explore the Danish camp under the disguise of a harper, his harp-playing must have been in the genuine professional manner of his time, otherwise it would have revealed to the Danish lovers of music that he was not what he pretended to be.

To become an eminent musician, one requires, besides an extraordinary talent, much time, freedom from disturbance, and perseverance,—conditions which are seldom at the command of royal personages. The middle classes are in this respect the most favoured,—as they are, in fact, in all intellectual pursuits. When King Solomon says: "Give me neither poverty nor riches," (Proverbs, Chap. XXX. v. 8), he speaks rather as a musician, or poet. A king requires riches as necessarily as a musician requires talent.

---

* 'Biographie von Ludwig van Beethoven, verfasst von A. Schindler;' Münster, 1845; p. 141.

COMPOSERS AND PRACTICAL MEN.

It is sad to think how some of our distinguished musical composers have had to struggle with poverty, when with a proper attention to business matters they might easily have been men of independent means. True, to be what is called a practical man requires a talent very different from that required by an artist; and an inferior artist may be,—nay, often is a far more practical man than a superior artist. But a superior artist is not necessarily devoid of the qualifications which constitute a clever man of business. To maintain that a highly gifted musical composer must needs be deficient in common sense as regards money transactions would be as unwarrantable as to assert that a musician who understands how to use the art as a milch-cow must necessarily be a bad musician. His love for the art, and his desire to achieve something great, not unfrequently animates the true artist to disregard, or even to sacrifice for its sake, his property, health, and other advantages which the practical man regards as the real happiness of life.

Whatever the composer produces less as a labour of love than for gain, by command, according to a plan prescribed to him, and under similar circumstances, is generally not the best he is capable of accomplishing. An artist must be allowed to create unfettered the work with which he feels the greatest inclination to occupy himself. But, if he possesses no property, he may starve before his work is finished. There are some painful instances on record of starving musical composers, who, with their admirable talents, might have saved themselves and others much trouble, if only they had thought it worth their while to be a little more practical.

Composers generally receive their worst pay for their best works. Their best works are generally those which made them celebrated; and when they have become celebrated, they are often well paid for insignificant or mediocre productions.

Composers sometimes appear to be much more unpractical than they really are. This may, for instance, easily be the case with those who strike out a new path in the art, or who aim at a reform, the disirableness of which seems questionable to all but themselves. However, occasionally it happens that an innovation, which is at first unpopular, comes by some unexpected cause rather suddenly in vogue, or at least finds many advocates; and in this case the originator of the innovation, who was regarded as an unpractical man, may attain the reputation of being of a remarkably practical turn of mind. When Richard Wagner, about thirty years ago, as a poor and obscure musician in Paris, was arranging operatic melodies for the cornet-à-piston to save himself from starvation, his notions about the opera of the future appeared to those few musicians to whom he communicated them, as a dream which to realize would be as impossible as it would be undesirable. At the present day he has many estimable musicians among his ardent admirers; he is honoured by kings, leads the life of a prince, and probably there are but few persons who would deny that he deserves to be called a practical man.

Several of our classical composers have shown that they could be shrewd men of business at periods when the pressure of want, or the desire for independence, urgently incited them to acquire property. Beethoven on one or two occasions formed the resolution of making it his special object to accumulate a sum of money, the possession of which would enable him to compose without regard to publishers and mercantile speculations. But the endeavour to carry out this resolution seems to have been generally of but short duration. In the year 1821, the music-seller Tobias Haslinger, in Vienna, compiled a tariff in which he enumerated the different kinds of compositions with the prices he was willing to pay for them, if Beethoven by signing the tariff would bind himself to give all his new compositions to Haslinger for publication. This tariff is so interesting that it shall be inserted here, although Beethoven, who at first expected from it a golden future, was soon dissuaded by his friends from entering into any contract of the kind.

INSTRUMENTAL MUSIC.

Symphony for full Orchestra - -	60 - 80	ducats.
Overture for full Orchestra - -	20 - 30	,,
Concerto for Violin with Orchestral accompaniment - - - - -	50	,,
Octett for different instruments - -	60	,,
Septett, ditto - - - - -	60	,,
Sextett, ditto - - - - -	60	,,
Quintett for 2 Violins, 2 Tenors, and Violoncello - - - - - -	50	,,
Quartett for 2 Violins, 2 Tenors, and Violoncello - - - - -	40	,,
Trio for Violin, Tenor and Violoncello -	40	,,

FOR PIANOFORTE.

Concerto for Pianoforte with Orchestral accompaniment - - - - -	60	,,
Fantasia, ditto - - - - -	30	,,
Rondo, ditto - - - - -	30	,,
Variations, ditto - - - - -	30	,,
Octett for Pianoforte with accompaniment of other instruments - - - -	50	,,
Septett, ditto - - - - -	50	,,
Quintett, ditto - - - - -	60	,,
Quartett, ditto - - - - -	70	,,
Trio for Pianoforte, Violin, and Violoncello	50	,,
Duett for Pianoforte and Violin - -	40	,,
Duett for Pianoforte and Violoncello -	40	,,
Duett for Pianoforte *à quatre mains* -	60	,,
Grand Sonata for Pianoforte alone -	40	,,
Sonata for Pianoforte alone - - -	30	,,

Fantasia for Pianoforte - - -	30 ducats.
Rondo for Pianoforte - - - - -	15 ,,
Variations for Pianoforte with accompaniment - - - - - -	10 - 20 ,,
Variations for Pianoforte alone -	10 - 20 ,,
Six Fugues for Pianoforte alone -	30 - 40 ,,
Pieces, such as Divertimenti, Airs, Preludes, Potpourris, Bagatelles, Adagios, Andantes, Toccatas, Caprices, etc., for Pianoforte alone, each -	10 - 15 ,,

VOCAL MUSIC.

Grand Mass - - - - - - -	130 ,,
Smaller Mass - - - - - - -	100 ,,
Grand Oratorio - - - - - -	300 ,,
Smaller Oratorio - - - - - -	200 ,,
Graduale - - - - - - -	20 ,,
Offertorium - - - - - - -	20 ,,
Te Deum Laudamus - - - - -	50 ,,
Requiem - - - - - - -	120 ,,
Vocal pieces with Orchestral accompaniment	20 ,,
An Opera Seria - - - - - -	300 ,,
Six large Songs with Pianoforte accompaniment - - - - - - -	20 ,,
Six smaller Songs, ditto - - - - -	12 ,,
A Ballad - - - - - - -	15 ,,*

It must be borne in mind that these terms were offered to Beethoven at the period of his life when he had already published his first eight symphonies and almost all his famous pianoforte sonatas, and other works, up to Op. 109, and when he therefore was in the zenith of his reputation in the eyes of the daily increasing number of lovers of music who were able to understand his genius. In fact, he afterwards received higher prices; for instance, the publisher Schott, in Mayence, paid him, in 1825, for the second Mass

* 'Biographie von Ludwig van Beethoven, verfasst von A. Schindler;' Münster, 1845; p. 246.

(D major) 1000 florins; for the ninth Symphony, 600 florins; for the Quartett Op. 127, fifty ducats; and for the Quartett Op. 131, eighty ducats. He was still better remunerated, on a certain occasion, by the publisher Diabelli, in Vienna, who having composed a Waltz for the pianoforte, wished Beethoven to write six or seven variations upon it, for which he offered to give him eighty ducats. Well, Beethoven sat down to compose seven variations. But, the longer he wrote, the more new ideas occurred to him, and the seven variations soon increased to ten, then to twenty, then to twenty-five. When Diabelli learnt that Beethoven had written twenty-five variations and was still continuing to add to their number, he became rather alarmed lest the work should grow too voluminous for practical use. However, he did not succeed in stopping the composer until after the thirty-third variation. The entire set was published by Diabelli in 1823, under the title '33 Veränderungen über einen Walzer von A. Diabelli, von Ludwig van Beethoven, Op. 120.'

What must one think of Beethoven's knowledge of money matters when in a letter to a friend, in which he laments his reduced circumstances, he asks for advice how he can obtain "money for a bank-note;" while all he has to do is to cut off from his bond a coupon, and to have it cashed by the nearest money-changer.* Beethoven, owing to his unpractical habits, required much money, although he lived but frugally. For instance, it happened that he had to pay rent for three or four residences at a time, because he had neglected to give warning at the old residence when he hired a new one. Fortunately for him, some of his admirers among men of position and wealth interested themselves about his personal comfort. In an honourable and delicate way they ensured him an annual income in addition to the gains accruing to him by the sale of his works. The result was that he actually left some money at his death. He died (to use an English expression) worth one thousand pounds.

---

* 'Biographische Notizen über L. van Beethoven, von Wegeler und Ries;' Coblenz, 1838; p. 34.

If the correspondence of some of our most celebrated composers with their publishers were made known, we should probably find therein unvarnished statements which would surprise us, inasmuch as they would reveal disappointments which it is now difficult to reconcile with the celebrity of those composers. The obstacles which some of our classical composers have encountered in getting their works printed are very remarkable. J. S. Bach himself engraved on copper-plates his esteemed work 'The Art of Fugue;' only thirty copies were struck off, as sufficient to supply the demand; and, after the death of the old master, his exceedingly practical son, Emanuel, offered the plates for sale at the value of the copper plates.* It is painful to reflect that some composers who lived in straitened circumstances obtained little or nothing for certain of their works which have enriched their publishers. Franz Schubert had to struggle for his daily bread. When the 'Erl-King' was sung by his friend Vogl for the first time in public, at a concert in Vienna in the year 1821, it produced sensation, while other compositions by Schubert which were performed on the same occasion, met with a cool reception. Schubert published the 'Erl-King' at his own expense, with the assistance of some friends. But, as his needy circumstances soon compelled him to sell the copyright of this song, which was then but little known, his gain was very small, even if compared with the profits which some arrangers have derived from transcribing the song for the pianoforte. Although the conditions which he proposed to the publishers were always modest, they were generally rejected as being exorbitant. How cautiously the publishers treated him, may be seen from a letter which Peters, in Leipzig, wrote to Hüttenbrenner, a friend of Schubert. As this letter is also interesting inasmuch as it affords a glance into the speculations of a practical man who makes the art his business, it deserves a place here, although it is rather long. The translation, which is from the German, is as literal as possible :—

* 'Historisch-Kritische Beiträge zur Aufnahme der Musik, von F. W. Marpurg.' Vol. II., Berlin, 1756; p. 575.

"Having been extremely busy since I received your letter of the 18th of October, I trust you will excuse the tardiness of my reply.

"I am very much obliged to you for your communication respecting Herr Schubert. Several of his vocal compositions are favourably known to me, and give me confidence in your recommendation of this artist. It will be a great pleasure to me to assist in a wider diffusion of the works of this composer than the Vienna music-sellers are capable of effecting. But, before I enter into any obligation, allow me to give you a little sketch of my business arrangements.

"At the moment when I commenced my present business I resolved to distinguish myself advantageously as a publisher, never to print anything bad, but rather as much as possible to print only the best. It is impracticable to carry out this plan thoroughly; for I cannot obtain from the most distinguished artists alone as many manuscripts as I require. Besides, we publishers are also often compelled from policy to print many things which I at least would otherwise not print. Nay, we must publish even many slight works in order to provide for a certain public; for, if we confined ourselves to classical works only, we should have a very limited sphere of business; since, as is well known, the connoisseurs do not constitute the majority. Nevertheless, I have not been influenced by desire for gain to patronize the more lucrative but trashy fashionable trifles; I have always taken care that also the works for the great majority of the people should never be bad. Always keeping my favourite aim in view, I have chiefly striven to issue superior works; and this my endeavour will in future become more and more apparent, since every year increases the number of my valuable connections, which my financial resources permit me to maintain.

"These observations lead me to mention two obstacles which often frustrate my plan. The first is want of time, which almost continually curbs me. In order to obtain as many good works as possible, I must seek after connections with good artists, and I must strengthen these connections not only by endeavouring to satisfy the artists, but also by proving myself a publisher always ready at their service,—a mutual understanding which is convenient to both parties. My connection with most of those of my authors who are valuable to me,—as for instance, Spohr, Romberg, Hummel, etc.,—has grown into a friendly relation. I am, therefore, doubly compelled to accept all that such friends and good artists send me, although there is often much among it of which I know at once that I shall gain nothing by it. These obligations take up much of my time, not only because those artists give me constant occupation, but also because I require leisure for examining such works of other authors as I receive unexpectedly, as is the case with the present ones. Thus, the time remaining to me is seldom sufficient to enable me to undertake the publication of more works than I have in hand; and I am continually prevented forming new connections with composers from want of time.

"The second obstacle which renders a new connection difficult, and which proceeds from the facts above stated, is the novelty, and the name of a young composer unknown in my sphere of business. Very often I am reproached with not making known the works of new composers, and that a new composer cannot become known if the publishers do not undertake the publication of his works. This reproach is, however, quite undeserved as far as I am concerned; for I cannot do everything, and must keep to a fixed plan in order to succeed. My plan is to obtain the works of artists who are already celebrated. True, I print many other works besides; but if I can obtain enough of those, I must leave to other publishers the introduction to the public of new composers. These publishers are also able to do something, and many are glad to engage new composers, because they fear to pay the sums demanded by older and more valuable artists. But as soon as the new composer has obtained a name, and his works are known as being good, then I am his man; and then the publication of his works accords with my plan, which is calculated more with regard to honour than to gain. I will then rather pay a high price for his works than procure them in the beginning on low terms.

"You see, therefore, that it is difficult for me to meet at once your proposal respecting Herr Schubert, especially as my time is so much taken up. However, my opinion of him makes me reluctant to disregard altogether the wish of this young artist. As a middle course, I would, therefore, propose that Herr Schubert should send me some of his works which he desires to have printed, so that I may examine them; for, without having previously seen the manuscript, I accept nothing from a young composer who is but little known. If a great and well-known artist produces something bad, the blame falls upon him, because his name is my guarantee; but if I bring out something by a new artist which is not liked, the blame falls upon me; for, who compels me to print a composition of the merit of which I am not convinced? Here the name of the composer is no protection to me. Herr Schubert may be sure that in trusting his manuscripts to me, he places them in safe hands; there will be no misuse made of them. In case that I find them satisfactory, I shall retain of them as many as I find convenient; on the other hand, Herr Schubert must not feel hurt if I do not like one or other piece. I shall be quite candid, for candour is the surest way to lead to a right understanding.

"Furthermore, I must beg him to forward to me only his most successful works. True, he will not think of publishing anything which he does not consider a successful production. Be this as it may, a composer is always more successful with one work than with another; and I must have the best. I say I must have the best; not for the sake of gain, but for the sake of my reputation, when I introduce a composer to my public, which is very extensive. I have been very painstaking to make my establishment as complete as possible, and I now experience from many quarters the recompense that my firm enjoys in an extraordinary degree the confidence of others. People expect from me the publication of many good works; and if I bring out a new author, they soon give him their confidence, believing that he must be good because I had taken notice of him. No doubt, there have been mistakes; but I am becoming more and more cautious, in order that I may always ensure and strengthen my reputation, which to acquire I have taken so much trouble. For this reason I insist upon a new author giving me his best, in order that I may recommend him properly from the beginning, my recommendation being justified. Besides, the first impression often opens the road to the whole future; wherefore, to composers just beginning, the good advice to proceed with the publication of their works as cautiously as possible, cannot be too often repeated. They may venture much, but should have only little printed until their reputation is established.

"Spohr has hitherto brought out only 58 works; Andreas Romberg, 66; Bernhard Romberg, 38; while now many other artists who are much younger have already had printed above a hundred. Those well-known composers have written much more, which, however, they thought advisable to withhold from publication. If, by way of contradiction, you point out to me the fertile, and nevertheless valuable Mozart, Haydn, Beethoven, etc., I declare that such men are rare masters whom we ought certainly to regard as models, but that experience must first teach us whether the young aspirant is similarly gifted. Moreover, many of the earlier compositions of Mozart have never been printed.

"Now, have the kindness to confer with Herr Schubert upon my communication to you, and decide what is further to be done. As regards the terms, I beg you to inform me of them, because it is disagreeable to my feelings to make an offer for an intellectual production. Most likely there will not be any difficulty about settling the conditions. The perseverance with which my authors stick to me, sufficiently shows that they do well with me; this I can assert of myself to my own praise. Besides, the conditions of a young artist cannot be so high that they could not easily be conceded to. I believe that, as you intimate, of a new work by Herr Schubert, perhaps 300 copies might be sold in Vienna alone. But then it must be printed in Vienna. I do not think that I should sell there 100 copies, although I am in connection with all the music-sellers of that town. You will understand this quite well, and I need not explain the cause, but you may believe me that it is so; experience confirms it, and the exceptions are rare indeed.

I remain, with high esteem, etc.,

B. V. PETERS.

Leipzig, November 14th, 1822."

"Should Herr Schubert send me vocal compositions, I should prefer songs, each with a name, like Beethoven's 'Adelaide,' or others of the kind. There are so many songs now published that no sufficient attention is given to them if they have no names."*

During the years 1826-28, Schubert had still trouble in getting his compositions printed. This is evident from the tone of the replies to his solicitations as well as from the conditions demanded by the publishers. Probst, in Leipzig, in a letter to Schubert, dated August 26th, 1826, remarks:—"It was, no doubt, an honour to me, which I appreciate, to make your acquaintance through your letter of the 12th instant; and thanking you heartily for your confidence in me, I am quite willing to contribute, as far as lies in my power, to the spread of your reputation as an artist. I must, however, candidly confess that the peculiar direction of your intellectual productions, which often shows genius, but which is also sometimes rather strange, is not yet sufficiently and generally understood by our public. I, therefore, pray you to take this kindly into consideration when you send me manuscripts. A selection of songs, and pianoforte compositions for two or four hands, which are not difficult, and which are pleasant and easily comprehensible, would appear to me suitable for attaining your aim and my wish. When the way has been once opened, anything will do; but, in the beginning one must in some measure comply with the public taste," etc.

In another letter to Schubert, by the same publisher, written in 1827, he says: "However much pleasure it

* 'Franz Schubert, von H. Kreiszle von Hellborn;' Wien, 1865, p. 272.

would give me to incorporate your name in my catalogue, I must for the present renounce it, as I am overwhelmed with work owing to the publication of Kalkbrenner's *Œuvres complètes.* I also confess that the honorarium of eighty florins * for each manuscript seems to me rather high terms. I keep the works at your disposal, and remain," etc.

A year later, in 1828, he writes more encouragingly: "I have been sincerely grieved that a difference in our opinions, before my journey to Vienna, frustrated your esteemed application for the publication of your compositions through my firm. . . . . Have, therefore, the kindness when you have completed something which is a success, to send it here—especially songs, ballads, romances, which, without being devoid of originality, are easily comprehensible; also some pianoforte pieces for two performers, written in the same style. . . . . . As regards the honorarium, we shall readily come to an agreement, if you will only treat with me on a moderate scale; and you will find me always in these matters reasonable, provided the works are so that I can be pleased with them. The prices of the Vienna publishers might here fairly serve as a guide. Herr Lähne would pay you your honorarium in proper time punctually. Moreover, I must beg you to examine beforehand carefully the works which you intend me to have, and not to show them first to the Vienna publishers. Such business transactions must remain entirely between ourselves. I give you my solemn word that you shall never repent it if you favour me with your friendly confidence, and if, by selecting only such compositions for me in which you have been successful, you afford me the opportunity of exerting myself for the sake of your reputation."

Breitkopf and Härtel, the famous publishers in Leipzig, in a letter to Schubert, dated September 7th, 1826, cautiously suggest: "We reply with grateful thanks to your kind intention of sending us some compositions for

---

* £8.

publication, and we assure you that it would give us much pleasure to enter into a mutually advantageous business relation with you. But as we are yet quite unacquainted with the mercantile result of your compositions, and as we, therefore, cannot meet you by offering you a fixed pecuniary remuneration,—which the publisher can only fix and allow after the success of the work,—we must leave it to you whether you will make an attempt to form a connection with us which may perhaps be durable, and whether in order to facilitate this attempt you will be satisfied with a certain number of copies as remuneration for the first work, or works, which you may send us. We have no doubt that you will agree to the proposal, since with you as well as with us the object is less the publication of a single work, than the introduction to a continued connection. In this case we propose that you should send us first a few pianoforte pieces for one performer or for two. Should our hope of a good result be realized, so that we may be enabled to offer you for the subsequent works a proper remuneration in money, it will be a pleasure to us to render thereby your connection with us agreeable to you.

We remain, with the highest esteem, etc.,

BREITKOPF AND HÄRTEL." *

Somewhat later, when Schubert had become a little better known, he received more favourable replies. Schott, in Mayence, offered to publish several of his works, and to pay for them. In a letter dated April 28th, 1828, Schott, however, declined to accept the trio in E-flat major, which Schubert had mentioned in his list of finished manuscripts: "The trio," Schott remarks, "is probably large; and as we have recently brought out several trios, we must postpone to a later period the publication of compositions of this kind to avoid disadvantages for our business; and the delay would be against your interest." This trio (Op. 100) was afterwards bought by Probst, in Leipzig, for about two

* 'Franz Schubert, von H. Kreiszle von Hellborn;' Wien, 1865; p. 388.

pounds, paid with a grumble, and with the insulting remark: "In any case, I hope the Trio in question is not the 'Fantasia' which was performed on the 5th of February in Herr Slawick's concert at the Kärnthnerthor theatre; for that composition was unfavourably criticized in the Leipzig Musical Gazette, No. XIV., page 223."

Again, in a letter from Schott, dated October 30th, 1828, and received by Schubert about three weeks before his death, he is told among other business matters: "We shall soon print your Quintett; * but we must remark that the price put on this little work is too high. The pianoforte part takes up only six printed pages, and we surmise it to be by an oversight that we are asked to pay sixty florins † for it. We offer you thirty florins for it. . . . The pianoforte piece, Op. 101, certainly would not be too dear for us; but its unsuitableness for our sale in France is very vexatious. Should you compose occasionally something less difficult and yet brilliant, and also in an easy key, this you may send us, if you please, without further communication." ‡

Under these circumstances it is no wonder that after the death of Schubert there should have been some difficulty in defraying the expenses of his burial, which amounted to about seven pounds; while his effects, consisting of his dress, a bed, and some old music-books, were together valued at six pounds six shillings.

Mozart's pecuniary circumstances were scarcely more cheerful than Schubert's, considering how highly Mozart was appreciated by many during the last few years of his life. Having in his youth been guided by his prudent father to be careful in the management of his gains and expenses, he always wished to be careful, and sometimes troubled himself much about being practical, but evidently found it very difficult. When the publisher Hofmeister, in Leipzig, said to him: "Mozart, you must make concessions to the

---

* Op. 114. † £6.

‡ 'Franz Schubert, von H. Kreiszle von Hellborn;' Wien, 1865; p. 442.

popular taste, or I cannot buy anything more from you for publication!" Mozart replied: "Well, I must write what I think good, though I should starve." Some music-sellers, in an inexplicable way, succeeded in procuring manuscripts of his, for which they did not pay him anything.* His famous opera, 'Die Zauberflöte,' he wrote with the object of benefiting his friend, the embarrassed theatrical manager Schikaneder; and the statement of some writers, that Mozart gained only fifty thalers (about £7 10s.) by this opera, may therefore be correct. The King of Prussia offered him an appointment as Kapellmeister in Berlin, with a salary of 3,000 thalers. Mozart solicited an audience of his master, the Emperor Joseph II. and asked for his dismission. "Dear Mozart, you will leave me?" said the emperor. "No, your Majesty!" replied Mozart, touched by the hearty tone in which the Emperor spoke to him: "No, your Majesty, I remain!"

A friend, to whom Mozart soon afterwards related this occurrence, said: "But why did you not seize this favourable opportunity to ask for a fixed income?"

Mozart replied: "How could I at that moment think of money matters!"

He subsequently received an annual pay of 800 florins, with the title of Kapellmeister in the service of the Emperor. At his death, he left a debt of 3,000 florins. The copyright of 'La Clemenza di Tito' was offered to Breitkopf, in Leipzig, for sixteen ducats. Breitkopf having declined the opera, it was bought by his apprentice, A. Böhme, who with it laid the foundation of his prosperous publishing-house in Hamburg.

It must be admitted that among our modern composers several very practical men could be pointed out. Some, who are the offspring of rich bankers, may have inherited business-like habits in a natural course; this appears all the more probable since they belong to a race which is known to possess extraordinary talent for money-making.

---

* Biographie W. A. Mozart's, von G. N. von Nissen; Leipzig, 1828, p. 584.

It has long been a favourite project with distinguished musicians on the continent to visit England, to be there extremely practical, in order to accumulate as much money as they could in the shortest time possible, and then to retire to the fatherland to be happy ever after. Possibly the rumour concerning Handel's property, and his bequests, to which also Mattheson alludes in his annotations to the 'Memoirs of the Life of Handel,' * may have contributed to entice other continental musicians to try to make their fortune in England; and many have shown common sense enough in this attempt. Handel in London generally received for the copyright of an oratorio twenty guineas. The wealthy publisher, Walsh, gained £1500 by the publication of the opera 'Rinaldo,' a fact which elicited from Handel the remark: "My dear sir, it is only right that we should be upon an equal footing; *you* shall compose the next opera, and *I* will sell it." At any rate, so the story goes. Handel, after having lost, by his enterprise as manager of the Haymarket Theatre, all the money he had gained during a residence in England of about twenty-four years, which amounted to about £10,000, commenced anew, exerting himself as a practical man in another and more successful way. Handel died "worth" upwards of twenty thousand pounds.

Music-printing in the eighteenth century was not in the flourishing state which it has now attained. The composers had other sources of profit besides the sale of their manuscripts,—such as public performances, dedications of works to wealthy patrons of the art, or by having an appointment, with a fixed salary, in the service of a sovereign. To judge correctly of the capacity for business of a distinguished musician, it is necessary to take into consideration the usages of his time.

Haydn, on his first visit to London, in 1791, was engaged by Salomon for £500, for which sum he had to compose six symphonies, and personally to direct the performance of

* See above, page 23.

them at the concerts; and to resign the copyright of those six symphonies. Furthermore, £200 were guaranteed to him by Salomon for a benefit concert.

That Rossini could be practical in England, is evident from the following conversation of this composer with F. Hiller. It is given here in translation from the German. By way of preface to it, may be mentioned that Rossini, in Italy, received for an opera from twenty to thirty pounds. However, for the 'Barber of Seville' he received about eighty pounds.

Hiller. "Considering, Maestro, that you have grown up among singers and actors, and that you possessed a fine voice, it seems almost singular that you did not think of becoming an operatic singer."

Rossini. "I had no other intention, dear sir; but I also wished to learn my art more thoroughly than most of the singers with whom I came into contact at that time had learnt it. This was easy enough; at an early period I already officiated as *Maëstro al Cembalo;* then there came the period when the mutation of my voice interfered with my singing; my attempts at composition found favourable reception; and thus I fell almost accidentally into the career of the composer. I adhered to it, although I had from the beginning the opportunity of observing how incomparably better the singers are rewarded than we are."

Hiller. "Heaven knows! Beethoven has hardly received for all his works as much as Cruvelli obtains annually at the Grand Opera."

Rossini. "It was not quite so bad at that time as it is now; but that makes no difference. When the composer received fifty ducats, the singer received a thousand. I confess that I never could help feeling vexed at this injustice, and often have I given vent to my dissatisfaction in the presence of the singers. You ignorant fellows, I said, you cannot sing even so well as I can, and you gain more in one evening than I am paid for a whole score! But, what was the use of talking thus. Neither do the German composers get rich."

Hiller. "Certainly not, Maestro! But they obtain appointments which, though they are not lucrative, ensure the most important necessities of life. No German composer has ever gained so much by his operas that he could live upon the proceeds. However, it appears to be now better in this respect than it formerly was."

Rossini. "Incomparably better. The former Italian opera composers could write Heaven knows how many operas, and had nevertheless to struggle to make both ends meet. I was scarcely better off until I obtained an appointment with Barbaja."*

Hiller. "Tancredi was the first of your operas which proved a decided hit; how much did you get for it, Maestro?"

Rossini. "Five hundred francs. And when I composed my last Italian opera, 'Semiramide,' and insisted upon having five thousand francs for it, not only the theatrical manager, but the whole public regarded me as a sort of highwayman."

Hiller. "You have the consolation of knowing that singers, managers, and publishers have become rich through you."

Rossini. "A fine consolation! Except during my stay in England, I have never gained by my art so much that I could lay anything by; and the money which I made in London, I did not make as a composer, but as an accompanist."

Hiller. "Yet it was because you were a celebrated composer."

Rossini. "That is what my friends said, to persuade me to take to the new occupation. It may have been a prejudice with me, but I had a dislike to being paid for accompanying on the pianoforte, and I have submitted to it nowhere but in London. However, they were determined to see my nose, and to hear my wife. I had fixed for our co-operation at musical evenings the rather high terms of £50. We attended at about sixty of such evenings, and the pecuniary result was certainly worth the trouble. Moreover,

* Barbaja, the Impressario of the San Carlo Theatre at Naples.

in London the musicians will do anything to make money. I have witnessed there, queer doings."

Hiller. "There one scarcely trusts one's eyes, still less one's ears."

Rossini. "Thus, for instance, when I accepted my first engagement as accompanist at such a Soirée, I was told that Puzzi, the celebrated virtuoso on the horn, and Dragonetti, the celebrated double-bass player, would also be present. I thought they would play solo, but this was far from being the case, they had only been engaged to assist me in accompanying. Have you then written parts for all these pieces? I asked—'Oh, dear, no!' they replied, 'but we get well paid, and so we accompany with whatever comes into our head.' These attempts at improvised instrumental performances appeared to me, however, too venturesome; I therefore begged Dragonetti to restrict himself to twanging occasionally some Pizzicatos, whenever I should wink my eyes to him; and I suggested to Puzzi to fall in with his horn whenever a cadence occurred, which he, as a good musician, easily accomplished. Thus we went through it without very serious accidents, and everyone was contented."

Hiller. "That is capital! But the English, it appears to me, have made great progress in regard to music. They have at present much good music well performed and attentively listened to; that is, in public concerts. In the drawing-room, music is still painfully maltreated. Many persons without the least musical talent parade themselves with an incredible boldness, and give instruction in things of which they know little or nothing."

Rossini. "I knew in London a certain X., who as teacher of the pianoforte had amassed a large property. All he knew of music, however, was that he blew the flute a little, and that quite miserably. Another, who was greatly in demand as a teacher of singing, did not know even the notes. He kept his own accompanist, whose business it was first to hammer those pieces into his master, and afterwards to accompany him when he taught the pieces to the pupils. This singer possessed however a nice voice."*

For the sake of truth some business letters written by distinguished German composers to English publishers must be noticed here, although they redound to the honour of the writers as little as do some of the letters of the German publishers just cited. Not that they reveal a deficiency in common sense as regards business transactions; they exhibit the writers as rather too practical. Among the letters which the music-seller W. Forster, in London, received from Haydn, with whom he kept up a correspondence about the purchase of manuscripts for publication in England, the following, which was originally written in German, is selected as a characteristic specimen. It dates from the year 1788, and was published by S. A. Forster, a son of the music-seller, in his account of the correspondence which his father had with Haydn.

"My dear Mr. Forster,

Do not be annoyed with me that on my account you have had trouble with Mr. Longman. I will satisfy you another time on that point. It is not my fault, but that of the usurer Artaria. So much I promise you that so long as I live, neither Artaria nor Longman shall receive anything from me or through me. I am too honourable and upright to annoy or injure you. So much, however, you will yourself plainly understand that whoever will have six new pieces from me must give me more than twenty guineas. I did, in fact, some time ago conclude a contract with somebody who pays me for every six pieces one hundred guineas and more. Another time I will write you more; meanwhile I am with all respect,

Your obedient servant,

JOSEPH HAYDN."

Still less creditable to the writer are the following extracts from letters addressed by Beethoven to the publisher, R. Birchall, of London, who had bought the copyright

* 'Aus dem Tonleben unserer Zeit, von Ferdinand Hiller; Leipzig, 1868.' Vol. II., p. 22.

for Great Britain and Ireland of four works by Beethoven, viz.:—The pianoforte arrangement of the Battle Symphony, Op. 91; the pianoforte arrangement of the A major Symphony, Op. 92; the Sonata for pianoforte and violin in G major, Op. 96; and the B-flat major Trio for pianoforte, violin, and violoncello, Op. 97. The letters were originally written in English. They are too long for entire insertion here. To render the extracts fully comprehensible, it is necessary to state that Beethoven, after having received from Birchall the sum agreed upon for those works, unexpectedly demanded five pounds for the copying and postage of them; and when Birchall had shown him so much consideration as to satisfy him also on this point, Beethoven wrote to him as follows:—

"Vienna, October 1st, 1816.

"My dear Sir,

I have duly received the £5, and thought previously you would not increase the number of Englishmen neglecting their word and honour, as I had the misfortune of meeting with two of this sort. In reply to the other topics of your favour, I have no objection to write variations according to your plan, and I hope you will not find £30 too much; the accompaniment will be a flute, or violin, or a violoncello; you'll either decide it when you send me the approbation of the price, or you'll leave it to me. . . . . Concerning the expenses of copying and packing, it is not possible to fix them beforehand; they are at any rate not considerable, and you'll please to consider that you have to deal with a man of honour, who will not charge one sixpence more than he is charged himself. . . . . With all the new works which you will have of me, or which I offer you, it rests with you to name the day of their publication at your own choice. I entreat you to honour me as soon as possible with an answer, having many orders for compositions, and that you may not be delayed. . . . .

Your most humble Servant,

LUDWIG VAN BEETHOVEN."

These remarks of Beethoven elicited the following reply from Mr. C. Lonsdale, the manager at R. Birchall's.

"London, Nov. 8, 1816.

"Sir,

In answer to yours of the 1st October I am desired by Mr. Birchall to inform you he is glad to find you are now satisfied respecting the promise of paying you £5,—in addition to what you before received according to agreement, —but he did not think you would have delayed sending the receipt signed, after the receipt of the 130 ducats, merely because you had not received the £5, which latter sum was not included in the receipt. Till it arrives, Mr. Birchall cannot at any rate enter into any fresh arrangement, as his first care will be to secure those pieces he has already paid for, and see how they answer his purpose as a music-seller; and without the receipt he cannot prevent any other music-seller from publishing them. In regard to the airs with variations, the price of £30, which it is supposed you mean for each, is considerably more than he could afford to give,—even to have any hopes of seeing them repay him; if that should be your lowest price, Mr. Birchall will give up his idea of them altogether. . . . . . I am sorry to say Mr. Birchall's health has been very bad for two or three years back, which prevents him from attending to business; and as there are, I fear, but little hopes of his being much better, he is less anxious respecting making any additions to his catalogue than he otherwise would have been. He is much obliged to you for the offer of the Sonata and the Trio; but he begs to decline it for the reasons before mentioned. Hoping to hear soon respecting the paper sent for your signature.

I am, Sir,

For R. Birchall, etc.,

C. Lonsdale."

To this reasonable letter Beethoven replies (in English):

"Vienna, Dec. 14th, 1816.

"Dear Sir,

I give you my word of honour that I have signed and delivered the receipt to the house Fries and Co., some day last August, who, as they say, have transmitted it to Messrs. Coutts and Co., where you'll have the goodness to apply. Some error might have taken place, that instead of Messrs. C. sending it to you they have been directed to keep it till fetched. Excuse this irregularity, but it is not my fault, nor had I ever the idea of withholding it from the circumstance of the £5 not being included. Should the receipt not come forth at Messrs. C., I am ready to sign any other, and you shall have it directly with return of post.

If you find variations—in my style—too dear at £30, I will abate for the sake of your friendship one third, and you have the offer of such variations, as fixed in our former letters, for £20 each air. . . . . I anxiously hope your health is improving. Give me leave to subscribe myself,

Dear Sir,

Your very obedient Servant,

LUDWIG VAN BEETHOVEN." *

Beethoven being unacquainted with the English language was obliged to employ some person to write these letters for him. But, as he signed them, he must be held answerable for their contents. Had he been able to read them, he would probably have disapproved of the manner in which his business transactions were conducted by his interpreter.

During the later years of his life it was a favourite idea with Beethoven to visit England for the purpose of making money. In the year 1817 he corresponded (in German) with F. Ries, in London, on the subject, in consequence of an invitation from the Philharmonic Society.

* 'Jahrbücher für Musikalische Wissenschaft, herausgegeben von F. Chrysander.' Leipzig, 1863, p. 434.

The conditions under which he was willing to accept the invitation he carefully specified as follows:—

"1. I propose to be in London at the latest during the first half of the month of January, in 1818.

2. I promise to bring with me two new large symphonies, which shall become the exclusive property of the Philharmonic Society.

3. The Philharmonic Society pledges itself to pay me for the two symphonies three hundred guineas, and for my travelling expenses one hundred guineas. I expect that the journey will cost me much more than the sum which I ask, because I shall necessarily require a travelling companion.

4. In order that I may be enabled to occupy myself at once uninterruptedly with composing those large symphonies, the Philharmonic Society binds itself to pay 150 guineas of the above sum in advance, so that I may procure without delay a travelling carriage and other travelling equipments.

5. The conditions proposed by the Philharmonic Society as regards my non-appearance in any other public orchestra than its own, about not conducting the orchestra, and about suchlike matters for the advantage of the Society, I consent to unreservedly. My feeling of honour would have dictated them to me as a matter of course.

6. I dare to hope that the Philharmonic Society will oblige me with its assistance in the preparation and promotion of one benefit concert, or perhaps more. . . .

7. I must beg that the conditions, or the agreement to the above, shall be written in the English language, signed by three Directors of the Philharmonic Society in the name of the Society, and forwarded to me."

Failing health prevented Beethoven from undertaking the journey. The Philharmonic Society, believing him to be in want, which was far from being the case, in a delicate way presented him with £100. Indeed, Beethoven had every reason to feel gratified by the generous attention shown to him by those Englishmen who were able to appreciate his merits. In the year 1817, some of his London admirers gave him great pleasure by sending him a new grand-piano of Broadwood's manufacture; and in 1826, the kind-hearted

Mr. J. A. Stumpff, in London, a German by birth, and a harp-maker in by no means affluent circumstances, made him a present of Arnold's edition of Handel's works, in forty volumes folio,—a gift which was taken to the bedside of the dying composer, and which soothed his last days of suffering.

Also Haydn received from England touching marks of veneration. Some instances of homage offered by enthusiastic amateurs, must have caused him amusement on account of their singularity, if for no better reason. The worsted-spinner W. Gardiner, of Leicester, forwarded to him a present of six pairs of cotton stockings in which he had worked the notation of some popular melodies by Haydn,—such as the air "My mother bids me bind my hair;" the theme of the Andante in the Surprise Symphony; the tune of the Hymn "God preserve the Emperor," etc. W. Gardiner was himself a musical composer, his mode of composing being that of the Bavarian prince Joseph Clemens, who set about it "like the bees which extract honey from the most beautiful flowers, and mix it together." * Thus W. Gardiner "composed" a whole oratorio, which he made up of choruses and airs borrowed from various masters, and more or less distorted to suit them to their new place. Only the overture was wanting. He wrote to Beethoven to induce him to compose one for this oratorio, and offered to pay 100 guineas for it. Beethoven never answered the letter.† Had he been really as greedy of gain as in his correspondence with Birchall he appears to be, he would probably have accepted the offer, which was rather liberal. Nevertheless, had he accepted it, the result would very likely have proved the manufacturer a more practical man than the composer. Be this as it may, it is quite comprehensible that to Beethoven an attempt to associate him with musical jobbery must have been especially repulsive.

Perhaps no opera composer had a better chance of becoming a rich man than had Carl Maria von Weber.

---

* See above, p. 45.

† 'Music and Friends, by William Gardiner.' Vol. III., London, 1853, p. 378.

The success of 'Der Freischütz' was immense. The fascinating melodies of this opera were sung, played and whistled everywhere, by musical and unmusical people. It would be difficult to point out a civilized country in which 'Der Freischütz' has not been performed and listened to with rapture. Before the popularity of the opera was fully established, Weber offered the pianoforte score to the publisher Schlesinger, in Berlin, for sixty Frederick-d'ors (£51). Schlesinger thought the demand exorbitant, and offered two hundred and twenty thalers (£33), which Weber accepted.* Nevertheless, in consequence of the many performances of 'Der Freischütz' in various towns on the Continent, from which the composer derived some pecuniary advantage, the opera proved rather lucrative to him. Still, it was more remunerative indirectly than directly, inasmuch as its universal success induced Charles Kemble, the manager of the Theatre Royal, Covent Garden, to engage Weber to compose 'Oberon,' and to visit London for the purpose of conducting the new opera. Thus Weber had an excellent opportunity of exercising his aptitude for business. How he acquitted himself of the task, may be gathered from his rejecting at the outset the terms offered by Kemble,—which were £500, and all his expenses paid,—and proposing his own terms, which, with the help of some one acquainted with the English language, he had penned as follows:—

"At my arrival at London I will first of all preside at the piano in six representations of the 'Freischütz'; for the first five you will give me every night a pecuniary compensation of two hundred pounds, and the sixth as a benefit for me. During this time we will prepare 'Oberon' and I will preside at the piano also the first six representations at the same conditions. I must be assured that all this be settled in three months, otherwise I should claim an adequate indemnification. The music of 'Oberon' (Partition, and adapted by me for the Piano) is then your property for Great Britain. The poem and the music are mine for all the rest of Europe."

---

* 'Carl Maria von Weber, ein Lebensbild,' von Max C. M. von Weber; Leipzig, 1864. Vol. II., p. 270.

According to this proposal Weber would have realized in the course of three months £2,400. But he soon experienced that one may also be too practical. His shattered health rendered the journey to England exceedingly fatiguing, and the trouble, excitement and disappointments connected with the rehearsals and representations of 'Oberon,' and with the necessary preparations for his concerts, accelerated his dissolution. He died in 1826, when he had been about three months in London, and the proceeds of his toil during the time amounted to about £1,100, or less than half the sum which he at first demanded from Kemble.

The musical student, in perusing the master-works in his art, has continually occasion to admire the careful consideration which the composers have given to every bar so as to produce great effects by simple means, interesting variety in unity, thus achieving as nearly as possible a perfect work of art. Also, their remarks upon their compositions show how thoughtfully they laboured, considering and reconsidering every step they took. It is unnecessary to illustrate this fact by quotations, as instances will probably occur to the reader. Suffice it to notice a remark by Mozart, which shows how cleverly he contrived to make concessions to the popular taste, in as far as he could accomplish this without deterioration to his compositions as works of art. In a letter to his father, which he wrote from Paris, he thus describes the performance of a new symphony, which he had been requested to compose for the *Concert Spirituel* :—

"In the middle of the first Allegro is a passage of which I knew well that it would please. All the auditors were transported by it, and there was great applause. As I knew, when I wrote the passage, what its effect would be, I introduced it once more towards the end of the movement. Then they demanded a repetition of the entire Allegro. The Andante pleased also; but especially the last Allegro. As I had been told that it was the usual custom with the composers here in Paris to commence the last Allegro of a symphony, like the first, with the full orchestra, generally in unison, I commenced mine with only the first and second violins, *piano* through eight bars. Then came suddenly *forte*. Consequently, the auditors made first, as I had expected,—hush! and then the *forte* surprised them so greatly, that they applauded as a matter of course."

Is this not thoroughly practical in an artistic point of view?

MUSIC AND MEDICINE.

MUSIC is capable of exercising a favourable influence upon health, but it may also prove injurious. In order to know how to employ it with good result in certain illnesses, an exact acquaintance with its various effects is requisite. First of all, it ought to be borne in mind that music may serve as a remedy either by directly affecting the mind, or by acting primarily upon the body. In the former case its influence may be called psychical; and in the latter, physical.

Considering how much in the cure of certain illnesses depends upon the spirits of the patient, it will easily be understood that the affecting power of music deserves special attention. There are illnesses in which the attainment of a calm state of mind may be a most important condition for the recovery of the patient,—nay, instances are conceivable in which with this attainment the illness is already in a great measure removed. Some persons are much more susceptible of music than others; but there are few in whose heart it finds not some response, however slight. Indeed, the beneficial influence of music is almost universally felt, and is evidenced by examples the authenticity of which is indisputable. No other art is so capable of easily moving man to tears of grief, of exciting him in a moment to cheerfulness, of inspiring him with courage, and of making him forget his real or imaginary troubles and anxieties. Hence, with almost every nation we find the employment of music resorted to on occasions of sadness and mourning, at solemn celebrations and joyful festivities, in warlike exploits, in religious worship,—in fact, wherever a definite direction of a certain feeling is especially requisite.

Also the popular stories, of which a selection is given in the present work, testify to the universally-felt power of music. In many of the stories miraculous effects are ascribed to music. What stronger proof can be cited of its intense impression upon the human heart than the popularity of such conceptions traditionally preserved through centuries!

But also the direct influence which the cultivation of music may exercise upon the body is not insignificant, considered medically. Thus, for instance, singing, if judiciously practised, is conducive to health, inasmuch as it benefits the lungs and the chest; and the playing on certain musical instruments is salutary, while on others it is injurious. Moreover, in combination with dancing, music is likely to prove in some complaints an efficacious remedy. Of course, everything depends upon its judicious employment, if it is to serve medically. In order exactly to ascertain its efficacy it is advisable to examine its employment as we find it in different nations. Even the most uncivilized tribes ought not to be ignored in this enquiry, because the dictates of instinct are often not less suggestive than the speculations of reason.

Nations, or tribes, in a low state of civilization, as there are many still existing at the present day, have generally so-called "mystery-men," or "medicine-men," who combine in one person the avocation of the priest, physician, and musician, and who are also usually prophets, sorcerers, rain-makers, shrewd advisers,—in short, men who by their comparatively superior knowledge and skill obtain considerable influence over their ignorant and superstitious fellow-men.

The most ancient nations historically known were far more advanced in civilization than these our contemporaries. However, we find with them traces of the original existence of "mystery-men." With the Greeks, music, or the art of the Muses, originally comprised, besides the tone-art, several other arts and sciences; from which it may be conjectured that the earliest Greek musicians practised also the healing art like the mystery-men of our time. The ancient Egyptians, at an early period, had attained a considerably higher stage of development in the cultivation of music than many nations of the present day have achieved. This assertion will not appear exaggerated to any musician who has carefully examined the ancient representations of the variously-constructed instruments which were in use with the Egyptians, centuries before our Christian era. Equally suggestive is a statement of Herodotus, indicating the progress which the Egyptians had made in the healing art, nearly 500 years before our era. He remarks (Euterpe 84): "The art of medicine is thus divided amongst them: each physician applies himself to one disease only, and not more. All places abound in physicians; some physicians are for the eyes, others for the head, others for the teeth, others for the parts about the belly, and others for internal disorders." Such a high degree of cultivation of an art or science, in which each professor occupies himself especially with a particular branch in order to achieve the utmost possible perfection in it, is known at the present day only among the most civilized nations.

If, therefore, we desire to obtain an accurate idea of the primitive treatment of diseases by means of music, a reference to the usages of some rude tribes in uncivilized lands will be the proper step for acquiring the information.

Considering that the mystery-men alluded to are, as a rule, mentally the most gifted and the most crafty personages of the tribe to which they belong, and that they are especially familiar with the views, inclinations, customs, and weaknesses of their people, a detailed account of the social position and doings of these extraordinary individuals in different parts of the world might be very interesting. It would, however, be out of place here to describe them further than as they appear in their medical and musical capacities.

The mystery-men of the North American Indians, or the "medicine-men," as they are more usually called, are acquainted with the medicinal virtues of a great many different kinds of roots and herbs, of which they make use in their prescriptions, and for which they are paid.

Some of them enjoy a high reputation on account of their skill; and in general the medicine-man takes a high position among the people. Only when the common remedies of roots and herbs have proved unsuccessful does he resort to "medicine" or mystery. He arrays himself in a most grotesque dress, and provides himself with a rattle, commonly made of a gourd, which is hollowed and partly filled with pebbles. Thus equipped, he approaches his dying patient to cure him by a charm. He dances about him, singing songs of incantation, and producing a frightful noise by shaking his rattle. Catlin records a scene of an attempted cure of this description which he himself witnessed, as follows: "Several hundred spectators, including Indians and traders, were assembled round the dying man, when it was announced that the medicine-man was coming. We were required to form a ring, leaving a space of some thirty or forty feet in diameter around the dying man, in which the doctor would perform his wonderful operations; and a space was also opened to allow him free room to pass through the crowd without touching any one. . . . . He approached the ring with his body in a crouching position, with a slow and tilting step. His body and head were entirely covered with the skin of a yellow bear, the head of which—his own head being inside of it—served as a mask; the huge claws of which also were dangling on his wrists and ankles. In one hand he shook a frightful rattle, and in the other he brandished his medicine-spear, or magic wand; to the rattling din and discord of all of which he added the wild and startling jumps and yelps of the Indian, and the horrid and appalling grunts, snarls, and growls of the grizzly bear, in ejaculatory and gutteral incantations to the Good and Bad Spirits, in behalf of his patient, who was rolling and groaning in the agonies of death, whilst he was dancing around him, jumping over him, and pawing him about, and rolling him in every direction. In this wise the strange operation proceeded for half an hour to the surprise of a numerous and death-like silent audience, until the man died; and the medicine-man danced off to his quarters, and packed up, tied and secured from the sight of the world his mystery dress and equipments."* Should the exhausted patient unaccountably recover after such a ceremony, the lucky medicine-man will be seen for several days after the event on the top of a wigwam, extending his right arm, waving it to the gaping multitude, and boasting of his skill.

With the Indian tribes in Columbia and Vancouver Island the medicine-man, although he may become of great importance if he is clever, is liable to be put to death if he fails to cure his patient; it being presumed that he possesses the power, but not the wish, to cure. A strange procedure of one of these fellows in trying to cure a female who lay dangerously ill, was witnessed by an Englishman, who has given a circumstantial description of it, from which the following extract will suffice:—

"Towards night the doctor came, bringing with him his own and another family to assist in the ceremony. After they had eaten supper, the centre of the lodge was cleared and fresh sand strewed upon it. A bright fire of dry wood was then kindled, and a brilliant light kept up by occasionally throwing oil upon it. I considered this a species of incense offered, as the same light would have been produced, if desired, by a quantity of pitch-knots which were lying in the corner. The patient, well wrapped in blankets, was laid on her back, with her head a little elevated, and her hands crossed on her breast. The doctor knelt at her feet, and commenced singing a song, the subject of which was an address to the dead, asking them why they had come to take his friend and mother, and begged them to go away and leave her. The rest of the people then sung the chorus in a low, mournful chant, keeping time by knocking on the roof with long wands they held. . . . . As the performance proceeded, the doctor became more and more excited, singing loudly and violently, with great gesticulation, and occasionally making passes with his hand

* 'Illustrations of the Manners, Customs and Condition of the North American Indians, by G. Catlin.' London, 1848; Volume I., p. 40.

over the face and person of the patient, similar to those made by mesmeric manipulators." *

Likewise, in a cure effected in the case of a sick lad of the Wallawalla Indians, Columbia river, which Mr. Drayton witnessed, there appears to have been a kind of mesmerism used in combination with music. This case is also noteworthy inasmuch as it shows that the Indians have female physicians. The lad was lying on his back in a lodge and appeared to be in a dying state. Over him stood an old haggard-looking squaw, who was singing in great excitement, while about a dozen men and boys were accompanying her with their voices in a sort of chorus, the rhythmical effect of which they increased by striking sticks together at regular intervals. The music thus produced sounded unearthly to the foreign bystander. The squaw was all the time very busy about the lad, now bending over him and making all kinds of grimaces, and now baring his chest and pretending by her actions to be scooping out his disease, and now again falling on her knees before him and striving to draw out the evil spirit with both her hands. She blew into her hands and then moved them over the patient in a peculiar manner as if she were tossing the noxious spirit away into the air. Then again she would blow with her mouth on his neck downwards, making a quick sputtering noise; and at last she began to suck his neck and chest in different parts. Whatever may be thought of this operation, the boy certainly soon got better. Moreover, our informant concludes his account of the occurrence with the statement: "One singular custom prevailing here (with the Indians of Wallawalla) is that all the convalescents are directed to sing for several hours during the day."†

The Indian tribes in Guiana have mystery-men, called Piatzas, or Piaies, who constitute a powerful priesthood. In their incantations they use rattles, and also drums and

* 'Four Years in British Columbia and Vancouver Island, by R. C. Mayne.' London, 1862; p. 261.

† 'Narrative of the United States Exploring Expedition during the years 1838-42, by Charles Wilkes.' London, 1845; vol. IV., p. 399.

bells. When a person suffering from a protracted illness finds the commonly-used medicines of no avail, his refuge is to the Piatza, to induce him to drive out the evil spirit that must be the cause of the mischief. The Piatza carries the patient into the nearest forest, and having fastened his hammock to some tree across a pass, he commences the incantations, which he accompanies with the noise of his rattle. The rattle consists of a calabash partly filled with small pebbles. During his incantations no one is permitted to witness what he is doing, even the patient being enjoined to close his eyes and to keep them shut until the end of the ceremony. The Piatza draws a circle round the sick person and addresses the evil spirit.*

Again, the *Manchi*, or medicine-man of the Peguenches and other Indian tribes in the Argentine Provinces, is skilled in the use of herbs. If remedies of this kind prove ineffectual, mysterious ceremonies are resorted to. A sheep and a colt are killed, and are placed with vessels of a fermented liquor, called *chichala*, under trees close to a hut; the patient is carried out of the hut and laid on the sunny side of the trees. The *Manchi* and the women now dance in a circle round the trees, the animals, and the sick person. When the dancers are exhausted the *Manchi* fumigates the animals and the sick person three times, and then sucks the diseased part of the man with such force as to draw blood. After this, he sucks the heart of the colt and anoints the sick person with the blood of the animal. At the conclusion of these disgusting ceremonies, in the performance of which the *Manchi* affects to be in a trance, dancing is recommenced, and the patient is forced to join in it, supported by his friends. A general feast, in which the people consume the animals, concludes the ceremony.† The *Manchi* generally uses a kind of drum in his incantations.

The mystery-men of the Araucanian Indians are called *Gligua*, or *Dugol*, and some of them are distinguished by the

---

* 'Missionary Labours in British Guiana,' by the Rev. J. H. Bernau; London, 1847. p. 55.

† 'Two Thousand Miles' Ride through the Argentine Provinces,' by William MacCann; London, 1853. Vol. I., p. 111.

epithets *Guenguenu*, *Genpugni*, and *Genpuri* (*i. e.* "Master of the heavens, of epidemic diseases, of worms and insects,") and are supposed to have the power of curing every disease, of producing rain, and of preventing the ravages of worms and insects. The real medicine-men are called *Machi*,* and their method of curing is similar to that of the *Manchi* of the Argentine Provinces just described. The ceremony is, however, always performed in the night. The hut in which the patient lies is lighted with a great number of torches. In a corner of the room is placed, among branches of laurel, a large bough of cinnamon, to which is suspended the magic drum; and near to it is a sheep which is to be killed for sacrifice. A number of women sing aloud and beat upon little drums, while the *Machi* proceeds, with frightful gesticulations and horrible contortions of his body, to exorcise the evil spirit which is supposed to be the cause of the malady.† Sometimes he will suddenly exhibit in triumph a spider, a toad, or some other obnoxious animal, which he pretends to have extracted from the body of the sufferer.‡ A more detailed account of these impostors is unnecessary, especially as the works are mentioned which contain full descriptions of them.

The largest Indian tribes in Patagonia, the Moluches and the Puelches, have male and female sorcerers. Boys who suffer from epileptic fits, or from the St. Vitus's dance, are selected for this office, and are brought up in it. They have to adopt female apparel, which they continue to wear when grown up. These men, dressed like women, are supposed to have been destined for their profession by the demons themselves. They, likewise, assume the power of curing disease by means of incantations accompanied with the noise of rattles and drums.§

---

* *Machi* is evidently identical with *Manchi*.

† 'The Geographical, Natural, and Civic History of Chili,' by the Abbé Don J. Ignatius Molina; London, 1809. Vol. II., p. 105.

‡ 'The Araucanians,' by E. R. Smith; London, 1855; p. 235.

§ 'A Description of Patagonia and the adjoining parts of South America,' by Thomas Faulkner; Hereford, 1774; p. 115.

The close resemblance of certain practices of the medicine-men among uncivilized nations in different parts of the globe, is especially suggestive. Nor are the differences without interest.

Turning to Africa, we have musical-medical practitioners with the Negroes and Kafirs, whose art must have originated quite independently of that of the American medicine-men. The Negroes in Jamaica have sorcerers and physicians, called Obeah-men, whose ceremonies are probably of African origin, although they are in many respects similar to those of the Indian medicine-men. The Obeah-men, being well acquainted with the peculiar effects of the different poisonous plants, it is said, often make bad use of their knowledge.* When attending a sick person, the Obeah-man generally commences his cure with a dance, and he administers a powder, or a liquor, to his victim.†

The Negroes in Western Africa have professional musicians or minstrels, called in Senegambia, *Griots*; singing men, or bards, called *Jillikea*; Fetish priests who drum and dance as if they themselves were possessed of evil spirits; Priestesses of the Serpent worship, which has its principal temples in Whydah; Rain-makers; Wizards, called *Greegree-men*; and other "wise men," who are also physicians and musicians. The *Ganga*, in Loango, South Western Africa, are, according to the Abbé Proyard, priests as well as physicians: "When they come to a patient, they ask him where his ailment lies. They blow on the part affected: after that, they make fomentations, and tie up his limbs in different places with bandages. These are the preliminaries used in all diseases. They know nothing either of phlebotomy, or of medicine. .. . . They know a very salutary remedy, in their opinion, for all diseases; but this they only employ in favour of those who can afford the expense. When they are called in to a rich man, they take with them all the performers on musical instruments they

* 'Journal of a Residence among the Negroes in the West Indies,' by M. G. Lewis; London, 1845; p. 158.

† The word *Obeah* is probably identical with *Piaie*, mentioned above, page 89.

can find in the country. They all enter in silence; but, at the first signal which they give, the musical troop begin their performance. Some are furnished with stringed instruments, others beat on the trunks of hollow trees covered with skin,—a sort of tabor. All of them uniting their voices with the sound of the instruments round the patient's bed, make a terrible uproar and din, which is often continued for several days and nights in succession." *

The mystery-man in Benguela is called *Kimbanda.* He performs his ceremonies in the forest, in the presence of the people. Before him stands a calabash with a wide opening, in which are figures rudely carved, of wood or bone, which represent different kinds of wild animals. A rattle, which he holds in his hand, consists of a hollow calabash containing pebbles. He shakes his rattle and addresses the figures in a recitation, interspersed with questions concerning the ailments of his patient. An assistant, who is hidden in the neighbourhood of the figures, answers the questions in a hollow tone of voice, as if it came from the figures. However, for the accomplishment of the cure a sacrifice of a cow is generally demanded by those greedy figures; or even more, according to the means of the patient. The answers given by the figures are generally so indistinct that no one but the *Kimbanda* can understand them; and he communicates them to the people.†

The Somali, in Eastern Africa, have similar mystery-men, called *Tawuli;* and the natives of Zanzibar have the *Mganga*, who professes to heal the patient by expelling the demon by means of his singing and the shaking of his rattle. The mystery-man of the Kafirs of Natal likewise accompanies his recitations with a rattle. He is an extraordinarily dangerous and objectionable personage; for, when the cattle fall sick, or some other mischief happens, he is apt to declare that it has been caused by some evil-doer whom

---

* 'History of Loango,' by the Abbé Proyard; Paris, 1776. 'A General Collection of Voyages and Travels,' by John Pinkerton; London, 1808; Vol. XIV, p. 572.

† 'Reisen in Süd-Africa,' von Ladislaus Magyar; Pest, 1859; Vol. I., p. 26.

he can find out. He sings and dances towards several individuals in succession, and affects to examine them by his olfactory sense. Suddenly he touches one with the gnu's tail which he carries in his hand. He leaps over the head of the unhappy man, and points him out as the offender.* Also the Bechuana, in fact every Kafir tribe, has one or more of such personages, who are physicians and musicians, as well as priests, prophets, and rain-makers.

Considering the very low state of civilization of those natives of Australia who have not come into contact with the European settlers, it is especially interesting to learn their notions on the employment of music in the cure of disease. These aborigines are divided into numerous tribes, who have no chief, or leader properly speaking, except the *Crodgy*, or "wise man," who, besides being a quack, is also the conductor of their ceremonies. They not unfrequently suffer from rheumatic pains in their limbs, which they believe to be caused by some demon. To protect themselves against the demons, they carry about them charms consisting of bits of rock crystal, called "mundy-stones," which they value highly. They endeavour to drive away the demons by whirling round their head an oval-shaped board, called *moor-y-umkarr*, which is curiously ornamented, and is suspended to a string. It produces an unearthly, humming sound, sometimes soft, sometimes loud and roaring, according to the force with which it is whirled. The doctor, in curing a sick person, proceeds much in the same manner as the medicine-man of the North American Indians. He, however, uses no rattle; a bunch of green reeds held in the hand and shaken serves the same purpose. The small-pox is so greatly feared by the natives that they possess a special song, called *nguitkurra*, by the singing of which the disease is believed to be prevented, or checked in its progress. † A native from the vicinity

* 'The Kafirs of Natal and the Zulu Country,' by J. Shooter; London, 1857; p. 173.

† 'Outlines of a Grammar, Vocabulary, and Phraseology of the Aboriginal Language of South Australia.' By G. C. Teichelmann and C. W. Schürmann. Adelaide, 1840; part II.

of Port Jackson, whose wife was complaining of a pain in the stomach, was observed by a European traveller to cure her in the following manner: "After blowing on his hand, he warmed it at a fire, and then applied it to the part affected, beginning at the same time a song which was probably calculated for the occasion. A piece of flannel being warmed and applied by a bystander, rendered the warming his hand unnecessary; but he continued his song, always keeping his mouth very near to the part affected, and frequently stopping to blow on it, making a noise after blowing, in imitation of the barking of a dog. But, though he blew several times, he only made that noise once at every pause, and then continued his song. The woman always made short responses whenever he ceased to blow and bark."*

An English missionary in Tanna Island, New Hebrides, relates that when a native of that Island is taken ill, his friends believe that his illness is occasioned by some one burning his *nakah* (*i.e.* "rubbish"). They have "disease-makers" who are believed to have in their hands the power of life and death, and who are consequently much feared. Every kind of *nakah* is carefully buried or thrown into the sea, lest the disease-maker should pick it up, wrap it in a leaf, and burn it. When a native is taken ill, his friends blow on a conch trumpet, which signifies a supplication to the disease-maker to discontinue burning the rubbish. If the sick man recovers, the disease-man receives a present for having left off burning. The rubbish generally consists of some refuse of food.† The New Zealanders had formerly similar disease-makers, who were supposed to require a lock of hair, or some nail-parings, of the person whom they intended to afflict with disease.

Let us now turn to some tribes in cold regions of the North, to compare their musical ceremonies in the cure of illness with those in tropical countries.

---

* 'An Historical Journal of the Transactions at Port Jackson and Norfolk Islands.' By John Hunter. London, 1793; p. 476.

† 'Nineteen Years in Polynesia.' By the Rev. G. Turner. London, 1861.

The natives of Kamtschatka have persons called *Shamans*, who profess to be able to communicate with the spirits by arraying themselves in a grotesque garment, chanting, beating a drum, dancing, and working themselves up to a state of trance. They, on these occasions, drink an infusion of a species of fungus, which has an intoxicating power, and which sometimes makes them sleep afterwards for three or four days without interruption. Its effect must therefore be similar to that of opium. The Shamans of the Ostiaks, and of the Samoiedes, in Siberia, suspend to their dress metal representations of strange birds, fishes, and quadrupeds, with bones, teeth, and other frightful-looking things. In their incantations they shake the dress so that the metallic appendages produce clanging and tinkling sounds, the effect of which is increased by the Shaman's beating a drum, of the tambourine kind. Also the Laplanders, about a century ago, had such sorcerers, who used a drum called *rune-bomme*, or *gobodes*, the parchment of which was marked with mystic signs. The sorcerer was called *Noaaid*, or *Spagubbe*. Besides his magic drum he had a magic chain, about twelve inches in length, of tin and copper, which, when shaken, produced a shrill, tinkling noise. No journey, no business transaction was undertaken by the Lapp without his having previously consulted the Noaaid, who by means of a ring placed on the parchment of his drum, predicted the success of the undertaking. When he beat the drum, the vibration caused the ring to move to one or other of the mysterious signs marked upon the parchment; and from the position of the ring, he pretended to be able to divine the future. Moreover, he cured diseases by beating his drum to incantations and wild dancing. The Lapps believed that the defunct relations of the sick person attempted to draw him over to them; it, therefore, naturally suggested itself to his friends to engage the interference of the Noaaid, who professed to have intercourse with the spirits of the dead. The pagan Finns had the same notion, which is not surprising, considering that they and the Lapps are of one race. The sorcerers of the Finns recited songs, called *lugut*, when they attempted to exorcise the evil spirit of the patient, or to remove the witchcraft occasioning the mischief. These superstitions the Finnish races probably brought with them originally from Asia, where we still meet with them at the present day. It is remarkable that in time of remote antiquity, the priests of certain Eastern nations used tinkling instruments for the purpose of frightening away the demons. The ancient Egyptians shook the Sistrum; and the priests of the Copts and of the Abyssinian Christians observe still this very ancient custom. The Hebrew priests, at the time of Moses, had little bells attached to their robes for protection against evil influences; at any rate, it is recorded that the sound of Aaron's bell was to be heard "that he die not." (Exod. chap. xxviii., v. 35.)

A curious account of the employment of music in the cure of diseases in Chinese Tartary is given by M. Huc. He says: "When illness attacks any one his friends run to the nearest monastery for a Lama, whose first proceeding upon visiting the patient is to run his fingers over the pulse of both wrists simultaneously, as the fingers of a musician run over the strings of an instrument. . . . After due deliberation the Lama pronounces his opinion as to the particular nature of the malady. According to the religious belief of the Tartars all illness is owing to the visitation of a *Tchutgour*, or demon, but the expulsion of the demon is first a matter of medicine. The Lama physician next proceeds, as Lama apothecary, to give the specific befitting the case. The Tartar pharmacopœia rejecting all mineral chemistry, the Lama remedies consist entirely of vegetables pulverized, and either infused in water or made up into pills. If the Lama doctor happens not to have any medicine with him he is by no means disconcerted; he writes the names of the remedies upon little scraps of paper, moistens the paper with saliva, and rolls them into pills, which the patient tosses down with the same perfect confidence as though they were genuine medicaments." When the invalid is a person of property, the Lamas make extraordinary preparations for expelling the *Tchutgour*, for which the invalid has to give them dresses and other presents. The aunt of

Tokoura, chief of an encampment, visited by M. Huc, was seized one evening with an intermittent fever. "I would invite the attendance of the Lama doctor," said Tokoura, "but if he finds that there is a very big Tchutgour present, the expense will ruin me." He waited for some days; but, as the aunt grew worse and worse, he at last sent for a Lama. "His anticipations," M. Huc relates, "were confirmed. The Lama pronounced that a demon of considerable rank was present, and that no time must be lost in expelling him. Eight other Lamas were forthwith called in, who at once set about the construction, in dried herbs, of a great puppet, which they entitled *The Demon of Intermittent Fevers*, and which, when completed, they placed on its legs by means of a stick in the patient's tent. The ceremony began at eleven o'clock at night. The Lamas ranged themselves in a semi-circle round the upper portion of the tent, with cymbals, conch-trumpets, bells, tambourines, and other instruments of the noisy Tartar music. The remainder of the circle was completed by the members of the family squatting on the ground close to one another, the patient kneeling, or rather crouched on her knees, opposite the 'Demon of intermittent fevers.' The Lama doctor-in-chief had before him a large copper basin filled with millet, and some little images made of paste. The dung-fuel (*argols*) threw, amid much smoke, a fantastic and quivering light over the strange scene. * Upon a given signal, the clerical orchestra executed an introductory piece harsh enough to frighten Satan himself, the lay congregation beating time with their hands to the charivari of clanging instruments and ear-splitting voices. The diabolic concert over, the Grand Lama opened the Book of Exorcisms, which he rested on his knees. As he chanted one of the forms, he took from the basin, from time to time, a handful of millet, which he threw east, west, north and south, according to the Rubric. The tones of his voice, as he prayed, were sometimes mournful and suppressed, sometimes vehemently

---

* Dried dung, which constitutes the chief, and indeed in many places the sole fuel in Tartary, is called *argols*.

loud and energetic. All of a sudden he would quit the regular cadence of prayer, and have an outburst of apparently indomitable rage, abusing the herb puppet with fierce invectives and furious gestures. The exorcism terminated, he gave a signal by stretching out his arms, right and left, and the other Lamas struck up a tremendously noisy chorus, in hurried, dashing tones; all the instruments were set to work, and meantime the lay congregation, having started up with one accord, ran out of the tent, one after the other, and, tearing round it like mad people, beat it at their hardest with sticks, yelling all the while at the pitch of their voices, in a manner to make ordinary hair stand on end."

Then they returned to the tent, and repeated the same scene. After they had done this three times, they covered their faces with their hands, and the Grand Lama set fire to the herb figure. "As soon as the flames rose, he uttered a loud cry, which was repeated with interest by the whole company. . . . After this strange treatment, the malady did not return. The probability is that the Lamas, having ascertained the precise moment at which the fever-fit would recur, met it at the exact point of time by this tremendous counter-excitement, and overcame it." *

The Burmese, especially those of the mountain region of south and east Burmah, have priests and sorcerers, called *Wees* and *Bookhoos*, who "pretend to cure diseases, to know men's thoughts, and to converse with the spirits. Their performances are fraught with awe and terror to a superstitious people. They begin with solemn and mysterious movements; at length every muscle is agitated, while with frantic looks and foaming mouth they utter oracles, or speak to a man's spirit and declare its responses." † In cases of severe illness which have resisted the skill of native medical art, the physician gravely tells the patient and relatives that it is useless to have recourse any longer to medicine.

---

* 'Travels in Tartary, Thibet, and China, during the years 1844-46,' by M. Huc; Vol. I., p. 76.

† 'Travels in South-eastern Asia,' by H. Malcom Boston, 1839; Vol. II., p. 197.

An evil *Natch* (" spirit ") is the author of the complaint, and requires to be expelled. This is accomplished by means of music and dancing, while the physician gives to the patient some medicine, pointed out to him as an infallible remedy by an accomplice in a kind of trance during the ceremony.*

That in certain complaints it may be beneficial to the invalid to dance to the sound of music, is owing to the exhilarating influence of the music as well as to the bodily exercise of the dancing.

The treatment of the Tarantism, or the derangement of the system caused by the bite of the Tarantula, a venomous spider in Apulia, Italy, has been so often described by medical and musical men, that a detailed account of it is hardly required here. Suffice it to notice the opinions entertained by some careful medical inquirers, respecting the efficacy of music and dancing in the cure of this illness. Nicolo Peroti, an Italian Archbishop, who lived in the fifteenth century, is supposed to have been the first who in his writings has drawn attention to the symptoms attributed to the bite of the Tarantula. Achille Vergari, a physician, in his treatise, entitled, 'Tarantismo, o malattia prodotta dalle Tarantole velenose,' Naples, 1839, says that not all these spiders are alike poisonous, but that some are so to a degree that a person bitten by them is sure to die almost immediately, notwithstanding all antidotes administered to him. According to Vergari, the Tarantula is found not only in South Italy, but also in Sardinia, the Caucasus, Persia, Abyssinia, Madagascar, the West Indies, and in several other hot regions. The poison consists in a fluid secreted in glands, which, when the spider bites, is pressed into the wound, and thus diffused throughout the body. The poison is most virulent during the dog-days, and during the period of breeding, especially if the spider is irritated, and if the person bitten is particularly susceptible for the action of the poison; under other circumstances it causes but little injury, or none at all. The only specific cure for the bite is believed to be music and dancing. The animating sound of the tune

* 'Six Months in British Burmah,' by C. F. Winter; London, 1858; p. 161.

known as the Tarantella subdues the depressing effect of the poison; the invalid feels invigorated by the music; he raises himself and begins to move his hands and feet to the time of it; and, be he old or young, though he may never before in his life have danced, he is irresistibly forced to dance until exhaustion compels him to desist. The dancing sometimes lasts three hours without cessation, and is repeated for three or four successive days. The most salutary time for it is the early morning, at sunrise, when the patient usually perspires, sighs, complains, and behaves like an intoxicated person. Occasionally, while dancing, he takes in his hands green branches, or ribbons of some particular colour; or he wants to be dressed in showy garments. The black colour he hates, and the sight of a person dressed in black irritates him greatly. The room in which the dancing takes place is ornamented with different bright colours, green branches, and looking-glasses. Some insist upon carrying weapons in their hands while dancing; others desire to be beaten; or they beat themselves; and so on. The musical instruments formerly used in playing the Tarantella are the violin, violoncello, guitar, flute, organ, lute, cither, shalm, and tambourine. Some of these instruments have now become obsolete; nor are the others always used in combination, but more frequently singly.

These statements were collected by Vergari from the observations of the most intelligent physicians and surgeons in Apulia, and other districts of the former kingdom of Naples.

De Renzi, a distinguished physician of Naples, sent, in the year 1841, to the 'Raccoglitore Medico,' published in Fano, the following account of a Tarantism witnessed by Doctor Samuele Costa. Giuseppe Mastria, a peasant from a small village in the southern district of the province Terra d'Otranto, twenty years of age, of robust bodily constitution, while mowing grass, in June, 1840, felt a sudden pain on his right arm, near the insertion of the Deltoid muscle, and saw that he was bitten by a speckled spider, the Aranea Tarantula. The wound having become livid, enlarged and spread the pain over the arm and the back of the neck. He was seized with anxiety and with pressure on the Præcordia, inclination to vomit, faintness, cold skin, and weak pulse. After some time, the warmth of the body increased, and the pulse became stronger. The patient experienced great thirst, heavy breathing, restlessness, and the impossibility of standing on his legs. When, however, the Tarantella was played to him, he suddenly became convulsive, jumped out of the bed, and danced briskly for nearly two hours. Tired and profusely perspiring, he consequently slept quietly and uninterruptedly. After several repetitions of the music in the course of three days, he entirely recovered.*

Dr. Martinus Kähler, a Swedish physician, who visited Apulia in the year 1756, for the express purpose of investigating the Tarantism thoroughly, came to the conclusion that it is not caused by the Tarantula, but that it is a peculiar hypochondria with hysteria, to which the inhabitants of the island of Taranto are especially subject on account of their mode of living, and from their food consisting principally of green vegetables, oysters, and periwinkles. Be this as it may, the complaint is, according to medical opinion, curable by means of music and dancing.

Thomas Shaw, who visited the Barbary States about the year 1730, mentions the *Boola-kaz*, a venomous spider in the desert of Sahara, the bite of which is cured thus: "The patient lies sometimes buried all over, excepting his head, in the hot sands, or else in a pit dug and heated for the purpose, in order, no doubt, to obtain the like copious perspiration that is excited by dancing in those who are bitten by the Tarantula."†

The Tigretiya of Abyssinia is in some respects similar to the Tarantism; it is, however, not caused by the bite, or sting, of any animal. The Tigretiya has its name from occurring principally in the Abyssinian district called Tigré.

---

* 'Allgemeine Musikalische Zeitung;' Leipzig, 1841, No. 17.

† 'Travels and Observations relating to Barbary,' by Thomas Shaw. 'A General Collection of Voyages and Travels,' by J. Pinkerton; London, 1808; Vol. XV., p. 635.

It is a kind of melancholy, the first symptoms of which usually are a gradual wasting away of the attacked person. Music and dancing are used as the most effective remedies for healing the sufferer.

A strange illness of the natives of Madagascar is described by the Missionary W. Ellis as "an intermittent disorder, with periods of delirium, a species of hysteria readily infectious." The sufferers perambulate in groups, singing, dancing, and running, accompanied by their friends, who carry bottles of water for them, as they generally complain of thirst,—which is not surprising, considering the state of excitement to which they work themselves up. Their whims being encouraged by the people, must rather impede the beneficial result which they might derive from singing and dancing, as far as concerns the restoration to a sound state of health. Their morbid affection of the nervous system is, however, especially interesting if compared with a similar derangement in European countries during the Middle Ages, of which some account shall presently be given.

The exercise of dancing to the sound of cheerful music is universally known to be, under certain circumstances conducive to the preservation of health. Thus, the traveller, H. Salt, relates that the Negro slaves in Mozambique "assembled in the evening to dance, according to the usual practice, for keeping them in health." * The same means were formerly resorted to by slave-owners in America. Likewise, during a voyage to the Arctic Sea, it has been found useful to order the sailors occasionally to dance on deck to the music of a barrel-organ, to keep them in health and good spirits.

On the other hand, there are instances on record of music and dancing having nourished morbid feelings and extravagant notions. At all events, certain Terpsichorean performances of religious fanatics can only be thus regarded. The most extraordinary exhibitions of this kind among Christian sects occurred on the Continent during the Middle Ages, and are described in an interesting little book, by

* 'A Voyage to Abyssinia, etc.' By Henry Salt. London, 1814; p. 33.

J. F. C. Hecker, entitled 'Die Tanzwuth, eine Volkskrankheit im Mittelalter; nach den Quellen für Aerzte und gebildete Nichtärzte bearbeitet,' (The Dancing Mania, an epidemic in the Middle Ages; compiled from original sources, for medical men and intelligent non-medical men. Berlin, 1832.) The author, a Doctor of Medicine, in Berlin, treats especially of the St. John's Dance and the St. Vitus's Dance, which, during the fourteenth and fifteenth centuries, were performed in Germany by perambulating fanatics who, in some respects, resembled certain Revivalists of our days. He carefully traces the origin of these morbid conceptions, the extravagant practices to which they led, and their gradual discontinuance during the seventeenth century. The persons afflicted with this nervous malady, men and women, wandered in troops from town to town and danced to the sound of musical instruments in the churches and streets. The authorities of some of the towns were of opinion that music and dancing alone could effectively cure this strange affection. They, therefore, hired musicians in order to bring on the dancing-fits the more rapidly; and they ordered strong, healthy men, to mix with the dancers with the object of compelling them to continue their violent exertions until they were quite exhausted,—a condition which was supposed to be a preliminary step to their restoration to health. Of the magistrates of Basle, for instance, it is recorded that in the sixteenth century they engaged some strong men to dance with a girl afflicted with the dancing mania, until she was recovered. One man substituted another, and this strange cure they continued about four weeks with scarcely any interruption, until the patient was exhausted and unable to stand on her legs. She was then carried to an hospital, where she completely regained her health.

The following miraculous occurrence, which is recorded in William of Malmesbury's 'Chronicle of the Kings of England' as having taken place in the year 1012, illustrates the fanaticism alluded to. The statement is by one of the poor sufferers :—

" I, Ethelbert, a sinner, even were I desirous of concealing the divine judgment which overtook me, yet the tremor of my limbs would betray me; wherefore I shall relate circumstantially how this happened, that all may know the heavy punishment due to disobedience. We were on the eve of our Lord's nativity, in a certain town of Saxony, in which was the church of Magnus the Martyr, and a priest named Robert had begun the first mass. I was in the church-yard with eighteen companions,—fifteen men and three women,—dancing and singing profane songs to such a degree that I interrupted the priest, and our voices resounded amid the sacred solemnity of the mass. Wherefore, having commanded us to be silent and not being attended to, he cursed us in the following words:—'May it please God and St. Magnus that you may remain singing in the same manner for a whole year!'—His words had their effect. The son of John the Priest seized his sister, who was singing with us, by the arm, and immediately tore it from the body; but not a drop of blood flowed out. She also remained a whole year with us dancing and singing. The rain fell not upon us; nor did cold, nor heat, nor hunger, nor thirst, nor fatigue assail us: we neither wore our clothes nor shoes, but we kept on singing as though we had been insane. First we sunk into the ground up to our knees; next to our thighs. A covering was at length, by the permission of God, built over us, to keep off the rain. When a year had elapsed, Herbert, bishop of the city of Cologne, released us from the tie wherewith our hands were bound, and reconciled us before the altar of St. Magnus. The daughter of the priest, with the other two women, died immediately; the rest of us slept three whole days and nights. Some died afterwards, and were famed for miracles; the remainder betray their punishment by the trembling of their limbs.

"This narrative was given to us by the Lord Peregrine, the successor of Herbert, in the year of our Lord 1013."

In our time, exhibitions of a morbid religious enthusiasm, called forth, or promoted by music, are less common with Christians than with Mohammedans. In the sacred dance of the Dervishes, the music, which is soft and plaintive, represents the music of the spheres; while the Dervishes turning in a circle round their superior, who sits quietly in the centre, represent the planetary system in its relation to the sun. So far, the procedures of these fanatics are intelligible enough; but the words of their songs are so mystic that probably the Dervishes themselves are unable to attach a reasonable meaning to them. Still more extraordinary is the behaviour of the Aïssaoua, a kind of Mohammedan fraternity in the Barbary States, who by means of music and dancing work themselves up to a state of ecstasy, in which they fancy themselves to be camels,—or, at any rate, in which they convey to others the impression that they are brutes rather than reasonable beings. As regards Christian sects, certain sacred evolutions of the Shakers, in the United States of North America, are not less extravagant than those of the Dervishes in Egypt or Turkey. Here too, music appears to have an injurious effect upon the people, inasmuch as it excites their morbid emotions.

Turning now to our literature on the medical employment of music, we find a number of treatises, the most important of which shall be briefly noticed by their titles. Of such only as are not easily attainable, some account of their contents shall be added.

'Medica Musica: or, a Mechanical Essay on the effects of Singing, Musick, and Dancing, on Human Bodies; Revis'd and corrected. To which is annex'd a New Essay on the nature and cure of the Spleen and Vapours. By Richard Browne, Apothecary, in Oakham, in the County of Rutland; London, 1729.'—This is the second edition, enlarged. The first edition was published without the name of the author.

'Die Verbindung der Musik mit der Arzneygelahrtheit, von Ernst Anton Nicolai.' (The Association of Music with the Science of Medicine, by E. A. Nicolai; Halle, 1745.)—Nicolai was Professor of Medicine at the University of Jena, in Germany.

'Reflections on Antient and Modern Musick, with the application to the Cure of Diseases; to which is subjoined an essay to solve the question wherein consisted the difference of ancient musick from that of modern time;'

London, 1749.—The author, Richard Brocklesby, was a physician in London.—A circumstantial account of the contents of this treatise is given in 'Historisch-Kritische Beyträge zur Aufnahme der Musik, von F. W. Marpurg;' Vol. II., Berlin, 1756; p. 16-37.

'Traité des Effets de la Musique sur le corps humain, traduit du Latin et augmenté des notes, par Etienne Sainte-Marie;' Paris, 1803.—This is an annotated translation of a dissertation written in Latin by Joseph Ludovicus Roger, and published at Avignon in 1758.

Desbout (Luigi): 'Ragionamento fisico-chirurgico sopra l'effetto della Musica nelle malattie nervose;' Livorno, 1780.—A French translation appeared in the year 1784, in St. Petersburg, entitled: 'Sur l'Effet de la Musique dans les Maladies nerveuses.'

Buc'hoz (Pierre Joseph): 'L'Art de connaître et de désigner le pouls par les notes de la Musique, de guérir par son moyen la mélancolie, et le Tarentisme qui est une espèce de mélancolie; accompagné de 198 observations, tirées tant de l'histoire que des annales de la médicine qui constatent l'éfficacité de la musique, non seulement sur le corps mais sur l'âme, dans l'état de santé, ainsi que dans celui de maladie. Ouvrage curieux, utile et intéressant; propre à inspirer le goût de cet art, qui est pour nous un vrai présent des cieux;' Paris, 1806.—A treatise with a similar title, by F. N. Marquet, appeared at Nancy in the year 1747.

Lichtenthal (Peter): 'Der musikalische Arzt; oder, Abhandlung von dem Einflusse der Musik auf den menschlichen Körper, und von ihrer Anwendung in gewissen Krankheiten,' (The Musical Physician; or, a Treatise on the influence of music upon the human body, and on its application in certain illnesses. Vienna, 1807.)—An Italian translation of this work appeared in Milan in the year 1811.

Schneider (Peter Joseph): 'System einer medizinischen Musik; ein unentbehrliches Handbuch für Medizin-Beflissene, Vorsteher der Irren-Heilanstalten, praktische Aerzte, und unmusikalische Lehrer verschiedener Disciplinen,' (A System of Medical Music; an indispensable guide for

Students of Medicine, Principals of Lunatic Asylums, Practical Physicians, and unmusical teachers of different methods. Bonn, 1835.) This comprehensive work, in two volumes, contains much information on the subject in question, interspersed with many remarks and citations which have little or no bearing on music considered medically. The last seventy-two pages of the second volume contain a sort of autobiography of the author.

To musicians, the most useful books among this class of literature are those which give good advice concerning the preservation of health.

F. W. Hunnius, a Doctor of Medicine in Weimar, wrote a book entitled 'Der Arzt für Schauspieler und Sänger' (The Physician for Actors and Singers. Weimar, 1798,) which, no doubt, has been useful to many. Another German publication of the kind, in which especial attention is given to the practice of musical instruments in so far as it affects the health, bears the title 'Aerztlicher Rathgeber für Musiktreibende' (Medical Adviser for those who cultivate Music) by Karl Sundelin, Berlin, 1832. The author, a Doctor of Medicine in Berlin, wrote his book with the assistance of his brother, who was a professional musician in the orchestra of the King of Prussia. This treatise is so noteworthy that the following account of it will, it is hoped, be of interest to the reflecting musician. Its table of contents is:—

"I. Of Singing. On the means of facilitating the practice of singing. Dietary and general rules for male singers, and for female singers. Of the different human voices.

II. Of the Clavier-Instruments, or Keyed-Instruments. The Pianoforte. The Organ. The Harmonica with a keyboard.

III. Of the Stringed Instruments. The Violin and the Viola (or Tenor). The Violoncello. The Double Bass. The Guitar. The Harp.

IV. Of the Wind Instruments. Means for facilitating the practice and dietary rules for players on wind instruments. The Flageolet and the Czakan. The Flute. The Oboe and the English Horn. The Clarionet and the Basset Horn. The Bassoon and the Contra-Fagotto. The Horn.

The Trumpet. The Trombone. The Serpent. General dietary and medical rules for those who cultivate music. Of the disturbances and injuries to the nervous system through disadvantageous influences by the practice of music. Care and treatment of particular diseased parts and structures. Of the chest and the lungs. The especial attention and care required by the organs of the voice. Of the diseases to which the mouth is subjected. The Teeth. The Lips. Of the Fingers. The Eyes and the Face. Prescriptions for some of the medicaments alluded to in the preceding dissertation."

The author is of opinion that the practice of music may be in many ways injurious to bodily health. However, he remarks, that since music is capable of expressing emotions which cannot be expressed by words or pictures, it relieves the heart of anything which is oppressive and distressing, and thus through the mind generally acts beneficially upon the body. He asserts that music has healed many a sufferer whose life was embittered by the fetters of melancholia, or the tortures of hypochondria. To persons suffering from indigestion and its harassing effects, he recommends a daily practice on some instrument which requires a rather fatiguing exertion of the body; such as the organ, on which hands and feet are occupied. His remarks on singing are judicious; but many of them would naturally suggest themselves to any thinking musician. No doubt, moderation in eating and drinking is recommendable, and the singer has to take care not to catch a cold; but it may be useful to him to be told by a medical man what kind of food is most conducive to the preservation of his voice, and how he can best protect himself against the injurious effects of sudden changes from heat and cold, to which professional singers are often exposed.

Pianoforte playing our medical adviser considers rather hurtful to health. The exertion of the hands and arms, while the position of the body remains nearly immovable, causes a stronger flow of blood to the chest than is natural. The pressure of the points of the fingers, where the nerves are especially sensitive, is apt to be injurious to the nervous system. This is still more the case in practising on instruments on which the strings are pressed down with the points of the fingers, as for instance on the violin; and also, though in a less degree, on instruments the strings of which are twanged with the fingers, as they are on the harp. The practice, however, causes the skin at the finger-ends to harden, and the touch becomes consequently less sensitive. Decidedly hurtful to the nerves is the sensation produced by the friction of the moistened fingers in playing the glass-harmonica and similar instruments. Among the wind instruments blown by being placed to the mouth, those which require a sudden and prolonged retardation of the breath, or a forcible compression of the air in the lungs, are especially liable, by constant practice, to prove injurious to health. The author has much to say on this subject, and he particularly warns against too continuous playing on the oboe, trumpet, horn, trombone, and serpent. As regards the clarionet, its practice, he says, is likely to be injurious on account of the quantity of air which it requires. The player is often compelled to take a deeper inspiration than is natural, and constantly to pay regard to being provided with a supply of air compressed in his lungs. Furthermore, considering that musical performances very frequently take place in artificial light, the eye-sight of the musician is apt to be disadvantageously affected. In this respect also the playing on some instruments is more injurious than on others. The Double Bass player, for instance, is compelled, from the size of his instrument, to have the musical notation placed at a greater distance before him than is naturally convenient for his sight, which renders it necessary for him to exert his eyes in an extraordinary degree. Thus much from Sundelin's 'Medical Adviser,' to which the following remarks may be added.

The musical instruments used by our forefathers, two or three centuries ago, were softer and more soothing in quality of sound than our present ones; at any rate, this was the case with the stringed instruments, and the wind instruments of the flute kind. Certain wind instruments of the trumpet kind had a very harsh sound; but these were intended especially to be played in the open air. Of the stringed instruments principally favoured in family circles—such as the lute, cither, clavichord, virginal, harpsichord, etc.,—almost all possessed a less exciting quality of sound than our present substitutes for them. The same was the case with the music composed for the instruments; it did not possess the passionate modulations which characterize much of our music of the present day. It was, therefore, evidently more conducive to social comfort, and consequently to health, than is our modern music, notwithstanding the progress which has been made in the cultivation of the art. Martin Luther said to an old hypochondriac schoolmaster who complained to him of his miserable feelings: "Take to the Clavichord!" Everyone acquainted with the character of the clavichord will probably admit that Luther's advice was judicious. The soft and unpretending sound of the clavichord is so expressive that the instrument may be said to respond to the sufferer as a sympathizing friend; while its successor, the loud and brilliant pianoforte, is apt to convey the impression of being cold and heartless, unless it is touched by a master-hand. Thus also the "trembling lute," and some other antiquated instruments appear to be remarkably suitable for consoling and calming the anxious heart.

The glass-harmonica is evidently hurtful to the health of the performer. We have seen that Sundelin attributes its injurious effect to the friction of the fingers upon the bowls, which revolve on a spindle. But it is a well-ascertained fact that the fascinating sound of this instrument exercises a distressing influence also upon persons who do not play it, but who often listen to it. Likewise, certain wind instruments of a so-called reedy quality of sound, as, for instance, the harmonium, are probably injurious rather than beneficial to the health of the players. Sounds of this nature are generally very pleasant when heard for a short time, but soon become harassing. They might be compared with confectionery, a little of which may be very palatable and innocuous, but which if made a meal of would probably produce sickness.

The effect of music upon animals is a subject for investigation so closely connected with an inquiry into the influence of music upon the human body, that some notice of it must not be omitted here. The investigation requires far more discernment than would appear at a first glance. Many of the anecdotes recorded respecting the effect of music upon animals are not properly authenticated; or rather, they are misrepresentations of facts not clearly understood by the observers. Nor is it surprising that this should be the case, considering how difficult it is to appreciate rightly the mental capacities even of our domestic animals, which we have constant opportunity of watching. Nothing is more common, even with intelligent observers, than to attribute to a dog certain motives for certain actions, which may possibly be the real motives, but which may also only appear to be the real ones. Acute and thoroughly unbiassed investigators, such as was for instance Gilbert White of Selborne, about a hundred years ago, are rare. At all events, many of the anecdotes given in works on Natural History, as illustrating the power of music upon animals, have evidently been copied by one author from another without any one of them having taken the trouble to ascertain by careful observation whether they are well founded. With quadrupeds it is probably generally more the rhythmical effect of the music than the tones which pleases them; while birds appear to be pleased by the tones rather than by the rhythm. All this requires more exact investigation than it has hitherto received; and surely it deserves the consideration of a Darwin.

In conclusion, attention may be drawn to a curious fact which is perhaps more interesting to musical antiquarians than to medical men. It is well known that the barbers in England, about three centuries ago, generally had some musical instruments in their shops for the amusement of their customers. In Germany it is still not unusual to meet with a musical barber. In former times the barbers were also surgeons and physicians to some extent. It would be interesting to trace the origin of their habit of cultivating the art of music. It is probably of high antiquity. May it not date from a remote period in which the physicians of European nations resorted to music and incantations like the medicine-men of uncivilized tribes of whom an account has been given in the beginning of this essay?

POPULAR STORIES WITH MUSICAL TRADITIONS.

THE intelligent reader need hardly be reminded that an insight into the peculiar notions respecting the beauty and power of music current among different nations may be of valuable assistance in the study of national music, inasmuch as it tends to throw light upon questions which appear obscure and inexplicable.

The following popular stories, like those which have previously been given in this work, are told exactly as they are heard from the mouth of the people. It is necessary that this should be mentioned by way of introduction to the stories, because the degree of interest which they may possess depends almost entirely upon the faithfulness with which they are recorded. For the same reason it must be stated that, although additions have been carefully avoided, it is otherwise with omissions, since it appeared desirable to abridge several of the stories by excluding passages which do not touch upon the subject of music. Should the reader find among the stories an old acquaintance with a somewhat different face than is familiar to him, he will, it is hoped, bear in mind that, just as there are varieties of a popular tune to be found in different districts of a country, so there are also different readings of a popular tale. Even the degree of education attained by the narrator, his personal character, and his peculiar views, will tend in some measure to modify the features of a story, although nothing extraneous may have been admitted into the incidents recorded.

THE ROYAL MUSIC-MASTER.

The modern Greeks have a long story, said to have been derived from Asia Minor, the substance of which is as follows:—

A mighty king in a distant land had a son who was an excellent flute player, but a bashful youth, and a woman-hater. The king, considering it all-important that his dynasty should be preserved, sends the young prince in a ship to a foreign court, to find, if possible, among the princesses a wife to his liking. The ship is wrecked, and all on board are drowned except the prince, who is thrown by the waves upon the shore of a beautiful island. Having dried himself, he meets a poor fisherman, with whom he changes clothes. Hiding his luxuriant hair under a bladder-cap, he sets out to the residence of the king of the island, into whose service he is taken by the master of the horse as a stable-boy. His chief occupation now is to fetch water for the horses from a spring in the garden of the palace. In the evening, when he is alone in the garden, he plays upon his flute so enchantingly that even the nightingales become silent in admiration. The King's daughter hears him, comes down into the garden, and, with the consent of her father, makes him her music-master. When he perceives that she really loves him, he loves her too, discloses to her that he is a King's son, and soon makes her his queen in his own dominions.*

THE HANDSOME MINSTREL.

The following story is told in Germany:—

A handsome minstrel plays under a window of the King's palace upon a golden instrument. His music is so alluring that the King, yielding to the entreaties of his daughter,

---

* 'Griechische und Albanische Märchen, gesammelt von J. G. v. Hahn.' Leipzig, 1864; Vol. I., p. 273.

invites the handsome minstrel to come up to him in his palace. The King's daughter soon learns to play on the instrument, and longs to possess a similar one. All the goldsmiths of the kingdom are applied to; but not one of them is able to construct such an artistic work. Thereupon the King's daughter becomes greatly dejected; and when the handsome minstrel learns the cause of her sadness he tells her that if she will marry him she shall have the golden instrument. But she rejects the offer with scorn.

Some days afterwards the handsome minstrel appears again under the window, playing on an instrument still more precious, and producing sounds most ravishing. The King's daughter is enchanted beyond measure; but the goldsmiths of the kingdom are still less capable of constructing such a wonderful work of art.

Then the handsome minstrel offers to give her both instruments if she will marry him. She cannot resist, and says, "Yes!" After the celebration of the wedding the handsome minstrel conducts his bride to his house, deep in the forest. The house is so small and poor, that the King's daughter, when she sees it, is overwhelmed with pride and remorse, and faints away. When she recovers she finds herself lying on a magnificent bed, and the handsome minstrel is a King.

THE DAISY LADY.

Among the Fairy Tales of the Hindus we meet with a story entitled 'Brave Seventee Bai,' which seems to contain the original key-note of the German 'Trusty Ferdinand.' * Seventee Bai (*i.e.* "The Daisy Lady") is the daughter of a Rajah. Bent upon roving about in the world, she assumes the dress and manners of a youth. Her rambles lead her into the garden of a beautiful enchantress whose name is Hera Bai (*i.e.* "The Diamond's Daughter.") This beautiful enchantress is described as being a child of the Great Cobra,

* See above, Vol. I., p. 84.

a serpent which plays an important part in many of the Hindu traditions. Here are to be found some striking coincidences between the superstitions respecting serpents popular among the country people in Germany and in Hindustan.

Well, Hera Bai, the beautiful enchantress, falls in love with Seventee Bai, who successfully maintains her disguise as a youth, but who cannot be prevailed upon to remain in the garden, averring that an important mission must be accomplished before the marriage takes place. The enchantress, finding persuasion unavailing, gives Seventee Bai a small golden flute. "Take this flute," she says; "whenever you wish to see me, or are in need of my aid, go into the jungle and play upon it, and before the sound ceases I will be there; but do not play it in the towns, nor yet amid a crowd." Seventee Bai puts the golden flute into the folds of her dress and proceeds on her wanderings. Sometime afterwards, when she is in need of assistance, she goes into the jungle, draws out of her dress the golden flute and plays. The beautiful enchantress appears, swinging in a silver tree, just as she appeared in the garden.

Again, on another occasion the beautiful lady immediately comes at the sound of the flute, inquiring, "Husband, what can I do for you?"*

In the Scandinavian Fairy Tales, collected by Asbjörnsen and Moe, we have a story entitled 'East o' the Sun and West o' the Moon,' in which a young country lass is taken into the cave of a shaggy White Bear, who afterwards turns out to be a lovely prince. When the White Bear has carried the lass to his home, which gleams with silver and gold, he gives her a silver bell and politely tells her that whenever she wants anything she has only to ring the bell, and her wishes shall be at once fulfilled.†

---

* 'Old Deccan Days; or Hindu Fairy Legends, current in Southern India, collected from oral tradition by M. Frere., London, 1868; p. 25.

† 'Popular Tales from the Norse, translated by G. W. Dasent.' Edinburgh, 1859; p. 27.

How effectively the magic flute and magic bells have been introduced into Mozart's opera 'Il Flauto Magico' is well known to lovers of good music,—or, which is the same, to admirers of Mozart.

THE INVISIBLE FLUTE-PLAYER.

A strange story is told by the peasants in Holstein of an invisible flute-player, who is said to have haunted, about fifty years ago, a farm-house situated near the river Elbe. Some of the children of the farmer who owned the house are still alive.

The mysterious affair commenced in a cabbage garden behind the house. There the people often heard flute-playing, but no one could make out whence it came. Gradually the invisible flutist intruded into the house. More and more frequently he came, until at last he took up his abode in the house altogether. Sometimes he played his flute in the sitting-room; sometimes in one of the bedrooms; at other times in the cellar, or in the garret. Occasionally also he paid a visit to a neighbouring house. The people on the farm became quite used to him; and when the children, or the servant lads and lasses, were disposed to enjoy a little dancing, they would just name a certain tune, or sing a bar or two of it, and ask him to play it; and directly they heard the desired tune. When the milkmaid was occupied in the dairy, she sometimes took an apple in her hand, for fun, and said: "Now, my boy, play me a nice air, and thou shalt have an apple!" In a moment the apple vanished out of her hand, and the music commenced.

In the course of time, however, the invisible flutist became very intrusive, and at last he proved quite a nuisance. One night he would amuse himself by breaking all the windows in the house; another night he had his gambols in the kitchen, turning everything topsy-turvy; and at midday, when the family had sat down to dinner, it sometimes happened that the large dish of stew before them, from which all were eating, was emptied in an instant by invisible hands. They would then jump up and run about the room, beating the air with their spoons. When they thought they had at last driven the fellow into a corner of the room, suddenly they heard him spitefully playing his flute in another corner.

In short, the annoyance became quite unbearable. There was no peace in the house. The farmer everywhere expressed the wish that he could find somebody who had the power to expel the invisible flute-player; he did not mind the expense. At last there came a clever man from the neighbouring town, who offered to settle the matter; he only wanted to know beforehand whether he should show and banish the flutist in his real figure, or in the figure of a poodle.

The farmer said: "I would rather not see him at all! Here are ten Thalers; all I want is to get rid of him, and to have peace in my own house."

By means of queer rhymes, and smoke, the clever man from town actually succeeded in driving out the troublesome guest, and no mysterious flute-playing has been heard since on the farm.*

THE BANISHED MUSICIAN.

At the bottom of the lake called "Das Langholter Meer," in the vicinity of the river Weser, south of Bremen, lives, according to popular tradition, a skilful musician who was banished there by a Pastor; but, the reason why he was banished to this place,—and indeed, why he was banished at all,—is not exactly known.

One day, in the winter, when the lake was all frozen over, two young lads happened to be keeping sheep in the neighbourhood; and when they saw the smooth ice, the tallest said to the other: "Come, let us not stand shivering here; let us go on the lake, and the musician shall play to us."

---

* 'Sagen, Märchen und Lieder der Herzogthümer Schleswig, Holstein und Lauenburg,' von Karl Müllenhoff; Kiel, 1845; p. 336.

Having said this, he went to the ice; his companion followed him, and they amused themselves for a while with sliding. It then occurred to them again that there was a musician at the bottom of the lake, and they called out in high glee: "If thou art still there below, old fellow, just strike up a tune, and we will dance to it."

But, how terrified they were when suddenly there arose from the bottom of the lake music such as they never had heard in all their life. It was the most ravishing music in the world!—Of course, they thought no longer of dancing, but left the lake as quickly as they could slide.*

THE WALRIDERSKE.

According to a tradition current in Northern Germany, especially near Holland, the Walriderske is a kind of a witch. Assuming the figure of some rough-haired animal, she visits the sleeper in the night, and presses herself upon his chest so as to prevent his moving any part of his body, scarcely permitting him to breathe. She creeps up to the sleeper from below, gradually crawling over his whole body. First he feels a pressure on his feet; then on his stomach; and at last on his chest. Meanwhile the tortured victim is unable to move even a finger. All he can do is to sigh and groan in almost intolerable anguish.

The apparition sometimes resembles a poodle, sometimes a cat, and at other times a strange-looking unknown beast particularly repulsive. Its colour is most commonly black; there are, however, also brown, and even white ones. Not unfrequently the sleeper feels the pressure without seeing the figure. In short, this unwelcome visitor is as bad as the worst nightmare, if not worse.

But, occasionally the Walriderske appears in the shape of a beautiful girl, and sings more charmingly than can be described. Indeed, from the oldest traditions still extant

---

* 'Aberglaube und Sagen aus dem Herzogthum Oldenburg, herausgegeben von Strackerjan;' Oldenburg, 1867; Vol. I., p. 190.

may be gathered that the Walriderskes ought to be regarded as superhuman beings; for, although they occasionally appear in human shape, and are in many ways like human beings, they live subject to other laws, and are endued with powers other than ours. It admits of no doubt that in the traditions respecting them much is to be found which has been derived from the pagan mythology of our ancestors relating to the Walküren, who rode or sailed in the clouds. The Walriderskes are frequently described as floating through the air and singing most sweetly. In Ostfriesland, England is the home assigned to these charming singers. They come from far over the sea to seek their sacrifice. Their boat is a sieve, such as the peasants in Ostfriesland use for straining milk, and which is called *Tähmse.* Their oars are human shoulder-blades.

A peasant of Barssel once, while on a moonlight night he was mowing his corn, towards midnight, became tired and threw himself down under a sheaf to sleep. He had not lain long when he heard at a distance a melodious song, which gradually came nearer and nearer until it was above the field where he lay. He looked up and saw sailing in the air a Walriderske who had come over from England. She descended, hid her *Tähmse* and oars under a sheaf, and went away in the direction towards Barssel. The peasant lost no time in appropriating to himself the things which the Walriderske had hidden. Towards morning she returned; and when she missed her *Tähmse* and oars, she began to sing so dolefully that the peasant felt sorry for her, and gave her back the things.

In the following night, when curiosity led him to go again to the place where this had happened, he found there, to his surprise, a large piece of the finest linen, evidently a present of the Walriderske. He took it home, and had it made into shirts. He wore the shirts without experiencing any harm; although his neighbours had warned him that he exposed himself to great danger by keeping the linen.*

* 'Aberglaube und Sagen aus dem Herzogthum Oldenburg, herausgegeben von Strackerjan;' Oldenburg, 1867; Vol. I., p. 375.

THE JEW IN THE THICKET.

Many popular tales could be noticed of instrumental performers who possess the power of making everyone dance. Not only men, but animals, and sometimes even inanimate objects are compelled to wheel around. Take for instance the following German tale, known as 'The Jew in the Thicket.'

Once upon a time there lived in a small village a poor peasant lad whose name was Heinrich, but whom his neighbours used to call Honest Heinrich, because he was as honest as he was poor. Whether he was so poor because he was so honest, or whatever else was the cause of his poverty, would now be useless to speculate upon. Enough that he found it expedient to improve his circumstances; and for this purpose he set out on a journey into the world, with only a few copper coins in his pocket.

After a while, his way led him to a lonely place near some hills. He thought he was quite alone, when unexpectedly a little grey man, very old-looking, accosted him and solicited alms. "Give me whatever thou hast in coppers," said the grey man, "and thou shalt have no cause to repent thy generosity; thou seest, I am old and infirm; but thou art young and robust, and wilt easily make thy way in the world."

When Honest Heinrich heard the grey man speak thus, it went to his heart, and he put his hand into his pocket, took out the copper coins,—which, in fact, constituted all the property he possessed in the world,—and gave them to the old beggar. Then cheerfully whistling he resumed his journey.

"Hallo! just wait a bit, my lad!" cried the grey man: "I know thou art an honest fellow, and deservest a helping hand to push thee on in the world; so thou mayst have three wishes, and they shall be granted to thee."

Then Honest Heinrich saw at once that he had to do with an Onnerersk, as the little folks are called who dwell under ground in golden halls deep in the mountains; so, having bethought himself for a moment, he touched his cap and said:

"Well sir, let me have a fiddle which when I play upon it makes everyone dance. And let me have a blow-pipe with which I am sure to hit everything I want to shoot. And my third wish shall be, if you please, that whenever I ask a favour of anybody, it will not be refused me."

All these wishes were readily conceded to Honest Heinrich, and it may easily be imagined what great advantages he now possessed in his endeavours to make his fortune in the world. The third wish especially proved invaluable to him. Neither was the fiddle to be despised; nay, it actually saved him from the gallows! and how this happened to come to pass, shall now be related.

After Honest Heinrich had proceeded on his way a mile or two, he came beside a thicket of thorns, in the middle of which sat a lovely little bird that sang even more beautifully than it was beautiful to look at. And near the thicket stood a Jew counting a bag of money, which was not exactly his own, for he had taken it from somewhere, so to say, without asking permission. Now, the Jew was in an awkward fix, for he could not move from the spot where he stood, because the lovely little bird had enchanted him with his melodious music. He had, however, a particular reason for moving on as quickly as possible, since it was not at all unlikely that somebody might follow him, overtake him, and say, "you are wanted; just come back with me to town!" Therefore, when he saw Honest Heinrich carrying a blow-pipe, he called out to him:

"A good piece of money I would gladly part with if thou couldst procure for me that charming bird."

Then Honest Heinrich took his blow-pipe, aimed, and hit the little bird: he only said "There!" and the charming little songster fell down into the thicket. Directly the Jew worked himself among the thorn bushes to take the bird out; meanwhile he made all kinds of excuses for not giving the piece of money which he had promised.

"O ho!" said Honest Heinrich, "that matter we shall easily settle!" Presently he took up his fiddle to try its effect upon the Jew. One stroke of the bow, and the Jew began to wabble;—another stroke, and he lifted up his right leg;—a third stroke, and the dancing began in earnest.

"O dear me!" cried the Jew, "leave off that confounded fiddling! The thorns hurt me dreadfully! Upon my honour, I shall be a dead man before I am safely out of the thicket!" But, Honest Heinrich was becoming warm with trying his newly-acquired instrument; so he only replied: "Never mind the thorns; all right!" and struck up a quicker tune. "O torture!" cried the perspiring dancer, "I am a ruined man! Here,—here is my whole bag of money,—all genuine coins,—take it,—only cease that fiddling!"

Honest Heinrich made what musicians call a brilliant cadence, which caused the Jew to throw a few somersaults, and then gave the finishing stroke, or in other words, the concluding chord. The Jew crept out of the thicket, handed over the bag to the fiddler, and made off as rapidly as he could into the wide world.

Honest Heinrich, on the other hand, took the direction towards the town with the intention of restoring the bag of money to its rightful owner. He was soon met by a man dressed in an unpretending kind of uniform, who, seeing the bag, in a friendly and almost playful way, gave Honest Heinrich a little tap on his shoulder, and said: "You are wanted; you must come with me to town." Then Honest Heinrich was taken to prison; and when the judge asked him about the bag of money, and he replied, "A Jew gave it me," the judge smiled and said, "A Jew? you will never make me believe that!" In short, Honest Heinrich was found guilty of robbery, and the judge sentenced him to be hanged.

There prevailed a strange taste in the town where this occurred. Whenever an execution took place, the people had a kind of festival. Days, nay, even weeks, before the interesting event, the wretched culprit was considered almost as a martyr. Whatever he said was carefully recorded, and made publicly known. Men of rank felt honoured when he shook hands with them; and when the awful hour for his execution had arrived, and he stood under the gallows, he would address the throng of people assembled as spectators. The women, of course, relished the exciting scene even more than the men, and cried with all their heart. Now, as Honest Heinrich was innocent, he did not like to have any fuss made about him ; so, when he stood under the gallows, he only asked that he might be permitted to play a "Last Farewell" upon his dear fiddle. The judge said he would not deny the last request of a dying sinner. "Pray, your worship!" cried the Jew, who had mingled with the spectators, and who rejoiced in his heart at the turn which the money affair had taken, "Pray, your worship, do not allow him his fiddle ; his music will do us mischief!" But the judge took no notice of the Jew, and said, "Play, my lad, but make it short ; we have not much time to lose."

Then Honest Heinrich took his fiddle and played. One stroke with the bow, and all the people began to wabble. Another stroke, and every one lifted up his right leg. A third stroke, and the dancing began in earnest. The judge, the clergyman, the doctor, the hangman, the Jew, women with their babies in their arms, ladies with their smelling-bottles in their hands ; in short, every one present, old and young, danced with the utmost exertion. Even the very dogs which had followed their masters, raised themselves upon their hind-legs and danced, profusely perspiring like all the people.

"Hold! stop! hold!" cried the exhausted judge, "Thy life is spared ; only put aside that dreadful fiddle!"

As soon as Honest Heinrich heard the judge's promise of acquittal he ceased playing and came down the steps from the gallows. At the foot of the steps he found the Jew lying prostrate on his back. "Confess directly," said Honest Heinrich, "how you came by the bag of money, or I shall give you a little private performance, with a brilliant cadence at the end, you know!" In a moment the alarmed Jew stood upon his legs again, and exclaimed, "Upon my honour, I stole it!"

Then they hanged the Jew upon the gallows. As for Honest Heinrich, he continued his wanderings in the world, and soon made his fortune. When he had become rich, he went home again to his village, and courted his neighbour's daughter, who had formerly jilted him when he was poor, but who loved him now dearly, not because he was rich (she said) but on account of his former poverty. Soon they married, and were happy ever after.

THE POPE'S WIFE.

There are several modifications current of the story of the Jew in the Thicket just told. A similar story which in olden time was popular in England, is given under the heading 'A Mery Geste of the Frere and the Boye,' in Ritson's Pieces of Ancient Popular Poetry, London, 1791. Again, a somewhat similar story is current in Greece. A lad has a flute given to him by some superhuman being. He goes to the market-place of the town, where piles of crockery are exhibited for sale. As soon as he begins to play, all the pots, jugs and basins fly about in the air and clash against each other until they are broken to pieces. The personage whom he compels to dance in the thorns is a priest. *

Perhaps the most tragic incident of this kind is the sad fate of the Pope's wife, related by the Wallachians. It need scarcely be said that it does not concern the Pope of Rome, who, as everyone knows, has no wife. But in Wallachia the common village priest of the Greek Church is called Pope, and may marry. He generally avails himself of the permission.

As regards Bakâla, whose music, as we shall presently see, killed the Pope's wife, various tricks of his are on record, which clearly show that he was a great fool, somewhat resembling the German Till Eulenspiegel, who had perhaps more happy ideas than many persons who have passed for wise.

Well, Bakâla, one fine day, took it into his head to ascend a high mountain, merely for pleasure, and for the sake of boasting. Arrived at the top of the mountain he

---

* 'Griechische und Albanische Märchen, gesammelt von J. G. v. Hahn;' Leipzig, 1864; Vol. I., p. 222, and Vol. II., p. 240.

was fortunate enough to make the acquaintance of a well-disposed spirit, who offered him a present from the clouds. The articles from which Bakâla was invited to select a keepsake looked mean and shabby, like those which people generally consign to the lumber-room. Bakâla, however, examined them carefully, and chose an old and dusty bag-pipe; for he imagined, as some people are apt to do, that he was madly fond of music. Moreover, the sound of the bag-pipe—this Bakâla soon discovered—had the power of making everyone dance.

When Bakâla had come down from the mountain he engaged himself as shepherd to a village Pope in the valley. Every day he led the sheep into the fields, and blowing his bagpipe he made them caper and jump into the air like grasshoppers. And when, one morning, his master had sneaked out before him into the fields, and had hid himself in some bushes of sloes and dog-roses to watch his servant's strange proceedings, Bakâla made the Pope dance as well as his flock.

The Pope was a soft-hearted sort of man. Quietness he loved above all things in the world; for its sake no sacrifice appeared to him too great. As to his wife, she was of a different disposition. To say the truth, she was just the reverse of her husband. She had more courage in her little finger than he had in all his limbs. His *Yes* was her *No*, and when he called a thing white she was sure to declare that she had long since found it to be very black indeed. Neither would she believe in the power of Bakâla's bagpipe. When the poor Pope, after his return from the sloes and dog-roses, showed her his tattered clothes and scratched limbs, all the sympathy he got from her was, "Tush! tush! nonsense! If I were as soft-hearted as some people are said to be, I might perhaps pity you."

"Well, my dear," replied the cowed husband, "you shall hear him to-night. I want to convince you"——

"Convince me?" cried the Pope's wife: "Fudge! I to be frightened by a bagpipe? Let him come on!"

Then the Pope thought that it was time to withdraw for the sake of quietness. But in the evening he took Bakâla aside, and desired him just to serenade their mistress for a little while under the window.

Before Bakâla commenced playing the Pope sat down on the ground and bound two heavy stones to his feet by way of precaution, while his wife busied herself in the upper story of the house. No sooner had Bakâla begun his performance than she danced so furiously that she made the whole house shake. Bakâla played faster and faster; her stamping grew louder and louder. She danced until she had actually stamped a hole in the floor, through which she descended into the lower story. The Pope peeped into the room; and when he saw what had happened he felt sorry, and he beckoned Bakâla to leave off playing. But, alas! he beckoned too late! The poor lady had danced herself to death.

Now, one might have thought the Pope would have dismissed Bakâla, telling him that his services were not any further required. But this is just precisely what he did not do. On the contrary, he kept Bakâla in his service, and treated him even better than before.*

THE TWO HUNCHBACKS.

The story of the two Hunchbacks is widely diffused. It is told in Ireland as well as in Germany and Italy; moreover it is said to be also current in Spain. There are, of course, many varieties of it in these countries. Compare, for instance, the Irish narrative of Lusmore, in 'Fairy Legends and Traditions of the South of Ireland, by T. Crofton Croker,' with the one given here, which has been obtained from the country people in Rhenish Prussia.

On St. Matthew's day, in the year 1549, a poor humpbacked musician was returning late at night to Aachen† from a village where he had been playing at a wedding.

---

* 'Wallachische Märchen, herausgegeben von A. Schott;' Stuttgart, 1845, p. 228.

† Aix-la-Chapelle.

Being in a half drowsy state, he took but little heed of time or place, and so he passed the Minster without concerning himself about anything particularly, just as the large clock in the tower boomed midnight. The sound startled him, especially as at the same time there arose in the air a strange whirring like the unearthly sound of owls and bats on the wing. It now occurred to him that this was the night of quarter-day, and he quickened his steps to escape the terrors of the ghost's hour and of apparitions. Nervously he turned into the Schmiedstrasse (Smith-street) as the nearest way to his home, which was in the Jakobstrasse (James-street). But on reaching the Fish Market,—what did he see! All the stalls glistened with innumerable lights, and about them were seated a large party of richly-dressed ladies, feasting on dainty viands served in golden and silver dishes, and drinking sparkling wine from crystal goblets. The musician, much frightened, endeavoured to hide himself in a corner; for, he had not the least doubt that he saw an assemblage of witches. But it was too late; one of the ladies nearest him had already observed him, and she conducted him to the table.

"Don't be frightened!" said the lady to the musician, who stood before her with chattering teeth and trembling knees: "Don't be frightened; but, play us some merry tunes, and thou shalt be paid for it."

The poor hunchback had no choice but to take up his violin, and to amuse the strange company as long as they pleased. Having quickly set aside the stalls with everything upon them, the witches—among whom the poor hunchback thought he recognised several ladies of high position from the town—whirled round in pairs to the sound of his fiddle. But the strangest thing was that the longer the fellow continued to play, the finer and fuller his performance appeared to him; so that he really thought he must be either dreaming, or there must be a whole band of violins and flutes placed behind him which joined in his performance.

Now the Minster clock struck a quarter to one; all the dancers instantaneously stopped, visibly exhausted, and everything was reinstated in its former order. Hesitating, the musician looked on, uncertain whether he ought to stay any longer, or whether he might go; when the lady who had engaged his services came up to him and said: 'Brave musician! thou hast done thy work to our content, and shalt now receive thy recompense."

While saying the words she pulled off his jacket, and, before he was aware of it, she had slipped behind him, and at one grasp relieved him of his hump. Who so happy as the disburthened fiddler? In thankfulness he was just going to throw himself on his knees before his benefactress,—when the clock struck One, and in a moment, ladies, lights, and dishes were gone, and the musician found himself at dark night standing alone in the middle of the Fish Market. Bewildered, he put his hand to his back, doubting lest the adventure had been merely a confused dream. But, no; it was reality! The hump was gone, and the happy fellow rejoiced in feeling as upright as man can be. Moreover, his joy was still increased when he took up his jacket, which lay before him on the ground. Perceiving it to be unaccountably heavy, and thrusting his hands into the pockets to ascertain the cause, he found that both pockets were filled with money. Doubly happy, he hastened home, and in thankfulness he made the next morning an offering of his fiddle to his Patron Saint, under whose image in the church he hung it as a glorious relic to be venerated by his children and his children's children for ever.

Now, the marvellous affair created, as may easily be understood, an immense sensation in the town. People went to the church to look at the fiddle; and whenever the lucky musician showed himself in public, a knot of curious idlers hovered around him, anxious to get a peep at his back. Moreover, his good fortune, as may likewise be easily understood, aroused the envy of his rivals in his profession.

The most envious of these professional brothers possessed himself a tolerably respectable hump, which annoyed him all the more, since he was not less vain than envious. His estimation of his personal appearance was, however, exceeded by that of his musical accomplishments.

"How surprised they will be!" said he to himself: "If that wretched scraper could please them, I am sure I have only to treat them with a few of my inimitable flourishes, and I shall be a straight man and a man of property in no time!"

It was at midnight of St. Gerhard's day when the vain virtuoso repaired to the Fish Market. The old clock of the Minster had already boomed the last stroke announcing the twelfth hour, when he arrived at the place. He actually found there a large party of ladies, just as he expected, and they invited him to play. Confidently he stepped forward, and having bowed with a smile which he was wont to assume whenever he appeared before the public, he threw his fiddle-stick across the strings and extemporized a few rapid passages up and down, to show at once his superior skill. But, how wretchedly provoking! Never in his life had he produced such miserable tones; they sounded so execrably thin and poor, as if the strings had been stretched over a piece of solid wood instead of a violin. Enraged, he renewed his exertions, but only to render the matter worse; for, now he produced a noise so horribly ear-piercing that he thought there must be standing behind him a whole chorus of whistling and screeching sneerers accompanying his performance.

Highly exasperated, he tucked his violin under his arm, and walked up to the dancing witches. Then boldly addressing one of the richly-attired ladies, in whom he believed he recognised the wife of the burgomaster of the town, he said:—

"Ah, Madam! I wonder what your husband, our respected burgomaster would say if he knew of your night-excursions on the broom-stick! But that is your own affair. All I care for is my due reward, if you please."

With these words he threw off his jacket and turned round. The lady quickly uncovered a silver dish, from which she took the hump of the former musician, and before the vain virtuoso was aware of it, she had pressed it on his back beside the other hump.

The clock had struck One, and the witches were already on their broom-sticks riding through the air homewards, when the musician recovered from his shock. He slowly put his hand to his back, hoping that perchance he might only have had a bad dream. But no! it was all right,—or rather all wrong. There remained now nothing for him to do but to take up his jacket and make the best of his way home. But the jacket felt so unusally heavy;—could there, perhaps, be gold in it to make up in some measure for the cruel infliction? Eagerly he rummaged the pockets; but what should he find? A few heavy stones and rubbish.*

THE PARSON'S ADVICE.

This tale of the Manx people is almost literally copied from 'The History and Description of the Isle of Man, by George Waldron, London, 1744.'

"A man, one day, was led by invisible musicians for several miles together; and not being able to resist the harmony, followed till it conducted him to a large common, where a great number of people were sitting round a table, and eating and drinking in a very jovial manner. Among them were some faces which he thought he had formerly seen; but he forbore taking any notice, or they to him; till, the little people offering him drink, one of them whose features seemed not unknown to him, plucked him by the coat, and forbade him, whatever he did, to taste anything he saw before him. 'For, if you do,' added he, 'you will be as I am, and return no more to your family.'

The poor man was much affrighted, but resolved to obey the injunction. Accordingly, a large silver cup, filled with some sort of liquor, being put into his hand, he found an opportunity to throw what it contained on the ground. Soon after, the music ceasing, all the company disappeared, leaving the cup in his hand; and he returned home, though much wearied and fatigued. He went the next day and communicated to the minister of the parish all that had

---

* 'Deutsche Märchen und Sagen, gesammelt von J. W. Wolf.' Leipzig, 1845; p. 472.

happened, and asked his advice how he should dispose of the cup: To which the parson replied, he could not do better than devote it to the service of the church. And this very cup, they say, is that which is now used for the consecrated wine in Kirk Merlugh."

RELICS OF THE GOBLINS.

The old tradition embodied in the preceding story from the Isle of Man, is also current,—with various modifications,—in the north of Germany, in Denmark, and in Sweden. Afzelius, in his interesting account of Swedish popular superstitions, mentions some curious notions on this subject. The country people in Sweden still preserve an old belief that if a person drinks of the contents of a beaker, offered to him by the goblins inhabiting the mountains, he loses all recollection of the past, and must become one of them. Several cups are said to have been purloined from these mysterious beings by persons who stealthily avoided partaking of the proffered liquor. Some are still shown in churches, to which they were presented by the purloiners; and it is asserted that these oddly-shaped vessels were formerly used in the Communion Service.

The goblins in Sweden have their principal meetings at midnight before Christmas, and their amusements consist chiefly in music and dancing. They generally assemble in those isolated spots among the mountains where are found large stones resting on pillars, around which they delight to dance. It is considered decidedly dangerous to encounter them at their pastimes on Christmas Eve.

Many years ago,—some say it was so far back as in the year 1490,—a farmer's wife in Sweden, whose name was Cissela Ulftand, distinctly heard, on Christmas Eve, the wild music of the goblins who had assembled not far from her house. The farm in which the good woman lived is called Ljungby, and the group of curiously-placed stones around which the goblins had congregated is well known to many people; indeed, almost everyone in Sweden knows the Magle-Stone.

Well, when Mistress Ulftand heard the music, she spoke to one of her farm-servants, a strong and daring young fellow, and induced him to saddle a horse and to ride in the direction of the Magle-Stone, that he might learn something about the mysterious people, and tell her afterwards all he had seen. The lad rather liked the adventure; he lost no time in mounting his horse, and was soon galloping towards the scene of the music and rejoicing. In approaching the Magle-Stone, he somewhat slackened his speed; however, he drew quite near to the dancers.

After he had been gazing a little while at the strange party, a handsome damsel came up to him and handed him a drinking-horn and a pipe, with the request that he would first drink the health of the King and then blow the pipe. The lad accepted both, the drinking-horn and the pipe; but, as soon as he had them in his hands, he poured out the contents of the horn, and spurring his horse he gallopped off over hedges and ditches straight homewards. The whole company of goblins followed him in the wildest uproar, threatening and imploring him to restore to them their property; but the fellow proved too quick for them, and succeeded in safely reaching the farm, where he delivered up the trophies of his daring enterprise to his mistress. The goblins now promised all manner of good luck to the farmer's wife and her family, if she would return to them the two articles; but she kept them, and they are still preserved in Ljungby as a testimony to the truth of this wonderful narrative.

The drinking-horn is of a metallic composition, the nature of which has not been exactly ascertained; its ornaments are, however, of brass. The pipe is made of the bone of a horse. Moreover, the possession of these relics, we are told, has been the cause of a series of disasters to the owners of the farm. The lad who brought them to the house died three days after the daring enterprise, and the day following, the horse suddenly fell down and expired. The farm-house has twice burnt down, and the descendants of the farmer's wife have experienced all kinds of misfortunes, which to enumerate would be not less laborious than painful. It is only surprising that they should still keep the unlucky horn and pipe.

THE GOLDEN HARVEST.

This is a genuine Dutch story. A long time may have elapsed since the hero of the event recorded was gathered to his fathers. Howbeit, his name lives, and his deeds will perhaps be longer retained by the people in pleasant remembrance than the deeds of some heroes who have made more noise in the world.

An old village crowder, whose name was Kartof, and who lived in Niederbrakel, happened once, late in the night, to traverse a little wood on his way home from Opbrakel, where he had been playing at a dance during the wake. He had his pockets full of coppers, and felt altogether mighty comfortable and jolly; for the young folks in Opbrakel had treated him well, and the liquor was genuine Old Hollands. But, there is nothing complete in this world, as the saying is, and as old Kartof was presently to experience to his dismay, when he put his hand into his pocket for his match-box. Had he not just filled his old clay pipe in the pleasant expectation, amounting to a certainty, that he should indulge in a comfortable smoke all the way home? And did he not feel, with a certain pride, that he deserved a good smoke after all his exertions with the fiddlestick? But what use was it to rummage his pockets for the match-box! It certainly was not there, and must have been lost or left behind somewhere.

"The deuce!" muttered old Kartof, "If I had only a bit of fire now to light my pipe, I should not care for anything else in the world, I am sure!"

Scarcely had he said these words, when he espied a light gleaming through the bushes. He went towards it, but it was much further off than it at first appeared to him;

indeed, he had to go more than a hundred yards into the brush-wood before he came up to it. He now saw that it was a large fagot burning, around which a party of men and women, joined hand in hand, were dancing in a circle. "How odd!" thought old Kartof; but being a man accustomed to genteel society, he was at no loss how to address them politely; so, taking off his hat, he said:—

"Ladies and Gentlemen! Excuse me. I hope I am not intruding too much if I ask the favour of your permission to help myself to a little fire to light my pipe."

He had not even quite finished his speech, when several of the dancers stepped forward and handed him glowing embers in abundance. Now, when approaching him they perceived that he carried a violin under his arm, they importuned him to play for them to dance, intimating that he should be well rewarded for his services. "Why not?" said old Kartof: "It is only about midnight, and I can sleep to-morrow in the day-time; it will not be the first time that I have gone to bed in the morning."

While talking in this way, he tuned his instrument; and soon he struck up his best tunes, one after the other. But, though he played ever so much, he could never play enough, the dancers were so insatiable! Whenever his arm sank down from sheer fatigue, they threw a golden ducat into the sound-hole of his violin, which pleased him immensely, and always animated him to renew his exertions, especially also as they did not neglect to refresh him occasionally with a remarkably fine-flavoured Schiedam, from a bottle so oddly-shaped that he had never seen anything like it, so funny it was. He could not help smiling whenever he looked at the bottle.

Gradually his violin became heavier—of course, that was from the golden ducats which the dancers continually threw into it. But also his arm became heavier, and at last old Kartof felt altogether too heavy, sank softly down, and fell asleep.

How long he lay in this state no one knows, nor is ever likely to know. But, thus much is certain, when old Kartof awoke the day was already far advanced, and the sun shone brightly upon his face. He rubbed his eyes and looked about, doubtful whether he was a man of property or whether he had only dreamt of golden ducats. There was the violin lying in the grass near his feet. He hastily took it up;—it felt as light as usual. He shook it;—no rattling of ducats. He held it before his face and peeped into the sound holes;—to be sure, there was something in it, yellow and glittering like gold. He shook it out on the grass;—what should it be?—a score or two of decayed yellow birch-leaves.

Disappointed, old Kartof rose to his feet to look around whether he could not find the place where the fire had been.

Yes, there it was! Some embers were still glimmering in the ashes. This appeared to him more odd than anything else he had experienced. But old Kartof, after all, took the matter quietly enough. He lighted his pipe, and taking up his violin set out on his way home, resolving as he went never to go to that confounded place again after twelve o'clock at midnight.*

GIPSIES.

There prevails in popular traditions much mystery respecting gipsies. No wonder that this should be the case, since these strange vagabonds are in most countries so very different from the inhabitants in their appearance and habits; and their occupations are often so well calculated to appeal to the imagination of superstitious people, that a gipsy is regarded by them almost as a sorcerer. His better-half not unfrequently pretends to be a soothsayer, and he is often a musician. However different the gipsy hordes which rove about in European countries may be from each other in some respects, they

---

* 'Niederländische Sagen, herausgegeben von J. W. Wolf;' Leipzig, 1843; p. 466.

are all fond of music, magic, and mysterious pursuits. Among the gipsy bands in Hungary and Transylvania talented instrumental performers are by no means rare; and in Russia, the gipsy singers of Moscow enjoy a wide reputation for their musical accomplishments. It is told, —not as a myth but as a fact,—that when the celebrated Italian singer Signora Catalani heard in Moscow the most accomplished of the gipsy singing-girls of that town, she was so highly delighted with the performance that she took from her shoulders a splendid Cashmere shawl which the Pope had presented to her in admiration of her own talent, and embracing the dear gipsy girl, she insisted on her accepting the shawl, saying that it was intended for the matchless cantatrice which she now found she could not longer regard herself.

There is a wildness in the gipsy musical performances, which admirably expresses the characteristic features of these vagrants. Indeed theirs is just the sort of music which people ought to make who encamp in the open air, feed upon hedgehogs and whatever they can lay hand on, and profess to be adepts in sorcery and prophecy.

The following event is told by the peasants in the Netherlands as having occurred in Herzeele. A troop of gipsies had arrived in a valley near that place. They stretched a tight rope, on which they danced, springing sometimes into the air so high that all who saw it were greatly astonished. A little boy among the spectators cried: "Oh, if I could but do that!"—

"Nothing is easier," said an old gipsy who stood near him: "Here is a powder; when you have swallowed it, you will be able to dance as well as any of us."

The boy took the powder and swallowed it. In a moment his feet became so light that he found it impossible to keep them on the ground. The slightest movement which he made raised him into the air. He danced upon the ears of the growing corn, on the tops of the trees,—yea, even on the weather-cock of the church-tower. The people of the village thought this suspicious, and shook their heads, especially when they furthermore observed a disinclination in the boy to attend church. They, therefore, consulted with the parson about the boy. The parson sent for him, and got him all right on his legs again by means of exorcism; but it was a hard struggle to banish the potent effects of the gipsy's powder.*

The gipsies were formerly supposed to be descendants of the ancient Egyptians. The German peasants call them Taters,† a name indicating an Asiatic origin; and it has been ascertained that they migrated from Western India. The roving Nautch-people in Hindustan are similarly musical and mysterious.

THE NAUTCH-PEOPLE.

The Nautch-people in Hindustan are not only singers and dancers who exhibit their skill before those who care to admire and to reward them; but they possess also dangerous charms.

In a popular story of the Hindus, called 'Chandra's Vengeance' we are told of a youth who, on hearing the music of the Nautch-people at a great distance, is irresistibly compelled to traverse the jungle in search of them. When, after twelve day's anxious endeavour to reach them, he discovers their encampment, Moulee, the daughter of the chief Nautch-woman, approaches him singing and dancing, and throws to him the garland of flowers which she wears on her head. He feels spell-bound, and the Nautch-people offer him a drink which, as soon as he has tasted it, makes him totally forget his family and his dear home. So he remains with the Nautch-people, and wanders with them about the country as one of the company.

Again, in a Hindu story called 'Panch-Phul Ranee,' a Rajah, or King, is enchanted by the Nautch-people, so that he finds his happiness in roving with them from place to place, and in beating the drum for the dancers. His enchantment is accomplished in this way: He had set out

---

* 'Niederländische Sagen, herausgegeben von J. W. Wolf;' Leipzig, 1843; p. 648.

† *Taters* is evidently synonymous with *Tartars.*

on a journey, leaving his wife and infant son behind. One day he happened to fall in with a gang of Nautch-people, singing and dancing. He was a remarkably handsome man, and the Nautch-people, on seeing him approach, said to each other "How well he would look beating the drum for the dancers!" The Rajah was hungry and told them that he required some food; whereupon one of the women offered him a little rice, upon which her companions threw a certain powder. He ate it, and the effect was that it made him forget his wife, child, rank, journey, and whatever had happened to him in all his life. He willingly remained with the Nautch-people, and wandered about with them, beating the drum at their performances, full eighteen years. His son, the prince, being now grown up, could no longer be detained from setting out in the world in search of his beloved father. After many fruitless attempts the prince discovered his father among the Nautch people,—a wild, ragged-looking man whose business it was to beat the drum. The joyful prince summoned the wisest doctors in the kingdom to restore the Rajah to his former consciousness; but their exertions did not at first prove at all successful. In vain did they assure the old drummer that he was a Rajah, and that he ought to remember his former greatness and splendour. The old man always answered that he remembered nothing but how to beat the drum; and, to prove his assertion, he treated them on the spot with a tap and roll on his tom-tom. He really believed that he had beaten it all his life.

However, through the unabated exertions of the doctors, a slight remembrance came gradually over him; and by-and-by his former mental power returned. He now recollected that he had a wife and a son. He also recognized his old friends and servants. Having reseated himself on the throne, he governed as if nothing had ever occurred to interrupt his reign.*

* 'Old Deccan Days; or Hindu Fairy Legends, current in Southern India.' Collected from oral tradition, by M. Frere. London, 1868; pp. 139, 273.

THE MONK OF AFFLIGHEM.

The aim of the present series of popular stories demands that some notice should now be taken of such musical legends as breathe a thorough Christian spirit. Several of these are, as might be expected, very beautiful; but they are familiar to most readers. One or two which are less well known may, however, find a place here.

The legend of the Monk of Afflighem bears some resemblance to the beautiful tradition of the Seven Sleepers. If it fails to interest the reader, the cause must be assigned to the simple manner in which it is told rather than to the subject itself.

Towards the end of the eleventh century occurred in the Abbey of Afflighem, in Dendermonde, East Flanders, a most wonderful event, the pious Fulgentius being at that time the Abbot of the monastery.

One day, a monk of very venerable appearance, whom no one remembered to have seen before, knocked at the door of the monastery, announcing himself as one of the brotherhood. The pious Abbot Fulgentius asked him his name, and from what country he had come. Whereupon the monk looked at the Abbot with surprise, and said that he belonged to the house. Being further questioned, he replied that he had only been away for a few hours. He had been singing the Matins, he said, in the morning of the same day in the choir with the other brothers. When, in chanting, they came to the verse of the ninetieth psalm, which says: "For, a thousand years in thy sight are but as yesterday!" he pondered upon it so deeply that he did not perceive when the singers left the choir, and he remained sitting alone, absorbed by the words. After he had been a while in this state of reflection, he heard heavenly strains of music, and on looking up he saw a little bird which sang with a voice so enchantingly melodious that he arose in ecstacy. The little bird flew to the neighbouring wood, whither he followed it. He had been only a little while in the wood listening to the heavenly song of the bird; and now, in coming back he felt bewildered,—the appearance of the neighbourhood was so changed he scarcely knew it again.

When the pious Abbot Fulgentius heard the monk speak thus, he asked of him the name of the Abbot, and also the name of the King who governed the country. And after the monk had answered him and mentioned the names, it was found to the astonishment of all that these were the names of the Abbot and the King who had lived three hundred years ago. The monk startled, lifted up his eyes, and said: "Now indeed I see that a thousand years are but as one day before the Lord." Whereupon he asked the pious Abbot Fulgentius to administer to him the Holy Sacraments; and having devoutly received them, he expired.*

THE PLAGUE IN GOLDBERG.

The inhabitants of Goldberg, a town in Germany, observe an old custom of inaugurating Christmas, which is peculiar to themselves. Having attended divine service, which commences at midnight on Christmas Eve, they assemble at two o'clock to form a procession to the Niederring, a hill situated close to the town. When the procession has arrived at the top of the Niederring, old and young unite in singing the Chorale *Uns ist ein Kindlein heut geboren* ("For us this day a child is born"). As soon as this impressive act of devotion is concluded, the town band stationed in the tower of the old parish church performs on brass instruments the noble Chorale *Allein Gott in der Höh sei Ehr* ("All glory be to God on High"), which in the stillness of the night is heard over the whole town, and even in the neighbouring villages.

The origin of this annual observance dates from the time when the town of Goldberg was visited by a deadly plague called *Der schwarze Tod* ("The black Death"). According

---

* 'Niederländische Sagen, herausgegeben von J. W. Wolf;' Leipzig, 1843. P. 230.

to some accounts the awful visitation occurred in the year 1553; at all events this date appears to have been assigned to it on an old slab embedded in the wall of the parish church of Goldberg; but the inscription has become so much obliterated in the course of time, that no one can make out the year with certainty. Thus much, however, is declared by all to be authentic: The plague spread throughout the town with frightful rapidity. The people died in their houses, in the streets, everywhere, at night, and in the day-time. Some, while at their work, suddenly were stricken and fell down dead. Some died while at their meals; others while at prayers; others in their endeavours to escape the scourge by hastening away from the doomed town. Indeed, it was as if the Angel of Death had stretched out his hand over the place, saying "Ye are all given up to me!"

The plague raged for some weeks, and then quietness reigned in Goldberg. The few survivors had shut themselves up solitarily in their houses, not knowing of each other; for, no one now ventured into the street; neither did anyone open a window, fearing the poisonous air; for the corpses were lying about, and there remained none living to bury the dead.

Such was the condition of Goldberg in the month of December, just before Christmas. On Christmas Eve one of the solitary survivors, deeply impressed with the import of the holy festival, attained the blessing of a firm trust in the wisdom of the inscrutable decrees of Providence. He thought of the happy time of his childhood when his parents lighted up for him the glorious Christmas tree; and this recalled to his mind the simple and impressive Christmas hymn which his mother had taught him to recite on the occasion. Strengthened by devout contemplation, he ventured to open the window. The night was beautiful, and the air wafted to him so pure and delicious that he resolved to leave his prison. At the second hour after midnight he went out of the house, and bent his steps through the desolated streets towards the Niederring. Arrived at the top of the hill he knelt down and sang from the depth of his heart the Christmas hymn.

His voice was heard by another solitary survivor, who perceiving that he was not, as he had supposed, the only person still living in Goldberg, gained courage and likewise from his hiding place repaired to the Niederring, and kneeling down joined the singer with sincere devotion. Soon a third person made his appearance, slowly drawing near like one risen from the grave. Then a fourth, a fifth, until the number of them amounted to twenty-five; and these were all the inhabitants of Goldberg who had escaped the ravages of the Black Death.

The Christmas Chorale sung in the refreshing mountain air wonderfully invigorated their desponding spirits. They arose and solemnly vowed henceforth to unite in Christian fellowship, with reliance upon the wisdom of the divine ordinances. The next day they buried their dead; and when their vow became known in the neighbourhood, many good people were drawn to Goldberg. The town soon revived, and prospered more than ever.

The inhabitants have not forgotten the visitation which befel their forefathers, but remember it in humiliation; and this is a lasting blessing.*

* 'Deutsche Volksfeste, von F. A. Reimann;' Weimar, 1839; p. 218.

FICTIONS AND FACTS.

Knowledge is, of course, to superstition as light is to darkness; still, some nations endowed with a lively imagination, although they are much advanced in mental development, cling to the superstitions of their forefathers, since the superstitions accord with their poetical conceptions, or are endeared to them by associations which pleasantly engage the imaginative faculties.

Besides, in countries where the inhabitants frequently witness grand and awful natural phenomena, their poetical conceptions are likely to be more or less nourished by these impressive occurrences, however well acquainted they may be with their natural causes.

It is therefore not surprising that many superstitious notions, such as have been recorded in the preceding stories, should be found in civilized nations.

Moreover, in some countries, a more careful research into the old traditions harbouring among the uneducated classes of the people has been made, than in other countries. It would, therefore, be hasty, from the sources at present accessible, to judge of the degree of mental development attained by individual nations. The Germans are not less rational than the English; nevertheless, a far greater number of Fairy Tales have been collected in Germany than in England.

An enquiry into the musical traditions of the different European races is likely to increase in interest the more we turn to the mythological conceptions originally derived from Central Asia, and dispersed throughout Europe at a period on which history is silent, but upon which some light has been thrown by recent philological and ethnological researches.

A word remains to be said on the musical myths of modern date. We read in the biographies of our celebrated musicians facts which would almost certainly be regarded as fictions, were they not well authenticated. On the other hand, it would not be difficult to point out modern myths referring to the art of music. Tempting as it might be to cite the most remarkable examples of this kind, and anecdotes relating to musicians in which fiction is strangely mingled with fact, it is unnecessary to notice them here; for, are they not written in our works on the history of the art and science of music?

DRAMATIC MUSIC OF UNCIVILIZED RACES.

THE first music of a dramatic kind originated probably in the passion of love. Savages, unacquainted with any other dramatic performances, not unfrequently have dances representing courtship, and songs to which these dances are executed. However rude the exhibitions may be, and however inartistic the songs may appear,—which, in fact, generally consist merely of short phrases constantly repeated, and perhaps interspersed with some brutish utterances,—they may nevertheless be regarded as representing the germ from which the opera has gradually been developed. Dancing is not necessarily associated with dramatic music; the dances of nations in a low degree of civilization are, however, often representations of desires or events rather than unmeaning jumps and evolutions.

Even in the popular dances of nations in an advanced state of civilization love is generally the most attractive subject for exhibition by action and music. The Italian national dances,—the *Saltarello*, the *Monferrino*, and several others,—have an unmistakable meaning; or, as Mac Farlane says, "there is a story in them which at times is told in a very broad, significant, and unsophistical way. The story is a sort of primitive courtship, varied by the coyness or coquetry of the female dancer, and animated by the passion and impatience of the wooer."* The same may be said of the Spanish Bolero and Fandango.

---

* 'Popular Customs, etc., of the South of Italy,' by Charles Mac Farlane, London, 1846; p. 68.

The excitement of the chase appears to be another cause of the origin of dramatic music. The savage, in pursuing the animals which he requires for his subsistence, experiences successes and disappointments which are to him highly interesting, and the recollection of which he enjoys. He naturally feels proud of results which he could not have achieved without agility and shrewdness, and he delights in showing to his friends how he proceeded in accomplishing his feat. Besides, savages have a strong instinct for imitation, almost like monkeys. Hence their fancy for counterfeiting the habits of certain animals which they chase and with the peculiarities of which they are generally well acquainted.

The aborigines of Australia have a dance in which they imitate the movements of the Kangaroo. The women sing, and produce a rhythmical accompaniment by beating two pieces of wood together; while the men, who represent the Kangaroos, produce sounds peculiar to these animals. The North American Indians have an Eagle Dance, a Bear Dance, and even a Dog Dance. The natives of Kamtschatka have a dance in which they cleverly imitate, not only the attitudes and tricks of the Bear, but also its voice. The peasants in Finland, in the beginning of the present century, still occasionally performed a similar dance, or rather action. The Aleutian Islanders, who have various pantomimic dances executed with masks frightfully ugly, have also a favourite representation in which a sportsman shoots a beautiful bird, and afterwards cries for grief at having killed it; when, suddenly, the beautiful bird revives, changed into a beautiful woman. The sportsman, of course, falls over head and ears in love with her, and thus all ends well.* This story is enacted with recitations accompanied by some musical instruments.

Next to love and the chase, it is probably war which elicited the first attempts at dramatic music. To recall to the memory by a lively description with gesticulations, the

---

* 'Voyage pittoresque autour du Monde, par M. Louis Choris;' Paris, 1822; p. 9.

valiant deeds, clever stratagems, and glorious achievements of the warriors after the battle, must have been always a fascinating entertainment to the victorious combatants. The Dyaks in Borneo, who preserve the heads of their slain enemies suspended near their hearths as ornamental trophies, perform a war-dance in which some of the combatants, gaily decorated, cleverly act a scene by seizing swords and handling them in various expressive ways. The Scalp-Dance of the North American Indians, performed in celebration of a victory, may be described as a kind of histrionic entertainment, which generally takes place at night by torchlight. The singular procedure of the Maori warriors in New Zealand in a certain dance, of projecting all of them their tongues simultaneously at fixed intervals, appears to be a pantomimic expression of defiance or contempt for the enemy.

The Corroborie Dance of the natives of Australia had perhaps also originally reference to warlike exploits, although this does not appear at once evident to European witnesses. Twenty or more men paint their naked dark bodies to represent skeletons, which they accomplish by drawing white lines across the body with pipe-clay, to correspond with the ribs, and broader ones on the arms, legs, and the head. Thus prepared they perform the Corroborie at night before a fire. The spectators, placed at some distance from them, see only the white skeletons, which vanish and re-appear whenever the dancers turn round. The wild and ghastly action of the skeletons is accompanied by vocal effusions and some rhythmical noise which a number of hidden bystanders produce by beating their shields in regular time.

Traces of dramatic music in its most primitive condition may also be discovered in representations of occurrences and scenes like the following:

Wilhelm Steller, in his 'Description of Kamtschatka' (published in the German language in the year 1774), says that the inhabitants of that country possess an astounding talent for imitating the manners and conduct of strangers whom they happen to see. During their long evenings one of their chief amusements consists in acting extempore comedies, in which the habits of any foreigners with whom they have become acquainted, are cleverly mimicked and ridiculed.

The missionary W. Ellis remarks of the Polynesian Islanders that "they had songs which, when recited on public occasions, were accompanied with gestures and actions corresponding to the events and scenes described, and which assumed in this respect a histrionic character. In some cases, and on public occasions, the action represented a kind of pantomime."* Other travellers have given more detailed accounts of these performances. During Captain Cook's first voyage round the world, Banks and Solander, who accompanied him, witnessed in one of the Society Islands, in the year 1769, a comedy with music and dancing, performed by the natives, the subject of which was the adroitness of a thief, and his subsequent capture. At Cook's second circumnavigation, during the years 1772-75, he was treated by the Society Islanders with a somewhat similar comic opera called *Teto* (*i.e.* "The Thief"). G. Forster, who was with Cook, remarks that the dialogue, which of course he was unable to understand, seemed to be closely connected with their actions. One of them kneeled down, and another beat him and plucked him by the beard. Then two others were treated by the torturer in the same unceremonious manner; until one of them seized a stick and gave him a sound thrashing in return. This formed the conclusion of the first act, and the players withdrew. The commencement of the second act was announced by the musicians beating their drums. There were actresses as well as actors engaged in the performance.† A more detailed account of the dramatic attempts of the Polynesian Islanders is given by W. Mariner, who, during his sojourn with the natives, had the best opportunity of becoming

* 'Polynesian Researches,' by William Ellis; London, 1827. Vol. I., p. 285.

† 'A Voyage round the World, in His Britannic Majesty's Sloop "Resolution," commanded by Captain James Cook, during the years 1772-75;' by George Forster: London, 1777. Vol. I., p. 398.

acquainted with their customs and amusements. His observations, which refer especially to the Tonga Islanders, show that the actors recite sentences which are answered by a chorus of singers. There is a great variety in their movements and groupings. Occasionally they sing slowly, and afterwards quickly for about a quarter of an hour. Sometimes they form a semicircle, assume a bending position, and sing in a subdued tone of voice a soft air; which is soon again followed by a loud and vehement recitation.*

Grotesque dresses and adornments are, of course, an essential attribute in these entertainments. Neither are buffoons wanting. According to B. Seeman, the entertainment called *Kalau Rere*, which he witnessed in the Fiji Islands, "with its high poles, streamers, evergreens, masquerading, trumpet-shells, chants and other wild music, is the nearest approach to dramatic representation the Fijians seem to have made, and it is with them what private theatricals are with us. They are also on other occasions very fond of dressing themselves in fantastic, often very ridiculous costume; and in nearly every large assembly there are buffoons. Court fools, in many instances hunchbacks, are attached to the chief's establishment."†

Also the Negroes in Senegambia and Upper Guinea have buffoons, who delight the people with their antics and acting in processions and public festivities. Buffoons are popular even in Mohammedan countries, where dramatic performances are generally considered objectionable. Morier states that in Persia the princes, governors of provinces, etc., as well as the King, have a band of *Looties*, or buffoons, in their pay, who are looked upon as a necessary part of Persian state. They attend at merry-makings and public festivals, and some of them are endowed with great

* 'An Account of the Natives of the Tonga Islands, in the South Pacific Ocean, compiled and arranged from the extensive communications of Mr. William Mariner, several years resident in those Islands, by John Martin;' London, 1817. Vol. II., p. 309.

† 'An Account of a Government Mission to the Fiji Islands, in the years 1860-61;' by Berthold Seeman; Cambridge, 1862. P. 116.

natural wit. This was, for instance, the case with a certain buffoon named Looti Bashee. "His dress, when he came to the ambassador, was composed of a felt hat, the crown of which was made like ours, but with two long ears projecting before, and two behind. Others of his troop were dressed in the same way; all looked grotesque, and I conjectured that nothing could give one a better idea of Satyrs and Bacchanalians, particularly as they were attended by a suite of monkeys headed by a large ape, which were educated to perform all sorts of tricks. They carried copper drums slung under the arm, which they beat with their fingers, making a noise like castanets; others played the tambourine; and when all this was put into motion, with their voices roaring in loud chorus, the scene was unique."*

Sir Robert Ker Porter witnessed at Bagdad, in the beginning of the present century, a kind of musical drama performed by men and boys, the latter being dressed like females. "This amusement," he remarks, "is the only one of a theatrical complexion known among the people. It is often called for by the female part of the inhabitants; but I am told that with the men it is now very rare, the Pasha so setting his face against it as to forbid the avowed existence of hirable dancing-boys in his capital."† There is a Turkish theatre at Pera in which Turkish plays, adapted from the Italian, are acted by Turkish actors, and Turkish women appear unveiled upon the stage.‡ The women in the hareem, who in their diversions are only permitted to employ slaves of their own sex, occasionally make them act melodramas, the subject of which is generally a love story.

The Indians in Mexico have some characteristic dances in which scenes are pantomimically enacted referring to Montezuma and to the conquest of Mexico by the Spaniards.

---

* 'A Second Journey through Persia, Armenia, and Asia Minor, etc.,' by James Morier; London, 1818. P. 104.

† 'Travels in Georgia, Persia, Armenia, etc.,' by Sir Robert Ker Porter; London, 1822; Vol. II., p. 272.

‡ 'Travels in Greece, Russia, etc.,' by Bayard Taylor; London, 1859; p. 282.

In most of the entertainments, of which examples have just been given, the music must necessarily partake of a dramatic character. Generally, the tunes are not selected at pleasure, but certain tunes belong to certain representations. The dramatic effect of the music depends, however, chiefly upon its execution, which naturally changes according to the action which it accompanies. Thus, if the actors represent a sentimental or heart-rending scene, their vocal effusions will naturally be in a subdued tone, and the sympathizing musicians will touch their instruments delicately and slowly. If, on the other hand, the actors represent some exciting or heart-stirring scene, they will naturally raise their voices, and the musicians will play louder and faster as a matter of course. In fact, when their pulse beats quicker, the rhythmical flow of their music, however rude and inartistic it may be, becomes more animated unpremeditatedly. Such is the most primitive condition, or the commencement of the development of dramatic music. Let us now examine it in a somewhat more advanced stage of cultivation.

The Javanese, who among the islanders of the Indian Archipelago are renowned for their skill in the dramatic art, generally use fabulous traditions from their own history, or Hindu legends, as subjects for their performances, which are acted exclusively by men. A full band of musicians generally accompanies the drama. The instruments mostly belong to the class called Instruments of Percussion, but several of them are constructed with plates of metal which produce a series of sweet tones, arranged according to the pentatonic scale. Some of the Javanese airs, which have been collected by Europeans, are very expressive, and it might be instructive to musical enquirers, if some really musical European visitor in Java would faithfully commit to notation the orchestral accompaniments of some of the most popular Javanese dramas. Madame Ida Pfeiffer relates that she was treated in the house of a Rajah, at Bandong, with a kind of pantomime in three acts, the third of which represented a combat. "The music that accompanied the combat," she remarks, "was very noisy and discordant; but, on the defeat of the one party, a soft plaintive melody arose at some distance off. The whole performance was really pretty and expressive." * Sir Stamford Raffles, and other travellers, give similar descriptions, and have besides much to say about the clever puppet-shows of the Javanese, in which the characters of dramas are represented by puppets, or by their shadows.

The Siamese are fond of theatrical performances. According to Turpin's history of Siam, published in the year 1771, "whenever they burn the body of a minister or great man, a theatre is erected on the side of a river, where the actors appear habited according to their parts; and during three days they never quit the scene from eight in the morning till seven at night." De La Loubère, who visited Siam in the year 1687, says that the subjects of the dramas are "historical, in verse, serious, and sung by several actors who are always present, and who only sing reciprocally. One of them sings the historian's part, and the rest sing those of the personages which the history makes to speak; but they are all men that sing, and no women." About a century ago it appears to have been the custom to employ only men as actors, although there were female dancers. But, at the present day there are actresses, at any rate in the palace of the King, where Sir John Bowring saw them perform on several occasions. In one of these entertainments "the actors were all females, almost all girls. A few matrons, however, took the part of warriors, monkeys, priests; and the three manageresses, or prompteresses, were not only old and ugly, but seemed very spiteful, and on several occasions scolded and slapped the ladies who required correction. One of them had the drama written on black sheets in white letters before her, from which she prompted the singers of the recitative. The story began by the appearance of a monster monkey in a forest, which is visited by a number of ladies of rank, one of whom, after an unsuccessful struggle, the others having managed

* 'A Lady's Second Journey round the World,' by Ida Pfeiffer; London, 1855; Vol. I., p. 211.

to escape, the monster monkey contrives to carry off. She is redeemed by the interference of a priest, whose temple is in the forest. Afterwards we are introduced to a sovereign Court, where all the ceremonies are observed which are practised in daily life, the dresses being those ordinarily worn, and most gorgeous they are. . . . . There is a battle, and rewards to the victors, and a crowning of a king's son in recompense for his valour, and offerings to Buddha, and a great feast, etc." * The principal performers act, but do not speak. The tale is told in recitative by a body of singers, accompanied by various instruments. The band assisting generally consists of about twenty members who play on wind instruments of the oboe kind, gongs, large castanets above a foot in length, and several sonorous instruments of percussion constructed with slabs of wood, or plates of metal, somewhat similar to those of the Javanese before mentioned.

The Cochin-Chinese are remarkably fond of dramatic entertainments, which are generally of an operatic character commemorating historical events. An English gentleman who witnessed the performance of some of these plays remarks of the actors: "Their singing is good, when the ear has become accustomed to it; and the modulation of voice of the females is really captivating."† Sir George Staunton was evidently surprised to find that a kind of historical opera, which he heard in the town of Turon (called by the natives Hansán) contained recitatives, airs, and choruses, which were, he says, "as regular as upon the Italian stage." He adds: "Some of the female performers were by no means despicable singers. They all observed time accurately, not only with their voices, but every joint of their hands and feet was obedient to the regular movement of the instruments." ‡ The band consisted of stringed

* 'The Kingdom of Siam.' By Sir John Bowring. London, 1857; Vol. II., p. 325.

† 'A Voyage to Cochin-China.' By John White. London, 1824; p. 302.

‡ 'An Authentic Account of an Embassy from the King of Great Britain to the Emperor of China,' etc. By Sir George Staunton. London, 1797; Vol. I., p. 344.

instruments, wind instruments, and instruments of percussion. Sir John Barrow describes the theatre at Turon as "a shed of bamboo." He relates: "In the farther division of the building a party of comedians was engaged in the midst of an historical drama when we entered; but, on our being seated they broke off, and, coming forward, made before us an obeisance of nine genuflexions and prostrations, after which they returned to their labours, keeping up an incessant noise and bustle during our stay. The heat of the day, the thermometer in the shade standing at 81 deg. in the open air, and at least 10 deg. higher in the building, the crowds that thronged to see the strangers, the horrible crash of the gongs, kettle-drums, trumpets, and squalling flutes, were so stunning and oppressive that nothing but the novelty of the scene could possibly have detained us for a moment. The most entertaining, as well as the least noisy part of the theatrical exhibition, was a sort of Interlude, performed by three young women for the amusement, it would seem, of the principal actress, who sat as a spectator in the dress and character of some ancient Queen, whilst an old eunuch, very whimsically dressed, played his antic tricks like a scaramouch or buffoon in a Harlequin entertainment. The dialogue in this part differed entirely from the querulous and nearly monotonous recitation of the Chinese, being light and comic, and occasionally interrupted by cheerful airs which generally concluded with a chorus. These airs, rude and unpolished as they were, appeared to be regular compositions, and were sung in exactly measured time. One in particular attracted our attention, whose slow melancholy movement breathed the kind of plaintiveness so peculiar to the native airs of the Scotch, to which indeed it bore a close resemblance."

Probably the air was founded on the pentatonic scale, which is common in the music of the Chinese and Javanese, and of which traces are to be found in the Scotch popular tunes.

"The voices of the women are shrill and warbling, but some of their cadences were not without melody. The instruments at each pause gave a few short flourishes, till the music gradually increased in loudness by the swelling and deafening gong. Knowing nothing of the language, we were of course as ignorant of the subject as the majority of an English audience is of an Italian opera." *

A curious mode of paying the actors, which prevails in Cochin-China, may be mentioned here. An Englishman who was present at a theatrical performance in the town of Kangwarting, relates that the Quong, or governor of the province, bore the expense of the entertainment. The musical drama was performed in a large shed before a great concourse of spectators. "The Quong was there squatted on a raised platform in front of the actors with a small drum before him, supported in a diagonal position, on which he would strike a tap every time any part of the performance pleased him; which also was a signal for his purse-bearer to throw a small string of about twenty cash to the actors. To my taste, this spoiled the effect of the piece; for, every time the cash fell among them there would be a silence, and the next moment a scramble for the money; and it fell so frequently as almost to keep time with the discordant music of the orchestra. The actors were engaged by the day, and in this manner received their payment, the amount of which entirely depended upon the approbation of the Quong and the number of times he encored them by tapping his drum. I could see that many of them paid far more attention to the drum than they did to their performance; though I suppose, the amount thrown to them is equally divided. Sometimes the string on which the cash was tied, unluckily broke, and the money flew in all directions; by which some of the bystanders profited, not being honourable enough to hand it up to the poor actors." †

The Burmese have dramas performed by men, and also comedies represented by means of marionettes, or puppets. In the latter entertainments the figures are cleverly managed by persons situated beneath a stage which is hidden by a

* 'A Voyage to Cochin-China in the years 1792 and 1793,' by John Barrow. London, 1806; p. 295.

† 'A Seaman's Narrative of his Adventures in Cochin-China,' by Edward Brown. London 1861; p. 221.

coarse curtain. The dialogues between these figures are much relished by the common spectators. At any rate, as they are apt to elicit uproarious mirth, they may be supposed to be often irresistibly comic. The real dramatic performances of the Burmese are acted by professional players, generally in the open air. The principal characters of the piece usually consist of a prince, a princess, a humble lover, a slave, and a buffoon. The female characters are represented by boys dressed in female attire. The dresses are handsome and gorgeous. However, the best theatrical performances take place in a building. On these occasions, there are two musical bands, one being placed on each side of the scene. The principal musical instruments of such an orchestra are of the percussion kind, containing a series of sonorous slabs of wood, or plates of metal, and somewhat resembling the Javanese instruments, but being attuned according to a diatonic order of intervals, instead of the pentatonic order. Also a curious contrivance, consisting of a set of drums suspended in a frame, each drum having a fixed tone, is used on these occasions. Moreover, the Burmese orchestra generally contains several wind instruments of the oboe and trumpet kind, as well as cymbals, large castanets of split bamboo, and other instruments of percussion, which serve to heighten the rhythmical effect of the music. The story of the drama is usually taken from ancient Burmese history. Captain Henry Yule, who has given a more detailed account of the Burmese plays than any previous traveller, remarks that when he was at Amarapoora he procured copies of some of the plays which he saw acted, from which it was evident to him that, while the general plan of the drama, comprising the more dignified and solemn part of the dialogue, was written down at considerable length, the humorous portions were left to the extempore wit of the actors. The following scenes are from a drama commemorating an episode from the life of Odeinna, King of Kauthambi, a country in India. This drama, which was obtained by Captain Henry Yule, is a translation from the Pali, and the whole is in Burmese verse of four syllables.

(The scene opens in the Capital of Kauthambi. The king is seated on his throne, with his courtiers around him.)

King.—(*Addresses them*) "Great nobles and chiefs!"

Nobles.—"Phra, (Lord)!"

King.—"Are my subjects happy and prosperous?"

Nobles.—"Since Your Majesty's happy reign began, religion has shone forth with splendour; the seasons have been propitious; the earth has been bountiful; the rich and the poor, men and women, have enjoyed peace and prosperity, and the happy years have been to them as water to the lotus."

(*Scene closes.*)

*Himalaya Mountains.—Enter a Nát.**

Nát.—"Now I am a Nát! When, and in what body was I before? Ah! looking with a Nát's eyes and understanding, I perceive I was a hermit in these wilds. My companion, Alakappa, is still here. I will seek my friend."

(*Approaches a cave.*)

Hermit.—"Who art thou that comest suddenly to my cell in the garb and appearance of a Nát, with the nine jewels in thy crown?"

Nát.—"O holy Hermit, of a good lineage, who ever livest in the forest, tell me all thou desirest, so that nought may remain unsaid!"

Hermit.—"O Nát, who by stupendous merit has reached the exalted abode! I have nothing particular to ask; but numerous elephants come around my cell and do great damage. Be pleased to forbid this for the future."

Nát.—"O holy Hermit! I will give thee a golden harp, and by the virtue of its sounds, and thy songs accompanying, elephants will come or go as thou commandest."

From this passage it is evident that the Burmese ascribe to music a great power, and the same is also indicated in several other remarks occurring in the drama. It is, however, unnecessary here to give the entire drama, which

* '*Náts* are sprites corresponding to the Hindu *Dewas* whose place they take in the Burman Buddhist system. They are supposed to have been the objects of Burman worship in pre-Buddhistic times.

the reader will find in the interesting book above alluded to.* Suffice it to notice the following passages from a subsequent scene.

(The young Prince Oodeinna enters. The Hermit presents him with the golden harp and teaches him a tune and song. The Prince retires to a tree, ascends it, and plays. The wild elephants of the forest come around him, and are obedient to his voice and harp, etc.—)

Captain Yule remarks that "the comic stage-effects of the characters addressing the orchestra is very frequent," and there are several indications of the kind in the present drama. Take, for instance, the following:—

(Scene in the solitary wilds of Himalaya).

Enter an immense Bird.

BIRD (speaks).—"From the beginning of the world there have been numerous sorts of birds: cranes, ducks, crows, peacocks, and others. I am not of their sort. My power would extinguish them all. My home is amidst vast mountains and pathless forests, and ever and anon I descend from them. I will now go to the country of Kauthambi to seek for food. So now *(to the band)*, as I am about to fly, strike up a victorious melody, O leader of the orchestra!"

The bird commences his flight, and, soaring aloft, says:—

"This is a beautiful country, and full of golden palaces, and lovely gardens with gorgeous-coloured flowers and shrubs. Nevertheless, I must look out for something to eat. Thus, turning north and turning south, looking up and looking down, I spy outside the King's palace a piece of flesh, red, red as blood. It is mine, sure as the food in a monk's begging-dish; it cannot escape. I will stoop at it, seize it, and fly away; and now that I may easily reach the large tree in my own mountain from this country of Kauthambi, play a soft and simple air, O leader of the orchestra!"

---

* 'A Narrative of a Mission, sent by the Governor-General of India to the Court of Ava, in 1855,' by Captain Henry Yule. London, 1858; p. 368.

(The bird seizes the Queen, mistaking her red mantle for flesh, flies away with her to the mountains, and deposits her in a tree. The bird comes as if to devour her, when the Queen claps her hands at him, which frightens the bird, and he flies away).

This scene shows that the Burmese employ in their dramas loud and soft music, according to the events represented; and that the orchestra is conducted by a leader or music-director. The following example, from another scene, indicates the employment of the full orchestra *fortissimo* in conformity with the action.

Forest. A Hunter.

HUNTER.—"I and my dog will now go and kill whatever enemy appears. With my bow and my dog I care not what I encounter, elephants, deer, or what not; so come along *(to his dog)* brave Tiger. *(To the band.)* Now as I go on a grand expedition, burst forth like thunder!"

A detailed description of a kind of opera which was performed at Singapore is given by Charles Wilkes;* but, as the actors were transient visitors to. Singapore, who came from the neighbourhood of Madras, their play must have been a specimen of the popular Hindu dramas. Its title was 'The Results of Misplaced Friendship;' the words were recited in a "monotonous recitative," accompanied by a band of instrumental performers. As regards the plot of the piece, suffice it to say that it had a moral aim, and that a Brahmin and a clown were the most amusing characters of the Dramatis Personæ. The clown displayed much cleverness in mimicking a European in his dress and manners. The 'Select Specimens of the Theatre of the Hindus,' translated from the original Sanskrit, by R. H. Wilson, London, 1835, contain but few allusions to music; but these are ancient dramas, and the Hindus possess, as R. H. Wilson in his interesting Introduction points out, different kinds of theatrical entertainments. There was in

* 'Narrative of the United States Exploring Expedition, during the years 1838-42,' by Charles Wilkes; London, 1845; Vol. V.; p. 389.

former time no building appropriated to the public performance of dramas. The Kings had in their palaces a kind of music hall, called *Sangita Sálá*, in which were given entertainments consisting principally of music and dancing, and occasionally of dramatic representations.

Turning to Thibet, we meet with actors who are also singers, dancers, and acrobats. They perform in the streets, courtyards, and other open places of the towns, and their entertainments are enlivened by a musical band, and by the witticisms of their clowns. The actors generally wear masks.*

In China, dramatic performances, enacted by itinerant players, take place not unfrequently in the Joss-houses, or houses of religious ceremonies. The plays generally have reference to some remarkable event in the lives of the earliest Chinese Emperors, and almost always combine the comic with the tragic. The musical band occupies the back part of the stage behind the actors. The expenses of the entertainment are sometimes defrayed by private persons. Thus, on a certain occasion three performances were given in a town daily, for three days in succession, in honour of "The Mother of Heaven," a goddess who presides over the welfare of sailors; the defrayers of the entertainment being three merchants who had just received the returns of a lucky venture.† Female characters are represented by boys and eunuchs. The plot of a Chinese drama, which was performed at Tien-sing before the English Ambassador, in a temporary theatre erected opposite to his yacht, is described by Sir G. Staunton, as follows:—

"An Emperor of China and his Empress are living in supreme felicity, when on a sudden his subjects revolt. A civil war ensues, battles are fought; and, at last, the arch-rebel, who is a General of cavalry, overcomes his sovereign, kills him with his own hand, and routes the imperial army.

---

* 'Travels in Tartary, Thibet, and China, during the years, 1844-46,' by M. Huc; Vol. II.; p. 238.

† 'Twelve Years in China,' by a British Resident, (John Scarth), Edinburgh, 1860; p. 56.

The captive Empress then appears upon the stage in all the agonies of despair naturally resulting from the loss of her husband and her dignity, as well as the apprehension of that of her honour."

How interesting would it be to the student of National Music to possess an exact notation of the music belonging to this scene, and to ascertain in what manner the intense emotions and vehement passions represented are expressed in the Chinese musical compositions !

"Whilst she is tearing her hair, and rending the skies with her complaints, the conqueror enters, approaches her with respect, addresses her in a gentle tone, soothes her sorrows with his compassion, talks of love and adoration, and like Richard the Third with Lady Anne, in Shakespeare, prevails in less than half-an-hour on the Chinese Princess to dry up her tears, to forget her deceased consort, and to yield to a consoling wooer. The piece concludes with a wedding and a grand procession."*

The Japanese are fond of dramatic representations, and have special buildings for their performances. Captain Golownin describes the theatre in Matsmai, the capital city of the island of Yesso, as "a large and pretty high building. At the back is the stage, which, as with us, has a raised floor. From the stage to the front wall, where the entrance is situated, two rows of seats are placed for the spectators. In the middle, where we have the pit, there is a vacant space in which straw mats are laid down for the spectators. As this space is much lower than the stage, those in front do not intercept the view from those behind. There is no orchestra, either because the Japanese perform no music in their theatres, or because the musicians are reckoned among the actors."

The place for the orchestra was probably at the back of the stage, as in the Chinese theatre. Captain Golownin

---

* 'An Authentic Account of an Embassy from the King of Great Britain to the Emperor of China, etc., taken chiefly from the papers of His Excellency the Earl of Macartney,' by Sir George Staunton; London, 1797. Vol. II.; p. 31.

visited the building only in the day-time, and when the house was empty, the permission to see a piece performed having been refused to him by the government of the capital.

"Opposite the stage, where in our theatres are the Emperor's box and the galleries, there are only a bare wall and the door for the entrance. There were no ornaments in the interior; the walls were not even painted. The dresses and decorations are kept in a separate building. The subjects of their plays are chiefly memorable events in Japanese history; but they have also other representations which are of a comic nature, and which serve to amuse the public."* Moreover, the Japanese have annual religious festivals in which scenic representations take place, and which are very popular. The dramas usually commemorate the deeds of ancient heroes or a myth; some have for their subject a fanciful love-story; and some are especially designed to enforce a certain moral precept. According to Siebold and Fisher, many of the Japanese plays are very instructive and moral. They are often so constructed that not more than two actors appear on the stage during a scene. There are no actresses, the female characters being represented by boys. It is not unusual for the actors to pass through the pit on their way to the stage, in order to give the audience an opportunity to admire their appearance and costume as closely as possible.

Such dramatic music of extra-European countries as has been derived from Europe does not come within the scope of our present inquiry. It happens, however, not unfrequently that the European music is to some extent modified, by being interspersed with national tunes of the extra-European country into which it has been introduced, or by being performed in a peculiar manner. Whenever this is the case, it deserves the special attention of the student of national music.

The Tagals, or the aborigines of the Philippine Islands, have theatrical performances in bamboo buildings. The characters consist principally of fairies, demons, and other

---

* 'Japan and the Japanese,' by Captain Golownin (of the Russian Navy); London, 1853. Vol. II.; p. 149.

supernatural creatures; but, the musical part of these entertainments is said to contain much which has been borrowed from the Spaniards. Probably this is especially the case in Manilla. Besides the principal theatre, in which the actors are Spaniards, Manilla has two theatres of the natives. In South America we find, as might be expected, Spanish and Italian operas. In Lima the orchestra is deficient; Spanish dances, as the Bolero, Fandango, Don Mateo, are often performed instead of our ballets. At the theatre in Mexico, Spanish dances are frequently introduced between the plays. The Teatro de Tacon in Havana, said to be one of the finest edifices of the kind in the world, has singers who perform Italian operas, as in Europe. The female spectators sit in places separate from those of the men.

There can hardly be a doubt that many operatic entertainments, which are now secular, had originally a sacred character. The ancient nations performed religious dances with pantomimic representations. Also the Chinese at the time of Confucius thus enhanced their sacred ceremonies. The Burmese, at the present day, sing and dance by the coffin of a deceased priest. They are Buddhists. Funeral dances are common with several uncivilized races. Our Christian ancestors, during the earlier centuries of the Middle Ages, performed sacred dances in the church. The Christian priests of the Abyssinians still dance at certain religious ceremonies. In the Cathedral of Seville, boys, from the age of twelve to seventeen, dressed in an old Spanish costume, annually execute a ballet every evening during the Ottave del Corpus. Again, sacred dances with recitations, dialogues, and hymns are performed in several European countries during Christmastide. The Mysteries, Miracle Plays, or musical-dramatic entertainments on biblical subjects, so popular during the Middle Ages, have not entirely fallen into disuse. Passion-Plays are still occasionally performed by the peasantry in Bavaria, in the Tyrol, and in Moravia. The "Mayings," or popular rejoicings with music, dancing, and processions, remains of which are still to be found in England as well as on the Continent, had probably in pagan time also a religious character, as they were intended to welcome the approach of the sunny season. Turning to America, we meet in Peru with musical entertainments which were introduced among the Indians by the Spanish monks, who accompanied Pizarro's army, and who dramatized scenes in the life of Christ, and had them represented to facilitate by this attractive means the conversion of the heathen aborigines. These plays are no longer performed in the larger towns of Peru, but are still kept up by the villagers of the Sierra. Good Friday especially is celebrated by them in this manner; and on Palm Sunday an image of the Saviour seated on an ass is paraded through the principal streets of the town or village.* In Brazil we find on Hallelujah Saturday (between Good Friday and Easter Sunday) the popular ceremony of burning effigies of Judas Iscariot, the traitor, in company with dragons, serpents and demons; and there are besides several other religious celebrations in which music is employed in combination with fire-works and dramatic representations.

Comic scenes were not excluded from the old Mysteries of mediæval time. On the contrary, they appear to have been highly relished by the worshippers, and contributed much to the popularity of the entertainments. In Paris a building was erected, in the year 1313, principally for dramatic performances relating to the Passion of Christ and the Resurrection, enacted with music and dancing. Soon, attempts were made to vary these entertainments by the occasional introduction of some play founded on a myth, or on a wonderful event recorded in secular history, or also by the admission of profane comedies and farces. Although music, instrumental as well as vocal, did not constitute the chiefest point of attraction in these plays, it certainly contributed much to the impressiveness of the whole. † During the second half of the thirteenth century, Adam de la Hale wrote dramatic plays with songs, founded on secular

* 'Travels in Peru, by J. J. von Tschudi.' London, 1847; p. 377.

† 'Wesen und Geschichte der Oper, von G. W. Fink.' Leipzig, 1838; p. 53.

subjects. These plays, called Gieux (*jeux*), might perhaps be called operettas, since they contained dialogues interspersed with songs. In fact, although our opera may be said to date from about the year 1600, secular plays in which music and poetry were intimately associated were known long before that time. The ancient Greeks used in their dramas the vocal music of choruses and the instrumental accompaniment of flutes and other instruments, in close connection with the poetry. The latter art was, however, the principal one, while in our present opera *music* is the principal art.

As regards the secular dances of the ancient Greeks, it may be observed that some of them were similar to the pantomimic exhibitions which are still relished by several nations. The Pyrrhic dance, which was executed according to fixed rules, to the sound of the flute, depicted a combat of warriors. Lord Broughton, during his stay in Albania, was struck with the resemblance between some of the dances of the Albanians and those of the ancient Greeks. He notices especially the Pyrrhic dance.* The war-dance of the Jajis, a wild and hostile tribe in the mountainous districts of Afghanistan, is probably quite as picturesque and exciting as was the Pyrrhic dance. A European eye-witness of the war-dance of the Jajis states that it is performed by about twelve or fifteen men placed in a ring before a number of spectators who are arranged in a semi-circle. "The performers commenced chanting a song, flourishing their knives overhead, and stamping on the ground to its tones; and then each gradually revolving, the whole body moving round together and maintaining the circle in which they first stood up. Whilst this was going on, two of the party stepped into the centre of the ring and went through a mimic fight, or a series of jumps, pirouettes, and other movements of a like nature, which appeared to be regulated in their rapidity by the measure of the music; for, towards the close of the performance the singing ceased, and the whole party appeared twirling and twisting about in a confused mass amidst the flashing of their drawn knives, their

* 'Travels in Albania, etc., by the Right Hon. Lord Broughton.' London, 1855; Vol. I., p. 145.

movements being timed by the rapid roll of their drums. It was wonderful that they did not wound each other in these intricate and rapid evolutions with unsheathed knives. On the conclusion of the dance the whole party set up a shrill and prolonged yell, which reverberated over the hills, and was caught up by those in the neighbouring heights and thus prolonged for some minutes. Whilst all this was going on upon the heights around our camp, several parties of armed Jajis ranged in columns, three or four abreast, and eight or nine deep, followed each other in succession round and round the skirt of our camp, all the time chanting an impressive and passionate war-song in a very peculiar sonorous tone that seemed to be affected by the acoustic influences of the locality, which was a deep basin enclosed for the most part by bare and rocky eminences and hills." *

Not less characteristic, and equally descriptive, are the sword-dances of the Anazehs, in Syria, and of the warriors in Little Thibet, which are not unfrequently acted with too much reality, since the performers, having worked themselves up to a state of frenzy, are apt to forget that they ought only to feign fighting.

Some of the sword-dances still in use in European countries represent scenes with poetry and music. There is, for instance,—or, at any rate, there was still in the eighteenth century,—an ancient sword-dance occasionally performed in some villages of North Germany, in which the principal dancer, or "The King," addresses the people in a speech.† Here may also be noticed the "Fool Play" still popular in some villages of Northern England, which is described as "a pageant that consists of a number of sword-dancers dragging a plough, with music, and with one, sometimes two, in very strange attire; the Bessey, in the grotesque habit of an old woman; and the Fool, almost covered with skins, a hairy cap on, and the tail of some animal hanging from his back." And the

* 'Journal of a Political Mission to Afghanistan, by H. W. Bellew.' London, 1862; p. 143.

† 'Das deutsche Volk, geschildert von Eduard Duller.' Leipzig, 1847; p. 183.

sword-dance performed in the North Riding of Yorkshire, from St. Stephen's Day till New Year's Day. "The dancers usually consist of six youths dressed in white ribands, attended by a fiddler, a youth with the name of Bessey, and also by one who personates a Doctor. They travel from village to village. One of the six youths acts the part of the King in a kind of farce which consists chiefly of singing and dancing, and the Bessey interferes while they are making a hexagon with their swords, and is killed."*

The Cavalcade, or procession on horse-back, is supposed to have been originally connected with the Mysteries of the Middle Ages. It is still occasionally performed in Belgium, and its Flemish name is 'Ommegang.' A number of persons dressed in historical and fanciful costumes ride on horse-back and drive in carriages through the principal streets of the town in which the Cavalcade takes place, with the object of representing scenes from sacred or profane history, or allegorical subjects. The procession is made imposing by the splendid dresses of the principal characters, by the gorgeous gildings of their carriages, and the display of baldachins and flags. This show is supposed to have been introduced into the Netherlands by the Spaniards during their former possession of the country. At a certain religious festival, held in Malines in the year 1838, the entire Litany to the Virgin Mary was represented, each Invocation being written on a beautiful flag, carried by a beautiful and richly-dressed young girl, who was riding on a gorgeously-caparisoned horse led by men. The Invocations: "Queen of the Angels!" "Queen of the Patriarchs!" etc.,—were depicted by groups of characters in open carriages; each carriage, splendidly decorated, having the Virgin Mary seated on a high throne, while at her feet were placed picturesquely on steps the angels, patriarchs and prophets, all of whom were dressed in their appropriate costumes, and provided with their requisite attributes. Again, at a festival which was held at Brussels, in September,

* 'Observations on Popular Antiquities, by John Brand, revised by Henry Ellis.' London, 1813; Vol. I., pp. 396, 401.

1839, two parishes of the town arranged a grand Cavalcade, in which a scene was represented commemorating a political event from the history of Belgium. Many of the riders were dressed in mediæval costume, while some appeared in Oriental dresses. The sons and daughters of the most influential citizens generally undertake the representation of the principal characters in these processions. Music is, of course, an indispensable assistance for the solemnity of such pageants. However, as recitations are of secondary importance in them, or are even entirely omitted, the first attempts at dramatic music are less traceable in these remains of mediæval entertainments than they are in the rude amusements of savages noticed in the beginning of this survey.

It has probably already occurred to the reader that the "Opera of the Future," aimed at by Wagner, will be in some respect a return to the opera in its infancy, inasmuch as it will be devoid of the various artistically-written forms of composition which greatly contribute to the clearness and impressiveness of the music, and which Mozart has developed in his operas to the highest degree of perfection. Much might be said on this subject, were here the proper place for it. Enough if the facts which have been noticed convince the reflecting musician that the contemplated innovations alluded to might as well be termed retrocessions. Gluck was also a reformer of dramatic music, who aimed at truth in its noble simplicity; but, his objection to anything artificial in the opera did not mislead him to disregard the artistic beauties dependent upon form, which ensure the impressive total effect essential to a true work of art.

Furthermore, the examples given in the preceding pages will probably have convinced the reader that the origin of the opera can be traced more minutely in the first dramatic attempts of uncivilized races of the present time, than by a reference to the theatrical performance of the ancient nations. At any rate, the latter research does not render the former superfluous; they should go hand-in-hand.

A SHORT SURVEY OF THE HISTORY OF MUSIC.

The perusal of Chronological Tables illustrating the history of music must appear to many readers a dry occupation. Still, it enables the lover of music to obtain in a short time a comprehensive and clear view of the gradual development of the art from the earliest period of its cultivation recorded in history to the present day. Perhaps a coloured chart contrived like the "Stream of Time," which at a glance shows the great events in universal history, might answer the purpose even better. There is no disconnection in the progress of an art, though certain occurrences may appear to the superficial observer as being entirely accidental. A musical "Stream of Time" might exhibit in various colours the natural connection between the several branches of the art of music, and their modifications conspicuous in its history.

Or, this might be achieved by the representation of a tree. As in the genealogical tree which has been published of Johann Sebastian Bach the proper relation of the numerous members of his family is at once brought clearly before the eyes of the inquirer, so might the growth and spread of the different branches of the art of music be indicated, exhibiting distinctly their highest degree of culture, as well as their infancy and decay.

Diagrams of this kind are, however, only suitable for a very condensed historical survey. More detailed information is better conveyed by means of chronological tables, such as Carl Czerny has compiled in his 'Umriss der ganzen Musik-Geschichte' ('A Sketch of the whole History of Music'), published at Mayence, in the year 1851. Carl Czerny, of Vienna, was a very industrious man, who, although he gave pianoforte lessons during the whole day, nevertheless found time to write above nine hundred compositions, not to mention his innumerable arrangements of operas, oratorios, symphonies, and overtures. That he could engage in such laborious research as the preparation of his chronological tables must have required is certainly surprising, especially as he was a very practical man with regard to money-making, and there is probably no musical occupation less likely to yield pecuniary advantage than is the compiling of chronological tables. It used to be said of Czerny that he was in the habit of composing while he was giving pianoforte lessons. If this is no false rumour, it perhaps accounts for the enormous number of his compositions, as well as for the slight merit of most of them. But, chronological tables he may have compiled in this way without detriment to them, since they do not require to be written with feeling, even less with inspiration, but merely with careful discernment, and with perseverance. Be this as it may, he certainly was an eminent pianoforte teacher, as is proved by his having instructed Liszt, Döhler, and other distinguished pianists. His finger-exercises, or pianoforte-studies, have outlived his other compositions, and his chronological tables will probably be used for reference long after his finger-exercises have been supplanted by more modern ones.

As the object is to supply the lover of music with an historical survey, similar to that of Czerny, but on a smaller scale,—it may be useful to notice the plan adopted by Czerny.

He has divided his work into two Sections. The first Section records the ancient traditions respecting the origin of music, and gives an account of the music of the nations before the Christian era, of the music of our forefathers during the Middle Ages, and of the rise of our modern tone-art. This Section is arranged in eighteen Periods, thus :—

First Period.—The primitive Music of the Greeks until the time of the Trojan War (B.C. 2000—1200). Mythic and mythic-heroic Age. Beginning of the public games and contests.

Second Period.—From the Trojan War until Pythagoras (B.C. 1200—584). Gradual development of singing associated with poetry. Invention and improvement of different Stringed Instruments, Wind Instruments, and Instruments of Percussion. Encouragement given to artists by the bestowal of great honours.

Third Period.—From Pythagoras until Aristoxenus of Tarentum (B.C. 584—340). Highest development of all the Arts in Greece. The Art of Music founded on fixed rules.

Fourth Period.—From Aristoxenus until the Birth of Christ (B.C. 340—A.D. 1). New Musical System. Decay of the Arts.

Fifth Period.—From the Birth of Christ until Hucbald (A.D. 1—900). Gradual decay of the Ancient Music. Origin of the Christian Church-song.

Sixth Period.—From Hucbald until Franco of Cologne (A.D. 900—1200). The first attempts in Polyphonic Harmony. Invention of Musical Notation and Measure of Time.

Seventh Period.—From Franco of Cologne until Dufay (A.D. 1200—1380). Invention and development of Counterpoint.

Eighth Period.—From Dufay until Ockeghem, or Ockenheim (A.D. 1380—1450). The elder Netherlandish School. Developed Regular Counterpoint. Musical Notation fixed. Composers according to the new system of Harmony.

Ninth Period.—From Ockeghem until Josquin des Prés (A.D. 1450—1480). The newer or second Netherlandish School. Artificial Counterpoint. Beginning of the reputation of the Netherlandish masters. In Italy and Germany executive artists on the Organ, Clavichord, and other instruments, make their appearance.

Tenth Period.—From Josquin des Prés until Willaert (A.D. 1480—1520.) Commencement of the flourishing state of the Netherlandish masters, and their influence upon all European countries. Masters in Counterpoint arise in Germany. Meritorious teachers in Italy. French musicians attain reputation in other countries besides in France.

Eleventh Period.—From Willaert until Palestrina (A.D. 1520—1560). The Netherlandish masters institute Schools in Italy and develope the art of music with great success in that country. The Madrigal becomes the favourite kind of composition of the Venetian School.

Twelfth Period.—From Palestrina until Monteverde (A.D. 1560—1600). Commencement of the flourishing state of the Italian musical artists. Conclusion of the great Netherlandish epoch. Refinement of the stiff Netherlandish style. Romish School. Church Music of a high degree of perfection.

Thirteenth Period.—From Monteverde until Carissimi (A.D. 1600—1640). Commencement of Operatic Music. First attempts in the Recitative style, in the melodious song for a single voice (Monody) and in the Concertante style.

Fourteenth Period.—From Carissimi until Alessandro Scarlatti (A.D. 1640—1680). Improvements in the Recitative and in the Dramatic Melody. Origin of the Cantata and the Oratorio. Introduction of Concertante Instruments to the song. Neapolitan School.

Fifteenth Period.—From Alessandro Scarlatti until Leo and Durante (A.D. 1680—1720). Essential improvement in the Recitative and in Dramatic Music. Increase of the Orchestral Instruments. Development of Instrumental Music. Rise of great Composers in Germany.

Sixteenth Period.—From Durante until Gluck (A.D. 1720—1760). Flourishing state of the Neapolitan School. Reform in Melody. The highest art in Counterpoint in Germany. Oratorios. German Composers study in Italy, and write Italian Operas.

Seventeenth Period.—From Gluck until Haydn and Mozart (A.D. 1760—1780). Reform in the style of the Opera. Introduction of the Ensemble pieces and the Finales.

Rise of the French Opera. Development of Instrumental Music.

Eighteenth Period.—From Mozart until Beethoven and Rossini (A.D. 1780—1820). Great improvement of the Orchestra, and of Instrumental Music in general. Development of the German Operatic Style. Tone-artists of the Vienna School. Beginning of the popularity of the Pianoforte. Beethoven brings Instrumental Music to the highest degree of perfection. Flourishing state of the French Opera. With Rossini commences a new and effective epoch in Italian Operatic Music. Numerous Virtuosos on instruments. In the Opera, amalgamation of different styles. In the most recent time, an undecided direction.

Thus much about the Eighteen Periods noticed in Section I. of Czerny's work. Only the first seven periods are fully treated in this Section; the others form the subject of Section II., which is divided into Three Principal Epochs, thus:—

First Principal Epoch.—From the establishment of our Theory of Harmony until the commencement of the Opera (A.D. 1400—1600). Separation of the four chief nations: 1, France (with the Netherlands); 2, Italy (with Spain and Portugal); 3, England; 4, Germany (with Bohemia, Hungary, Poland, Sweden, and Denmark).

Second Principal Epoch.—From the commencement of the Opera until the development of Instrumental Music and Chamber Music (A.D. 1600—1700). Division of the Art of Music into Church Music and Operatic Music. First appearance of some distinguished performers on instruments. 1, Italy (with Spain and Portugal); 2, France (with the Netherlands); 3, England; 4, Germany (with Bohemia, Hungary, Poland, Sweden, and Denmark).

Third Principal Epoch.—From the development of Instrumental Music until the end of the Eighteenth Century (A.D. 1700—1800). Division of Church Music, Operatic Music, and Instrumental Music. 1, Italy (with Spain and Portugal); 2, France (with the Netherlands); 3, England; 4, Germany (with Bohemia, Hungary, Poland, Sweden, and Denmark).

After these Divisions and Sub-divisions follows an alphabetically-arranged Register of the names of the musicians who are mentioned in the different Periods and Epochs. But also here we have Divisions and Sub-divisions, so that the Register, in fact, consists of six Indices, each containing the musicians of a certain epoch or a certain country, from A to Z. The author says that the plan of the work renders this arrangement necessary; but, as he does not prove his assertion, students using the work for reference will probably arrive at the conviction that one general Index, containing all the names in alphabetical order, would be more convenient. Another disadvantage is that the Indices are entirely restricted to the names of musicians, no reference being made to important events relating to the history of music. In fact, the chief aim of the work is to notice a great many musicians. The number of composers, theorists, and performers entered amounts to 1713, of whom 236 belong to the ancient Greeks and Romans, 132 to the Middle Ages, and 1345 to European nations from A.D. 1400 to 1800. Many of these musicians have left no mark upon the history of their art, and their names have justly fallen into oblivion. These might better have been omitted. Of what use, for instance, can it be to the student to be supplied with the names of the musicians who played before Alexander the Great on the occasion of his marriage with Roxanen, at Samarkand, in the year B.C. 328? Especially among the 1345 composers who distinguished themselves during the four centuries from A.D. 1400 to 1800 are many who might now as well have been left at rest. What possible advantage can the student derive from a record of mediocre pianoforte composers whose productions were not held in much esteem even during their lifetime? On the other hand, it was prudent in the author not to extend his list beyond the year 1800. The distinguished musicians of the present century are known to readers who take an interest in the history of the art, and who are most likely to use the book. Anyhow, it would be a delicate task to admit the names of living musicians, some of whom may still become more celebrated than they are, while others may show that they really are not so clever as they at first appeared to be. It is impossible to assign his proper place in the history of his art to an artist before he is dead.

Czerny has had the happy thought of placing in a column before each chronological table short memoranda of the events in general history of the time when the composers lived. Nothing can be more advisable to a professional musician than to make himself familiar with this column of facts bearing directly upon his art. There can hardly be a doubt that other artists,—especially painters and sculptors,—generally possess more historical knowledge than musicians. Perhaps their occupation suggests to them more forcibly the value of such information. Be this as it may, the music of an intelligent musician is better than that of an ignorant, narrow-minded one; even for this reason, musicians ought to study universal history, were it not on account of the intimate connection of the cultivation of the arts with the progress of civilization.

Moreover, if we are exactly acquainted with the political and social conditions of the time in which a distinguished artist lived, we are the better able to appreciate his merits. Unfortunately, Czerny records the musicians under the date of their birth. Thus, many are mentioned in the century previous to that in which they flourished. Take for instance Handel and Sebastian Bach: both were born in the year 1685, and produced their great works during the first half of the eighteenth century. Now, if the plan of recording the musicians under the date of their birth had been throughout adhered to, the student might, as a general rule, surmise the time of their activity to have been about half a century later. But, of several celebrities the date of whose birth is unknown, Czerny gives some year in which they are known to have distinguished themselves, and this deviation from the plan leads to confusion in the chronological arrangement. True, it is impossible to determine exactly the year in which the musician in his lifetime exercised the greatest influence upon his art; but, this can be done as nearly as possible by adopting his fortieth or fiftieth year as that of his best period. Those who did not attain that age might be noticed under a date referring to the period when they most distinguished themselves, which was generally the case during the last few years of their life.

Again, the mention of the musicians of each country separately has too little advantage to justify the inconvenience thereby occasioned to the student. Cherubini, like Bellini and Donizetti, is classed with the Italian composers; he would, however, have been more properly placed with the German composers. Rossini, when he wrote 'Guillaume Tell,' was more German than some musicians born in Germany. Lulli, the founder of the old French opera is certainly more properly mentioned with the French musicians than with the Italian. Other examples could be pointed out which evoke the question whether such a complicated classification really serves a scientific purpose.

In the 'Chronology of the History of Music' offered in the following pages, in which Czerny's tables have been of great assistance, the aim has been to avoid the defects just noticed. It will be seen that only a brief survey of the most important events in the history of music has been attempted. When the student has ascertained these, he will probably choose to refer to some treatise on the history of music instead of a more extensive chronological table. But the latter may afterwards be of use to him inasmuch as it will assist him in recalling to his memory in proper order those facts with which he has become more minutely acquainted by reading the treatise.

As some account of the mythological traditions respecting the origin of music has already been given in the present work, * there is no necessity to advert to them here.

The recorded dates of the Greek music with which the survey commences must not be taken as authentic until we arrive at about the seventh century before the Christian era.

---

* Vol. I., p. 74.

CHRONOLOGY OF THE HISTORY OF MUSIC.

	B. C.	
Cadmus, from Phœnicia, and Cecrops, from Egypt, settle in Greece.	2000	Music, with other arts and sciences, is introduced into Greece from Western Asia and Egypt.
Abraham (1900). Joseph (1750). Moses (1550).	1750	The Jews have vocal music with instrumental accompaniment. (Gen., Chap. xxxi., v. 26, 27).
The oracle of Delphi.	1500	Hyagnis, in Greece, improves the flute and invents the Phrygian Mode.
Daedalus, Grecian sculptor and architect, invents the sails of ships, &c.		Marsyas, a distinguished flute-player, invents a new species of flute made of metal.
		Linus ventures upon a musical contest with Apollo, and is killed by him.
		"Then sang Moses and the children of Israel." (Exod. xv.)
The Argonauts, led by Jason, sail to Colchis.	1300	Orpheus, lyrist, singer, poet, and lawgiver, composes hymns.
Hercules. Theseus.		Amphion, lyrist, singer, and composer, improves the Grecian lyre.
Triptolemus introduces agriculture into Greece.		Musæus, lyrist, sets music to the words of the oracles.
Castor and Pollux, Grecian heroes.		About this time the Greeks instituted most of their public games in which musical contests formed part.
Tyrus, on the coast of Phœnice, founded by a colony of Sidonians.	1250	Olympus of Mysia, a celebrated flutist. Daphnis of Sicily. To him is ascribed the invention of the chalumeau, and of the bucolic poetry.

	B. C.	
Adrastus celebrates the first Pythian Games in honour of Apollo.	1250	Thamiris, singer and player on the kithara, a species of lyre, is chosen by the Scythians for their King on account of his musical accomplishments.
Amazons, or female warriors, from the Caucasus, invade Greece.	1240	Euneus, a distinguished singer and kithara-player of Greece. His descendants remain during many generations the privileged kithara-players at the public festivities in Athens.
Troy taken by the Greeks (1184).	1200	Agias, a celebrated Greek musician about the time of the destruction of Troy.
Grecian heroes: Menelaus, Agamemnon, Achilles, Ulysses.		The invention of the Dorian Mode is ascribed to Lamyras of Thracia; the invention of the Lydian Mode, to Carius; and the invention of the Ionian Mode, to Pythermus.
Trojan heroes: Priam, Hector, Paris, Æneas.		Celmis, a priest of Creta, invents (or probably improves) several instruments of percussion.
Codrus, the last King of Athens (1070). Abolition of Royalty.	1100	Ardalus, of Troezen, invents a new species of flute for accompanying vocal music.
King Saul. Cheops, the builder of the greatest Pyramid in Egypt.		The Greeks about this time possessed various kinds of stringed instruments and wind instruments, and the names of several musicians are recorded who improved the instruments, or introduced innovations in the construction of the popular ones.
	1050	David, King of Judah, musician and poet. Psalms.
King Solomon (1010-975).		King David institutes in Jerusalem a School for vocal and instrumental music (I. Chron., Chap. xv., v. 16).
Dido builds the city of Carthage on the north coast of Africa.	1000	Bardus, a King of Gallia, is said to have introduced music into Western Europe, and to have been the first of the singers known as the Bards.
Development of the Republics in Greece.	900	Homer, singer and poet, born probably in Chios. Iliad and Odyssey.

	B. C.	
Lycurgus reforms the Republic of Lacedæmonia, and gives laws to the Spartans.	850	Hesiodus, singer and poet, born in Boeotia. Simmicus, inventor of an instrument with thirty-five strings, called Simmikon or Simmicium. Thaletas, of Creta, musician and poet, composes in Sparta, under Lycurgus, the laws and war-songs for the voice. Phœcinus, of Greece, sketches the first musical rules.
Rome founded by Romulus (754).	800	Olympus, of Phrygia, flutist, invents the Enharmonic scale.
	720	Archilochus, of Paros, singer, poet, and instrumentalist.
		Important improvements in the music of the Greeks.
	700	Tyrtæus, of Athens, poet, singer, and trumpeter, composes war-songs for Sparta against Messenia.
	650	–TERPANDER, of Lesbos, lyrist, flutist, and composer. Important progress in the music of the Greeks.
Circumnavigation of the coast of Africa under Necho, King of Egypt (615).	625	Arion, of Lesbos, kithara-player, singer and poet, invents the Dithyrambs, or hymns of Bacchus, and improves the chorus-singing. He is recorded to have healed sick persons by means of music. The same is also recorded of Menias, a Greek musician, who lived about this time.
Nebuchadnezzar, King of Babylon, carries the Jews into captivity.	600	Stesichorus, of Sicily, composes choruses with instrumental accompaniment, besides airs to his poems.
		Alcæus, of Mytilene, singer, lyrist, and poet.
Solon, law-giver, in Athens.		Sappho, of Mytilene, female singer, lyrist, and poetess. To her is ascribed the invention of a stringed instrument called Barbitos.
The seven sages of Greece:—Solon, Thales, Periander, Cleobulus, Pittacus, Bias, Chilo.	570	The Romans, under the King Servius Tullius, introduce trumpets and horns of metal into their army.

	B. C.	
Cyrus conquers Lydia and dethrones Crœsus. Confucius, Chinese philosopher. Zoroaster in Persia.	550	About this time was performed in Athens, under Thespis, the first tragedy with choruses set to music.
Tarquinius Superbus, the last King of Rome, is expelled. Rome becomes a Republic (510). Cambyses conquers Egypt (509).	530	PYTHAGORAS, of Samos, philosopher, studies music in Egypt, founds in Greece a great School of music based upon mathematical principles; invents the monochord for measuring the sound; ascertains the harmonious Triad, the diatonic intervals, etc.
Battle of Marathon, in which the Greeks, commanded by Miltiades, defeat the Persians (490). Xerxes invades Greece (487). Battle of Salamis in which Themistocles defeats the Persians (480). Leonidas. Themistocles banished from Athens (471). Cimon defeats the Persians (466).	500	Lasus, of Achaia, writes treatises on the theory of music. Æschylus, born at Athens about 525, singer and writer of Tragedies. Simonides, of Ceos, born in 557, died 468, lyrist and poet. Pindar, born at Thebes, in Boeotia, about the year 520, flutist, lyrist, poet, and composer. Many hymns, odes, etc. Corinna, of Tanagra, in Boeotia, female singer and poetess. Several times gains the victory in contest with Pindar at the public games at Thebes. Anacreon, of Teos, lyric poet and musician. To him is attributed the invention of several stringed instruments. The Greeks had about this time several accomplished players on the kithara, flute, and other instruments, who introduced new and brilliant passages and embellishments into their performances.
Pericles, Greek General and orator.	450	The highest degree of perfection of the dramatic art in Greece through Æschylus, Sophocles, Euripides, and

	B. C.	
Herodotus, historian. Phidias, sculptor. Hippocrates, physician.	450	through the musical composer Damon, the singer Agathon, etc., at Athens. Democritus, of Abdera, philosopher, writes seven books on music.
Commencement of the Peloponnesian war between the Athenians and Spartans which lasts twenty-seven years (431).	430	Lysander, of Sycion, invents a more artistic instrumental accompaniment to vocal music. Alexandrides extends the compass of the Greek wind instruments.
Socrates (469-399). Alcibiades.	400	Timotheus, of Miletus, Asia Minor, singer, kithara-player and poet, composes many works, and improves the lyre.
Brennus, Chief of the Gauls, burns & sacks Rome (390).		Plato, philosopher, in his works treats also on music.
Demosthenes (384-322).	360	About this time, the first dramatic performances with music in Rome.
Diogenes (350). Alexander the Great, son of Philip of Macedonia (333).	350	Aristoteles, of Stagira, born in 384, philosopher and musician. In his works much about music.
Ptolemy I., King of Egypt, encourages the cultivation of sciences and arts in his kingdom, & founds a library in Alexandria.	310	ARISTOXENUS, of Tarentum, born in 340, philosopher and musician, founds a new School of music which is in opposition to the teaching of Pythagoras, generally accepted until that time. He writes many treatises on music. Division of the musicians into Musici, or the followers of Aristoxenus, who derive the rules of music from its effect upon the ear,—and Canonici, or the followers of Pythagoras, who derive them from mathematical laws.
Pyrrhus, King of Epirus, is defeated by the Romans (275).	300	About this period the Greeks made many improvements in the construction of their musical instruments.

	B. C.	
	300	Euclides, of Alexandria, born in 323, died 283, mathematician, writes on the theory of music and acoustics.
The first Punic war (264-241). The second Punic war (218-202). Scipio defeats Hannibal in Africa (202).	250	Archimedes, of Syracuse, born in 287, died 212, mathematician, is said to have invented the hydraulic organ. Ctesibius, of Alexandria, improves the pneumatic organ and alters it into a hydraulic organ. His son Hero still further perfects the instrument and describes it.
The first Macedonian war (200). The first library at Rome (167).	200	Aristeas, of Greece, a kithara-player, writes a treatise on kithara-playing.
Corinth and Carthage destroyed by the Romans (146). Greece and North Africa become Roman provinces.	150	Polybius, of Megalopolis in Arcadia, born about the year 204, historian, writes a treatise on the influence of music upon civilization.
Civil war in Rome (88). The Romans under Julius Cæsar invade Britain (55).	100	Alypius, of Alexandria, writes on musical notation by means of the letters of the Greek alphabet.
Julius Cæsar assassinated in the Senate-house (44). Cicero killed (43). Virgilius. Antonius and Cleopatra defeated (31).	50	Hermogenes (Marcus Tigellius), singer and instrumentalist of Greece, settles in Rome.
Augustus, Roman Emperor (30). Horace. Mæcenas.	30	Diodorus Siculus, of Agyrium in Sicily, historian, gives some account of the oldest music of the Egyptians and Greeks.
Titus Livius, historian. Ovidius, poet.	10	Vitruvius (Pollio M.), born in Italy, architect, writes on musical subjects.

	A. D.	
Hermann in Germany defeats Varus (9). The Romans under the Emperor Claudius invade England (40). London founded by the Romans (49).	1	Gradual decay of the Greek Music. The first Christian hymns (St. Matthew, chap. XXVI., v. 30; St. Mark, chap. XIV., v. 26; I Corinth., chap. XIV., v. 15; Ephes., chap. V., v. 19; Coloss., chap. III., v. 16; St. James, chap. V., v. 13, etc.).
	50	Pliny the Elder, born at Verona in the year 27, died in 79. Several books on music.
Destruction of Jerusalem by Titus (70). Herculaneum and Pompeii destroyed by an eruption of Vesuvius (79).	60	Nero, Roman Emperor from A.D. 54 to 68, musician, singer, flutist, lyrist. He sings and plays in public, and is said to have maintained 5000 musicians in his pay.
Tacitus, historian. Juvenal, poet. Martialis, poet. Pliny the Younger. Trojan, Roman Emperor (98).	80	Plutarchus, born at Chaeronea in Boeotia, about the year 40, biographer and philosopher. Several musical essays.
Introduction of Christianity into Ireland by St. Patrick (110).	100	Ptolemaeus (Claudius) born at Pelusium in Egypt, about the year 70, mathematician, geographer, astronomer, and musician. In his writings he endeavours to reconcile the musical theories of Pythagoras and Aristoxenus. He reduces the fifteen Modes of the Greeks to seven.
Fingal (Ossian) in Scotland (200) Persecutions of the Christians during the third century. Artaxerxes, king of Persia, conquers the Parthians, & founds the dynasty of the Sassanidæ (226).	200	From about the year 150 to 200, above a dozen authors are known in whose works some account is given of the music of the ancients.

	A. D.	
Probus, Roman Emperor, causes the vine to be planted on the banks of the Rhine and the Moselle (276).	250	The Fathers of the Church who give the first account of the sacred songs of the early Christians are Tertullian, Clemens of Alexandria, and Origen. Their writings date from the first half of the third century. The Christian communities had already during the first century in their religious observances, which in the beginning were held secretly, hymns sung alternately by a single voice and a chorus in unison. The melodies of the hymns were probably similar to those of the Greeks. At all events, the Modes in which they were sung, and the notation by letters of the alphabet, had been derived from the Greeks.
Constantine, Emperor, is converted to Christianity, and transfers the seat of his empire from Rome to Byzantine, henceforth called Constantinople (330).	330	Silvester I., Pope, institutes in Rome the first school for Church-song.
Division of the Roman Empire into Eastern and Western (364). Kingdoms formed by the Ostrogoths and Visigoths. The Huns migrate from Asia to Europe, and come in collision with the Goths (375).	350	Damasus, Bishop of Rome, born at Madrid in the year 314, introduces in Church the antiphonal singing of the Psalms by two choirs, and regulates the intoning of the Mass. St. Basilius (died 379) promotes sacred song in the Eastern (Greek-Christian) Church, and describes the Church-music of his time.
Theodosius the Great, Emperor of the Eastern Empire (379).	380	St. Ambrose, Bishop of Milan, from 374 to 397, born about 333 in Gallia, died in 398. Introduces the Ambrosian Song of Praise (Te Deum laudamus),

	A. D.	
	380	composes several hymns, and promotes the singing of the Psalms, in opposition to the old Greek music.
The Visigoths, or Goths of the West, under Alaric, invade Italy (400).	400	St. Augustine, Bishop of Hippo, born 354 at Tagasta, in Africa, died 430. In his works, writes much about music, and especially recommends Psalm-singing.
Rome is sacked and burnt by Alaric (410).		The Fathers of the Church, St. Chrysostom, Cyprian, and Hieronymus, with others, uphold the cultivation of Church-song, which is discouraged by many.
The Anglo-Saxons arrive in Britain (449). The Anglo-Saxon Heptarchy in Britain (457).	420	Macrobius writes on music according to the system of Pythagoras.
	500	Boethius, born 470 in Rome, died 526; writes several treatises on the music of the Ancients.
Silkworms are introduced into Europe from China (550).	550	Cassiodorus (Magnus Aurelius) born 480, died 575; musical author.
The Picts are converted to Christianity (565). The Visigoths, or Goths of the West, conquer the greater part of Spain (580).	590	GREGORY THE GREAT, Pope, 590 to 604, collects the Christian hymns, fixes the employment of them, improves the Singing Schools, appoints Cantores, Precentors, etc. The Gregorian Church-song used in place of the Ambrosian.
Foundation of the Kingdom of Mercia by Crida (582).	596	ST. AUGUSTINE, first Bishop of Canterbury, usually called the Apostle of the English, introduces into England with the Christian religion, the Church-song.
Mohammed, founder of a Religion (604).		Church-music contributes much to the diffusion of Christianity in heathen countries.
The Pope in Rome acknowledged as the head of the Church (607). University of Cambridge founded (631).	600	St. Isidore, Archbishop of Seville, in Spain, born at Carthagena about 570, died 636. Promotes the improvement of Church-music, and writes treatises on music.

	A. D.	
Conquests of the Arabs in Asia, as far as Hindustan. Jerusalem is taken by them (637). The Caliph Omar burns the Alexandrian library (640).	650	Jacob (Deacon), Stephan Eddi, Putta, Maban, and Acca (Bishop), were distinguished church-singers in England during the period from 620 to 700.
The Danes invade England (660). The Britons are driven into Wales (685).	660	Vitalianus, Pope, from 657 to 672, introduces the hydraulic organ into the Church for sounding the first tone of the Chorale as a guide to the singers. He sends two accomplished Roman singers to Gallia (France) for the purpose of improving the Church-song in that country.
Conquests of the Arabs in North Africa (688).	676	Johannes Damascenus, born at Damascus. Introduces in Church hymns, the melodies of which differ from the old Grecian.
The Saracens in Spain (713). Glass-painting & Mosaic in Italy (750). Pepin, King of the Franks (752-768).	700	BEDA VENERABILIS, born 673, died 735; an English Monk, to whom are attributed two important treatises on music. Benedict, an English Abbot, introduces chanting in choirs.
The Danes invade England (783). Harun al-Rashid, Caliph of Bagdad. Flourishing state of the sciences with the Arabs (786).	780	Alcuinus, or Albinus, an English Prelate, born 736, died 814; promotes Church-music.
Division of the Monarchy of Charlemagne (843).	800	Charlemagne, Emperor of Germany, introduces the Gregorian Church-song into all his dominions, and orders a collection to be made of the popular secular songs. Church organs come gradually into use.

	A. D.	
Alfred the Great defeats the Danes in England (880).	850	Notker, a Benedictine Monk of St. Gallen, in Germany, composes sacred songs called Sequentias Missales, which are introduced in the churches.
	886	Friar John of St. David's, the first Professor of Music at the University of Oxford, appointed by Alfred the Great.
Foundation of the University of Oxford by Alfred the Great (900) Foundation of the Kingdom of Hungary by the Magyars (about 900). University of Cambridge restored (915). Institution of Free-Masons in England (924).	900	HUCBALD, Monk of St. Amand, in Flanders, born about 840, died 932. First attempt to accompany an air with several voices in harmony. Notation, consisting of the syllables of the words placed in different positions between lines. The signs used for the purpose during the three preceding centuries were called Numæ.
The Russians, under Wladimir the Great, embrace Christianity (988).	950	St. Dunstan, Archbishop of Canterbury, introduces organs into English churches.
Poland becomes a Kingdom (1000). William of Normandy invades England (1066). The Moors in Spain (1091). Peter the Hermit. The first Crusade (1095).	1030	GUIDO OF AREZZO, a Benedictine Monk at Pomposa, born about 990 in Arezzo, died 1050. Improves the method of singing in use at his time, and the notation of Hucbald; designates the tones by the letters of the alphabet. He is supposed to be the inventor of the Solmisation of the Hexachord, or scale of six sounds, etc.
War between England and France (1113). Frederick I., called Barbarossa, in Germany (1152). The Sultan Saladin conquers Egypt (1187).	1100	NOTATION.—During the twelfth century originated our musical notation, the inventor of which is unknown. The first attempts in Counterpoint led to the employment of notes of different value (Mensural and Figural Notes). However, these innovations did not come into general practical use until about the year 1200.

	A. D.	
Magna Charta, or the Charter of English Liberty (1215).	1200	The most popular instruments of the Middle Ages were the Psalterium, Harp, Rotta, Viol, Lute, Organistrum, Regals, Recorder, Sackbut, Shalm, etc.
Distinguished Troubadours and Minnesänger during the twelfth and thirteenth centuries:— Guillaume IX., Count of Poitou; Blondel, with Richard Cœur de Lion; Sordello of Mantua, Peyrols, Bertrand de Lorm, Arnold of Maraviglia, Heinrich von Veldeck, Wather von der Vogelweide, Reimar der Aeltere, Reimar der Zweter, Ulrich von Lichtenstein, Heinrich von Morungen, Wolfram von Eschenbach, Hartmann von der Aue, Gottfried von Strassburg, Conrad von Würzburg, Johann Hadlaub.	1207	Contest of the Minnesänger at the Wartburg, in Saxony. The Minnesänger, who flourished in Germany, especially during the twelfth and thirteenth centuries, were identical with the Troubadours, or singers of secular, amorous, and martial ditties, which they accompanied with the harp, cither, guitar, or some other instrument. The original home of the Troubadours was Provence, in the South of France, where they originated about the beginning of the eighth century. Subsequently, at the time of the German Minnesänger, there were also Troubadours in Italy, Spain and England. Among them were many noblemen, and even princes.
The Kingdom of Granada founded by the Moors in Spain (1238). Foundation of the University of Vienna (1237).	1220	FRANCO OF COLOGNE, the first known musical author who treats circumstantially on the new theory of Harmony, and who, by expounding it systematically, greatly contributes to its diffusion. (Forkel, Fétis, and some other musical historians, maintain that Franco of Cologne lived during the second half of the eleventh century.)

	A. D.	
Cimabue, Giotto, Italian painters (1240). Termination of the Crusades (1248).	1240	Odington (Walter), an English monk, writes on music in a manner similar to that of Franco of Cologne, in Germany.
Parliament of Great Britain. First assembly of the Commons as a confirmed representation (1265).	1260	Hieronymus von Mæhren, in France, writes on the theory of music.
Venice and Genoa are powerful.	1280	ADAM DE LA HALE, of Arras, in France, writes compositions in four-part harmony, dramatic pieces, with songs, etc. He lived in Provence.
Invention of Gunpowder (1292). Italian poets and authors: Dante Alighieri (1265-1321); Petrarca (1304-1374); Boccaccio (1313-1375).	1290	Ægidius, of Zamora, a Spanish monk, writes on the invention of musical instruments.
Disunion in the Church. Popes in Avignon (1378).	1300	Gradual diffusion of the theory of Harmony, especially through Marchetto di Padua, about 1310, in Italy;—and through Jean de Muris, about 1325, in France.
The Turks victorious in Hungary (1396).	1390	Gerson (Johannes), a French monk, born 1363, died 1429. Musical author. Commencement of the period in which appeared numerous sacred vocal compositions, viz: Masses, Motetts (English Anthems), Offertories, Hymns, Psalms, Madrigals, etc. The Madrigals were in the form of the Motett, but often had secular words. Instrumental music was still insignificant.
Masaccio, Fiesole, Italian painters (1400). Conquest of France by Henry V., King of England (1420). Charles VII., of France (1422-1461).	1400	DUFAY (GUILLAUME), born about 1350 at Chimay, in Belgium, died 1432. The first Contrapuntist, properly speaking. Purer harmony than previously. Application in the notation of the White notes, which had been already invented before his time. Many Church compositions.

	A. D.	
Jeanne d'Arc burnt (1430). England loses all her possessions in France, except Calais (about 1440). Invention of Printing (1440).		Binchois (Egide), born in Picardy, contributes to the improvement of harmony and of musical notation. Composes much vocal music.
Constantinople taken by the Turks (1453).	1450	Dunstable (John), born about 1400 in Scotland, died 1458. Improves the harmony and the musical notation.
Watches invented at Nürnberg (1477). Inquisition in Spain (1480). Burgundy and Provence incorporated with France (1481). The Medici govern in Florence; flourishing growth of the arts & sciences (1402-1537).	1470	OCKEGHEM, or OCKENHEIM (Johann), born about 1430 in Hainault, Belgium; died 1513. Founder of the newer Netherlandish School, improver of harmony, and composer of Church music. Obrecht, or Hobrecht (Jacob), born about 1430 in Holland. Many compositions for the Church. Bernhard, a German residing in Venice, is said to have invented the organ pedal.
America discovered by Columbus (1492). Macchiavelli, historian (1469-1527). Ludovico Ariosto, poet (1474-1533). Leonardo da Vinci, painter (1444-1519). Tiziano Vecelli, painter (1477-1576). Rafael Sanzio, painter (1483-1520). Correggio (1494-1534). Albrecht Dürer (1471-1528).	1490	DÉPRÉS (Josquin des Prés), born about 1450 in France, died about 1521. Pupil of Ockeghem. Many Masses and other compositions for the Church. Tinctor (Jean), born about 1450 at Nivelles, died about 1520. Founder of a School in Italy. Many Church compositions. Gafforio (Franchino), born 1451 at Lodi, died 1522. Writer on the theory of music, and promoter of new rules of harmony. Adam von Fulda, born about 1450 in Germany. Writes a treatise on the newly-established theory of music, and composes music for the Church. Towards the end of the fifteenth century Chairs of Professorship for music were instituted in different towns

	A. D.	
Newfoundland, the first British Colony in America, discovered by Cabot (1497).	1490	of Italy, especially in Milan and Naples.
Copernicus, astronomer (1473-1543). Zwingli in Switzerland (1519). Gustav Wasa, king of Sweden (1523).	1500	In the beginning of the sixteenth century the Netherlandish music attains its highest reputation in Italy (at the time of the Popes Julius II. and Leo X.), in Spain, France, and Germany.
Henry VIII., King (1509-1547).	1502	Petrucci (Ottaviano), of Fossombrone in Italy, invents the printing of musical notation with movable types.
The highest degree of perfection of the art of painting in Italy.	1520	WILLAERT (HADRIAN), born about 1490, in Flanders, died 1563. Lived in Rome and Venice. Founder of the Venetian School. Composer of the first Masses for six and seven different voices, of Masses for two and three choruses, etc.
The Netherlandish School of Painting, founded by Johann van Eyk, about 1350:— Floris, Stradan, De Vos, Spranger, Peter & Franz Porbus, Steenvyk, Vanbort, P. & J. Breughel, Rubens (1577-1640). Snyders, Momper, David Teniers, De Crayer, Gerhard & Daniel Segers, Jordans, Rombouts, Anton van Dyk (1598-1641).	1530	Aaron (Pietro), born about 1480 in Florence. Contrapuntist, writer on the theory of music, and composer of Church music. Luther (Martin), born 1483 at Eisleben, in Germany, died 1546. Composes Chorales, and promotes congregational singing. Alterations in the old Church-songs for the Reformed Church. Introduction in German Churches of Chorales in the German language. Walther (Johann), born about 1490 in Saxony, died about 1555. German Mass, many Chorales, etc. Senfl (Ludwig), born about 1490, at Basle in Switzerland, died about 1560. Masses, Motetts, Chorales, etc. Agricola (Martin), born 1486 in Silesia, died 1556. Many vocal compositions, and a treatise on musical instruments.

The Dutch School of Painting, founded by Lucas of Leyden, born 1494:—Van Veen, Bloemart, Poelenburg, Wynants, Vertange, Hanesberge, etc.

Roman School of Painting; pupils of Rafael:— Giulio Romano, Penni il Fattore, Bagnacavallo, Del Vaga, Caravaggio, Gemigniani, Garofalo, etc.

Venetian School of Painting; pupils of Titian:— Del Piombo, Palma Vecchio, Lotto, Bordone, Pordenone, Schiavone, Bassano, Tintoretto, Poalo Veronese.

Florentine School of Painting; pupils of Da Vinci:— Luini, Salaino, Melzo, Fra Bartolomeo, Del Sarto, Peruzzi, Razzi, Michel-Angelo.

The Order of Jesuits founded by Ignaz Loyola (1540).

The Turks conquer Tripoli (1551).

Death of Rabelais (1553).

Philip II., King of Spain (1556).

A. D.

1530 Luscinius (Ottomar), properly Nachtigall, born 1487 at Strassburg, died about 1540. Treatises on music and on the musical instruments of his time.

Glarean (Heinrich Lorit), born 1488 in Switzerland, died 1563. Many essays on the History and Theory of Music.

Festa (Costanzo), born about 1490 at Rome. Many Motetts and other Church music. Regarded as the precursor of Palestrina.

1540 Berchem (Jacob), called Giachetto di Mantua, born 1499 at Antwerp, died about 1580. Many Masses, Motetts, etc.

Gombert (Nicolas), born about 1500 in the Netherlands, died about 1570. Many Masses, Motetts, and other sacred and secular compositions for four, five, and six different voices.

Arcadelt (Jacques), born about 1500 in the Netherlands, died about 1570. Teacher in Rome. Many Masses, Motetts, Madrigals, etc.

Clement (Jacques), called Clemens non Papa, born about 1500 in Flanders, died 1566. Masses and other sacred compositions.

1550 Goudimel (Claude), born 1510 in Flanders, died about 1572. Many Psalms, Motetts, and other sacred compositions, and also secular music. Much progress in Harmony. Founder of a Music School in Rome.

Morales (Christoforo), born about 1510 at Seville in Spain, lived in Rome. Many Masses, etc.

Est (Michael), born about 1510 in England. Many Psalms and Madrigals.

Tallis (Thomas), born 1520 in England, died about 1585. Many sacred compositions.

	A. D.	
Foundation of the University of Jena (1558). Holbein, painter (1494-1554). Calais is lost to England in the reign of Mary (1558).	1550	Lossius (Lucas), born 1508 in Germany, died 1582. Many Chorales, a treatise on music, etc.
Queen Elizabeth (1558-1603). English authors: Spenser, poet (1553-1598). Francis Bacon (1561-1626). Shakespeare (1564-1616). Marlow, Green, Beaumont, Fletcher, Massinger:—Dramatic poets and contemporaries of Shakespeare. Calvin in Geneva (1565). Hans Sachs, Meistersänger (1494-1576). Tycho Brahe, Astronomer (1546-1601). The Counts Egmont & Horn beheaded at Brussels (1568)	1560	Rore (Cyprian), called Vanrore, born 1516 at Malines, died 1565. Pupil of Willaert, in Venice. Many sacred and secular vocal compositions. Waelrant (Hubert), born 1517 in the Netherlands, died 1595. Many Church compositions. Improvement in the Solmisation. LASSUS (ORLANDUS), properly Roland de Latre, born 1520 at Mons, in Hainault, died 1594. A great number of Church compositions of every kind, of which 1572 are known. Kerle (Jacob), born about 1520 in Flanders. Many Masses, etc. *Zarlino* (Giuseppe), born 1519 at Venice, died about 1590. Many Church compositions. Great progress in Harmony. Several treatises on the Theory of Music. PALESTRINA (GIOVANNI PIERLUIGI DI), born 1524 in Palestrina, died 1594. Reform of the Italian Church music by means of purer harmony. Ennobling of the rude Netherlandish style. Many Masses, Hymns, Motetts, Litanies, Offertories, etc.—Palestrina's celebrated Mass, known as Missa Papæ Marcelli, which was performed in Rome in the year 1565, had the effect of altering the opinion of many of the ecclesiastics who at the Council of Trent, in 1562, advocated the banishment of all Figural music from the Church.

The first Puritans and Presbyterians (1571).

Massacre of St. Bartholomew (1572).

First circumnavigation of the world, by Drake (1577).

North-America English. Walter Raleigh (1584).

Portugal is conquered by the Spaniards in 1581, and remains a Spanish Province until 1640.

The Netherlands become independent (1581).

The Gregorian Calendar introduced into all the Roman Catholic States of Europe (1582).

Elizabeth, Queen of England, causes Mary, Queen of Scots, to be beheaded at Fotheringay Castle (1587).

Defeat of the Spanish Armada in the English Channel (1588).

A. D.

1570 Faber (Heinrich), born 1525 at Brunswick, in Germany, died 1598. Church compositions, and a treatise on music.

Lejeune (Claude), born about 1540 in the Netherlands, died about 1600. Masses, Psalms, etc.

Nanini (Giovanni Maria), born about 1540 at Vallerano, in Italy, died 1607. Teacher of Counterpoint; many Motetts for eight different voices, and other Church compositions.

1580 Morley (Thomas), born about 1540 in England, died 1604. Madrigals and other vocal compositions. Instruction book on music.

Opera. — About the year 1580, a number of professional musicians and amateurs associated in the house of Giovanni Bardi, Count of Vernio, at Florence, with the object of reviving in the drama the musical declamation of the ancient Greeks. To this association belonged the composers Emilio del Cavalieri, Giacomo Peri, Giulio Caccini, and the poet Ottavio Rinuccini. Their exertions resulted in the production of the first Lyric Opera, called 'Dafne,' the poetry of which was by Rinuccini, and which was performed at Florence in the year 1594. Soon followed the first Tragic Opera, 'Euridice,' the poetry of which being by Rinuccini, and the music by Peri and Caccini. The next Operas were 'Il Satiro' and 'La Disperazione di Filano,' both with music by Cavalieri. Meanwhile, Orazio Vecchi attempted to compose a kind of Comic Opera, entitled 'L'Anfiparnasso, Commedia Armonica,' which was performed at Modena in the year 1594. The songs of these operas partook of the character of the recitative, and they were accompanied by a few instruments.

	A.D.	
Janson, of Middlebourg, invents spectacles and telescopes (1590).	1590	Gabrieli (Giovanni), born about 1550 at Venice, died 1612. Many Church compositions.
Torquato Tasso (1544—1595).		Marenzio (Luca), born about 1550 at Brescia, died 1594. Motetts, Madrigals, etc.
		Bird (William), born 1546 in England, died 1623. Masses, Graduales, Madrigals.
First Edition of Bacon's 'Essays' published (1597).		Weelkès (Thomas), born about 1550 in England. Madrigals and other vocal compositions.
		Eccard (Johann), born about 1545 in Thuringia, Germany. Pupil of Orlando di Lasso. Many Church songs.
Edict of Nantes. Religious liberty (1598).		Gallus (Johann Peter), properly Händl, born about 1550 at Krain, in Austria, died 1591. Many sacred songs.
Incorporation by Royal Charter of the English East India Company (1600).	1600	Vittoria (Tomaso Ludovico della), born about 1560 in Spain, died about 1608. Many Church compositions.
		Dowland (John), born 1562 in England, died 1615. Virtuoso on the lute. Many vocal compositions.
Lopez de Vega, dramatic poet, in Spain (1562-1635).		Bull (John), born 1563 in England, died 1622. Organist. Vocal compositions and Organ pieces.
James VI. of Scotland, son of Mary Stuart, succeeds Queen Elizabeth of England as James I. (1603).		Vulpius (Melchior), born about 1560 in Germany, died 1616. Chorales and other sacred songs.
		Calvisius (Sethus), born 1556 in Thuringia, Germany, died 1615. Many Church compositions, and also theoretical works.
First French Colony in Canada (1604).		Schultz (Hieronymus), called Prætorius, born 1560 at Hamburg, died 1629. Motetts, etc.
First permanent British settlement in North America, formed by "the London Company" under charter from James I. (1607).		From about 1600 to 1725, the celebrated Violin Makers of Cremona, in Italy:—Amati, Guarneri, Stradivari, etc.

A. D.

Bacon publishes his Advancement of Learning (1605).

1600 The most popular instruments about the year 1600 were: The lute, cither, spinet, virginal, clavichord, flûte-à-bec, cornet, etc.

Guy Fawkes, Gunpowder Plot (1605).

Third recorded appearance of the comet afterwards known as Halley's Comet (1607).

1605 Viadana (Ludovico), born 1560 in Italy, died 1625. Many Church compositions, and the first Church concertos and Solo songs for the Church. Viadana is said to have invented, in the year 1605, the thorough-bass, or indication of the Harmony by marking the bass with figures; but this invention is also ascribed to Ottavio Catalano, born about 1595 in Sicily.

Thermometers are invented about this time by Drebbel, of Alkmaer, Paulo Sarpi, and Sanctorio.

Cervantes, author of Don Quixote, etc. (1547-1616)

English poets:—Milton, Dryden, Butler, Otway, Prior, Cowley, Denham.

The telescope is first applied to astronomical purposes by Galileo, at Padua. Discoveries of the satellites of Jupiter, and the spots in the sun (1610)

Tea is brought from India by the Dutch; it is introduced into England in 1666.

1610 MONTEVERDE (CLAUDIO), born 1565 at Cremona, died 1649. Masses, Madrigals, and also secular songs. The most important steps towards the development of the modern music by new licenses in the Harmony. Invention of the Tremolo of the violins, etc.

Cerone (Dominico Pietro), born 1566 at Bergamo, died 1620. Many theoretical treatises.

Prætorius (Michael), born 1571 in Thuringia, Germany, died 1621. Many Masses, Psalms, Hymns, and a musical treatise.

Walliser (Christoph Thomas), born about 1571 at Strassburg, died 1648. Church compositions, and a treatise on Harmony and on the Fugue.

1620 Frescobaldi (Gieronimo), born about 1580 in Italy, died 1640. Organist. Many Church compositions, Madrigals, Organ compositions, Fugues, Ricercari, etc.

Vieira (Antonio), born about 1580 in Portugal, died in 1650. Many Church compositions for eight different voices.

Allegri (Gregorio), born about 1580 at Rome, died 1652. Many Church compositions. The Miserere of the Vatican.

	A. D.	
The present authorized English version of the Bible is published, and is called "King James's Bible" (1611). Settlement of New York, in North America, by the Dutch (1614). Emigration of the Puritans to New England; they found New Plymouth (1620).	1620	Carissimi (Giacomo), born about 1582 at Padua, died about 1673. Many Masses, some of which are for twelve different voices, and other Church compositions. Improver of the Recitative. The first important Oratorios and Cantatas in Italy. Kapsberger (Johann Hieronymus), born about 1575 in Germany, died 1650. Lived in Italy. Church compositions, and Instruction books for playing the Lute and the Guitar. Gibbons (Orlando), born 1583 at Cambridge, died 1625. Many Church compositions, Anthems, Madrigals, etc.
Charles I. succeeds James I., King of England, after the death of the latter, in 1625. Disputes between King Charles I. and his Parliament. Civil war begins in 1642. Last general assembly of the Hanseatic cities of Germany. Lübeck, Hamburg and Bremen continue united.	1627	Schütz (Heinrich von), called Sagittarius, born 1585 in Germany, died 1672. Many Motetts, Psalms, and also Operas. In the year 1627 the Opera Dafne, by Rinuccini (see above, date 1580), having been translated into German by Opitz, and composed anew by Schütz, was performed in Dresden as the first German Opera. Mazzocchi (Domenico), born about 1590 at Castellana, in Italy. Oratorios, Madrigals for five different voices with instrumental accompaniments. Introduced signs of expression in the notation.
Kepler, Astronomer (1571-1630). Gustavus Adolphus dies on the battle-field at Lutzen (1632). Wallenstein assassinated at Eyer (1634). Rubens, Vandyck, Domenichino, painters (1620). Ben Jonson, dramatist (1620).	1630	Mazzocchi (Virgilio), brother of the preceding, born about 1595, died 1646. Many Church compositions. The first development of the melody in the present sense. Doni (Giovanni Battista), born 1593 at Florence, died 1674. Treatises on the music of the ancient Greeks and on that of his time. Jenkins (John), born 1592 in Kent, England, died 1678. Virtuoso on the Viola da Gamba. Many compositions for his instrument and also vocal music.

	A. D.	
Lope de Vega, Spanish writer (1620). Galileo is condemned by the Inquisition of Rome as guilty of heresy for upholding the Copernican system, and compelled to abjure it (1633). Richelieu founds the French Academy (1635.)	1630	Schein (Johann Hermann), born 1586 in Germany, died 1630. Chorales, Madrigals, Secular Songs, etc. Scheidt (Samuel), born 1587 at Halle, in Germany, died 1654. Contrapuntist. Many Church compositions as well as pieces for the Organ and Clavichord. Mersenne (Marie), born 1588 in France, died 1640. Treatises on Harmony, Acoustics, and Musical History.
Death of Cardinal Richelieu (1642). Louis XIV. (styled *Dieu-donné*), King of France (1643—1715). The Pendulum is applied to clocks by Richard Harris and the younger Galileo (1641).	1640	Lawes (Henry), born 1600 in England, died 1662. Psalms and Secular songs. Kircher (Pater Athanasius), born 1602 at Fulda, in Germany, died 1680. Several treatises on music.
Charles I. beheaded (1649).	1645	The first Italian Opera in Paris, ordered from Italy by Cardinal Mazarin.
Oliver Cromwell, Protector of the Commonwealth (1653). Portugal takes possession of the Brazils (1654). Calderon de la Barca, dramatic poet in Spain (1601—1687). Dutch and Flemish Painters:—Eykens, Sachtleven, Rembrandt, Douw Swanevelt, Wouvermann, Berghem, Paul Potter, etc.	1650	Sabattini (Galeazzo), born about 1610 in Italy. Litanies, Madrigals, and other vocal music. Dumont (Henri), born 1610 at Liege, Belgium, died 1684. Masses and other Church compositions. Innovation of the employment of instrumental accompaniments to the Mass. Child (William), born 1608 at Bristol, in England, died 1696. Psalms and other sacred vocal music, and secular songs. Simpson (Christopher), born about 1610 in England, died about 1670. Instruction book on the Viola da Gamba, on the Theory of Music, etc. Hammerschmiedt (Andreas), born

	A. D.	
Restoration of Charles II. (1660). Spain takes possession of Havannah (1662). The French, commanded by Turenne, victorious upon the Rhine (1663). Plague in London (1665). Great fire of London (1666).	1650	1611 in Bohemia, died 1675. Many Masses and other sacred compositions. Cesti (Marc-Antonio), born in 1620 at Florence, died 1681. Nine Operas. Progress in the development of operatic music. Eccles (John), born about 1620 in England. Several Operas, songs, etc. Lock (Matthew), born about 1620 in England, died 1677. Sacred music and dramatic compositions.
Flourishing state of France owing to her industry & commerce (1670). The Turks in Hungary invade Poland (1670).	1670	Stradella (Alessandro), born 1645 at Naples, died 1678. An Oratorio and some Operas. Kerl (Johann Caspar von), born about 1625 in Saxony, died about 1690. Masses and organ compositions. Meibom (Marcus), born 1626 in Schleswig, died 1711. Many Treatises on the Music of the Ancient Greeks.
Death of Molière (1673). De Ruyter, the Dutch Admiral, dies (1675).	1672	LULLI (GIOVANNI BATTISTA), born 1633 at Florence, died 1687 at Paris. Founder of the older French operatic music. Composed 19 Operas and 26 ballets. His first French Opera was performed at Paris in the year 1672.
William Penn founds Pennsylvania (1681). Vienna is besieged by the Turks (1683). Death of Corneille (1684). The Huguenots expelled from France (1685). Peter the Great, Czar of Russia (from 1682 to 1725).	1680	Frohberger (Johann Jacob), born 1637 at Halle, Germany, died 1695. Organist. Many compositions for the organ and the clavichord. Buxtehude (Dietrich), born about 1640 in Germany, died 1707. Many Organ compositions. Gasparini (Michael-Angelo), born at Lucca, in Italy, during the second half of the seventeenth century, died in 1732. Many Operas. Founder of a School of Singing at Venice. Steffani (Agostino), called Gregoria Piva, born about 1650, at Venice, died 1730. Masses and other sacred compositions, Operas, vocal duets.

	A. D.	
William III., Prince of Orange, and Mary (daughter of James I.) his wife, declared King and Queen of England (1688). Charles XII. King of Sweden from 1697 to 1718. Alsace becomes French (1697). Death of Racine (1699). Locke, philosopher, English (1632-1704).	1690	Baj (Tomaso), born about 1650, at Bologna, died 1714. Many sacred compositions. A Miserere for the Vatican, which is sometimes performed instead of that by Allegri. Corelli (Arcangelo), born 1653 at Fusignano, in Italy, died 1713. Violinist. Many concertos, etc. Blow (John), born 1648 at Nottingham, died 1708. Many anthems, psalms, etc. Purcell (Henry), born 1658 in London, died 1695. About 17 English Operas, secular songs, anthems and other sacred compositions. Krieger (Adam), born 1646 at Nürnberg, died 1725. Operas, etc.
Charles XII., King of Sweden, at war with Denmark, Poland, and Russia. He forces the King of Denmark to conclude a peace with him, and defeats the Russians on the banks of the Narva (1700). Queen Anne (1702). Battle of Blenheim, or Höchstadt, gained by the Duke of Marlborough & Prince Eugene over the French and Bavarians (1704). Gibraltar taken by the English (1707).	1700	SCARLATTI (ALESSANDRO), born 1659 at Trapani, in Sicily, died 1725. Composed 115 Operas, 200 Masses, several Oratorios, many sacred and secular cantatas, etc. Invention of the Recitative with orchestral accompaniment; of a greater combination of orchestral instruments than hitherto; of the Da-Capo, or repetition of the theme; and of several other essential innovations. Desmarets (Henri), born 1662 at Paris, died 1741. About 8 Operas. Brossard (Sébastien de), born 1660, probably at Strassburg, died 1730. Many Masses, a Dictionary of Music. Brossard's Dictionary, which was published in 1703, is generally regarded as the earliest work of its kind. Tinctor, however, already in the fifteenth century compiled a collection of the definitions of the musical terms in use at his time; and Janowka published at Prague a Musical Dictionary in Latin, two

	A. D.	
Union of England and Scotland by Treaty (1707). Peter the Great defeats Charles XII. at Pultowa (1709).	1700	years previous to the appearance of Brossard's work, which is in French. Fux (Johann Joseph), born 1660 in Austria, died about 1732. Composed 17 Operas, 26 Masses, 3 Requiems, 1 Stabat Mater, 10 Oratorios, above 170 other sacred compositions; likewise, instrumental pieces, a work on the theory of music (Gradus ad Parnassum), etc.
Herculaneum discovered (1711). Peace of Utrecht (1713).	1710	Gasparini (Francesco), born about 1665 at Lucca, died 1727. Many Operas, Cantatas, etc. Teacher in counterpoint of Domenico Scarlatti and Marcello.
Death of Fénélon (1715). Defoe, author of 'Robinson Crusoe.'		Lotti (Antonio), born about 1665 at Venice, died 1740. Nineteen Operas, many church compositions and madrigals.
Saunderson and Brook Taylor, English mathematicians.		Vivaldi (Antonio), born about 1670 at Venice, died about 1743. Twenty-six Operas, violin concertos, and many other instrumental pieces.
Prior, Congreve, and Parnell, English Poets.		Bononcini (Giovanni), born about 1672 at Modena, died 1750. Composed about 23 Operas. For a time rival of Handel in London.
George, Elector of Hanover, becomes King of England, as George I. (1714).		Couperin (François), born 1668 at Paris, died 1733. Organist. Many organ and clavecin (harpsichord) compositions.
Prince Eugene defeats the Turks at Peterwardein in Austrian Slavonia (1716).		Keiser (Reinhard), born 1673 at Leipzig, died 1739. Many Operas, many Oratorios and other sacred compositions, etc. He is said to have composed 116 Operas, partly to German, and partly to Italian words.
Prince Eugene defeats the Turks at Belgrade (1717).		Pepusch (Johann Christoph), born 1667 at Berlin, died 1732. Cantatas and other sacred music. Leveridge (Richard) born 1670 in London, died 1758. Operas and songs.

Charles XII., King of Sweden, is killed at the Siege of Fredericksball, in Norway (1718).

English authors: Pope (1688—1744); Swift (1667—1744); Young (1684—1765); Thomson (1700—1748); Fielding (1707—1754); Johnson (1713-1784); Goldsmith (1728—1774); Sterne (1713—1768); Hogarth, painter (1698—1764).

Death of the Duke of Marlborough, born 1650 (1722).

Death of Peter the Great (1725).

George II., King of Great Britain, succeeds his father, George I., who died, aged 68 (1727).

Fahrenheit, improver of the thermometer (1724).

Réaumur, improver of the thermometer (1731).

The Jesuits are expelled from China (1724).

Isaac Newton (1642—1727).

Swift publishes his 'Gulliver's Travels' (1726).

A. D. 1720

Caldara (Antonio), born 1678 at Venice, died 1763. Sixty-seven Operas, many Masses and other sacred compositions.

Astorga (Emanuale), born 1681 at Palermo, Sicily, died 1736. Several Operas, a Requiem and many other sacred compositions.

Geminiani (Francesco), born 1680 at Lucca, died 1762. Violinist. Many compositions for his instrument.

Scarlatti (Domenico), son of Alessandro Scarlatti, born in 1683 at Naples, died about 1760. Clavicembalist. Many compositions for his instrument.

Rameau (Jean Philippe), born 1683 at Dijon, died 1764. Composed 36 Operas, many motetts and other sacred vocal compositions, as well as pieces for the organ and for the clavecin (harpsichord). Several theoretical works. A new System of Harmony. Progress in operatic music.

Mattheson (Johann), born 1681 at Hamburg, died 1764. Seven Operas, 24 Oratorios, several other sacred compositions, and a great many works on the theory and history of music.

Telemann (Georg Philipp), born 1681 at Magdeburg, in Germany, died 1767. Composed 44 Operas, many Oratorios and other sacred compositions, secular instrumental pieces, etc.

Heinichen (Johann David), born 1683 in Saxony, died 1729. Operas, sacred and secular compositions. Treatise on the Theory of Music.

Walther (Johann Gottfried), born 1684 at Erfurt, died 1748. Organ compositions, chorales, and a Musical Dictionary.

About this time, the first Pianofortes were constructed by Christofali, in Italy, and by Schröter, in Germany.

Pope publishes his 'Essay on Man' (1729).

Thomson publishes his 'Seasons' (1730).

Arbuthnot and Sir Hans Sloane, English physicians (1730).

Le Sage, author of 'Gil Blas' (1730).

Jonathan Swift, Dean of St. Patrick's, poet and miscellaneous writer (1730).

Harrison, an Englishman, constructs a chronometer of great precision (1735). His fourth chronometer is used at sea in 1764, and he receives a reward of £20,000.

Frederick III., Elector of Brandenburg, and Duke of Prussia, in an assembly of the states, puts a crown upon his own head, and upon the head of his consort, and is proclaimed King of Prussia, by the title of Frederick I. (1701).

German poets and authors:—

Elias Schlegel, Gellert, Hagedorn, Rabener, Rammler, Kleist, Weisse, Bürger,

A. D.

1730 Marcello (Benedetto), born 1686 at Venice, died 1739. Composed fifty Psalms, several Oratorios, Masses, etc.

Porpora (Nicolo), born 1687 at Naples, died 1767. Great singing teacher. Composed fifty Operas, many Masses, etc.

Tartini (Giuseppe) born 1692 at Pirano, died 1770. Violinist and composer. Author of a Treatise on Harmony.

Leo (Leonardo), born 1694 at Naples, died 1756. Composed forty-eight Operas, several Oratorios, Masses, and other sacred music. He wrote for his Operas larger overtures than previous composers had done.

Carey (Henry), born about 1690 in England, died 1743. Many songs. He is supposed to have composed in the year 1740 the English national air of 'God save the King.'

HANDEL (GEORG FRIEDRICH), properly Händel, born 1685 at Halle, died 1759 in London. Composed fifty-one Operas (forty-three having Italian words and eight having German words), twenty English Oratorios, many cantatas, motetts, anthems, a Mass, four Te Deums, concertos, instrumental compositions for the organ, harpsichord, etc.

The concertos of that period consisted of orchestral pieces with or without an organ concertante; or of violin-quintetts with double-bass; or also of pieces for the harpsichord accompanied by a quartett of stringed instruments, etc.

During the eighteenth century, most of the German Opera composers of distinction wrote chiefly to Italian words. Every German town in which a Sovereign resided had an Italian Opera. The German art of singing began to flourish

A. D.

1730 only about the year 1760. Even Mozart wrote but two Operas to German words. The German composers (Handel, Gluck, Hasse, Mozart, etc.) studied dramatic music in Italy.

BACH (JOHANN SEBASTIAN), born 1685 at Eisenach, in Germany, died 1750 at Leipzig. Composed several Oratorios, many Masses, a great many motetts, cantatas, chorales, etc.; many compositions for the organ, clavichord, clavicembalo (harpischord), and for the orchestra. The first book of his Preludes and Fugues for the clavichord, entitled 'Das Wohltemperirte Clavier,' dates from the year 1722, and the second book from the year 1740. He composed the Passion according to St. Matthew, about the year 1728; the great Mass in B minor, about 1734; the Art of Fugue, in the year 1748.

Stölzel (Gottfried Heinrich), born 1690 in Bohemia, died 1749. Several Operas, Oratorios, Masses, and Treatises on the Theory and History of Music.

Pergolesi (Giovanni Battista), born 1710 at Jesi, died 1736. Composed 7
1740 Operas, a Stabat Mater, several Masses, offertories, etc.

Durante (Francesco), born 1693 at Naples, died 1755. Composed Masses and other sacred music, secular madrigals, pieces for the clavicembalo, etc.

Durante, was with Leo, the founder of the famous Neapolitan School.

Feo (Francesco), born 1699 at Naples. Operas, Oratorios, Masses, Psalms. Feo is especially remarkable for being regarded as the master whom Gluck particularly admired and studied.

Greene (Maurice), born 1698 in London, died 1755. Many sacred compositions and some English Operas.

Hölty, Stollberg, Voss, Gleim, Jacoby, Uz, Gerstenberg, Gotter, Claudius, Gessner.

Frederick William I, King of Prussia, son of Frederick I. (1713.)

First attempt of Steam Navigation, by Jonathan Hulls (1736).

John Wesley, founder of the sect of Methodists (1730).

George Whitfield, founder of the sect of Calvinistic Methodists, preaches in London in the open air (1738).

The Methodist Society is fully established (1740).

Italian Painters of this period:—Rotari, Casanova, Landi, Grassi, Appiani Bossi, Sabatelli Ermini, Alvarez, Camoccini, etc.

Frederick II., King of Prussia (from 1740 until 1786).

First Silesian war (1740-1742).

Second Silesian war (1744-1745).

	A. D.	
Maria - Theresa, Empress of Germany, Queen of Hungary and Bohemia (1740). Francis I., Duke of Lorraine, marries Maria-Theresa, and is elected Emperor of Germany (1745). During the reign of Frederick II. or 'Frederick the Great,' the Prussian monarchy is made to rank among the first powers in Europe. Battle of Dettingen gained by George II. over the French (1743). The electric shock is discovered at Leyden (1745). German poets: Salis, Matthison, Pfeffel, Kind, Langbein, Seume, Schubert, Tiedge, etc. Lima and Callao are destroyed by an earthquake which buries 18,000 persons in the ruins (1746).	1740	Quanz (Johann Joachim), born 1697 at Hanover, died 1773. Flute-player, and teacher of Frederick II. of Prussia. Many compositions, and an instruction book for the Flute. Graun (Carl Heinrich), born 1701 in Saxony, died 1759. Composed 30 Operas, several Oratorios, Masses, cantatas, etc. Hasse (Johann Adolf), born 1699 at Hamburg, died 1783. Composed 52 Operas, 11 Oratorios, several Masses, a Requiem, 4 Te Deums, various other sacred compositions, symphonies, sonatas for the clavichord, concertos, etc. Galuppi (Baldassaro), born 1703 at Venice, died 1785. Composed 55 Operas, several Masses, motetts, and other sacred music. Sammartini (Giovanni Battista), born about 1700 at Milan, died 1775. Many Masses and other Church music, many symphonies, quartetts, trios, and other instrumental compositions of every kind. Sammartini wrote about 2,800 works, and his style is considered as being the precursor of that of Joseph Haydn. From about the middle of the eighteenth century, the sonata-form in instrumental compositions (sonatas, symphonies, quartetts, etc.) becomes much developed, especially through Joseph Haydn.
Linnæus, naturalist (1750). The Academy of Sciences at Stockholm, and the Royal Society at Göttingen, are founded (1750).	1750	The flourishing period of the Italian operatic music dates from about the year 1700 to 1780. The most celebrated writers of libretti were Apostolo Zeno and Metastasio. The most celebrated female singers: Faustina, Cuzzoni, Mattei, Scotti, Grassi, Gabrieli, Agujari, Danci, Allegrante, Storace, etc.

Samuel Johnson commences the publication of his 'Rambler' (1750).

Lady W. Montague, and Lord Chesterfield, miscellaneous writers (1750).

New style introduced into England (1752)

Death of Montesquieu (1755).

Great earthquake at Lisbon (1755)

Voltaire at the Court of Frederick of Prussia (from 1750 until 1753).

Benjamin Franklin, in America, invents the lightning conductor (1755).

Conquest of India under Colonel, afterwards Lord, Clive (1757).

Death of General Wolfe at the Battle of Quebec (1759).

The Seven Years' War in Germany (1756-1763).

A. D.

1750 The most celebrated male singers: Lovattini, Guarducci, Farinelli, Nicolini, Guadagni, Millico, Pacchiarotti, Morelli, Marchesi, Salimbeni, Crescentini, etc.

Martini (Giovanni Battista), Padre, born 1706 at Bologna, died 1784. Many sacred compositions, History of Music, School of Harmony, and other literary works on music.

Perez (Davide), born 1711 at Naples, died 1778. Composed 31 Operas.

Jomelli (Nicolo), born 1714 at Aversa, died 1774. Composed 40 Operas, 4 Oratorios, several Masses, Requiems, etc.

Rousseau (Jean Jacques), born 1712 at Geneva, in Switzerland, died 1778. Author. Some French Operas. Many Treatises on Music. Musical Dictionary. Invention of the melodrama ascribed to him.

Arne (Thomas Augustus), born 1710 in London, died 1778. Composed 23 Operas, 3 Oratorios, and many other vocal pieces, etc.

Boyce (William), born 1710 in England, died 1779. Organist. Several dramatic compositions, an Oratorio, sacred songs, many organ pieces.

Bach (Friedemann), son of J. S. Bach, born 1710 at Weimar, died 1784. Compositions for the organ, clavichord, and harpsichord.

Bach (Carl Philipp Emanuel), son of J. S. Bach, born 1713 at Weimar, died 1788. Oratorios, cantatas, sacred songs, many compositions for the clavichord. Instruction Book for playing the clavichord.

1760 Fiorillo (Ignazio), born 1715 at Naples, died 1787. Several Operas, an Oratorio, a Requiem, Masses.

George III., King of Great Britain, grandson of George II. (1760).

Moses Mendelssohn, philosopher.

Winckelmann, antiquarian.

Garrick, actor.

Joseph II., Emperor of Austria (1765).

Mesmer, a German physician, publishes his 'Theory of Animal Magnetism' (1766).

Blackstone publishes his 'Commentaries on the Laws of England' (1767)

Corsica becomes French (1768).

Napoleon Buonaparte born at Ajaccio, in Corsica (1769).

Death of Emanuel Swedenborg, founder of a new religious sect (1772).

Sheridan publishes his first drama, 'The Rivals' (1775).

Pestalozzi founds the Reformatory School at Neuhoff, in Switzerland (1775).

Adam Smith publishes his 'Wealth of Nations' (1776)

A. D.

1760

Alembert (Jean-le-Rond d'), born 1717 in Paris, died 1783. Author of a System of Composition, and of other theoretical works on music.

Marpurg (Friedrich Wilhelm), born 1718 in Prussia, died 1795. Organ and clavichord compositions. Treatises on the Theory of Music.

Mozart (Leopold), father of the great Mozart, born 1719 at Augsburg, died 1789. Composed 4 Operas, 12 Oratorios, many symphonies, and other instrumental and vocal music. Also a Violin School.

Gerbert (Martin), Abbot, born 1720 in Austria, died 1792. History of sacred music.

Benda (Georg), born 1721 in Bohemia, died 1795. Composed 14 Operas, some melodramas, cantatas, and instrumental music.

Kirnberger (Johann Philipp), born 1721 in Thuringia, Germany, died 1783. Composed fugues and other pieces for the clavichord and pianoforte. Author of several works on the theory of music.

1770

The Pianoforte begins to supersede the clavichord and clavicembalo (English harpsichord).

Piccini (Nicolo), born 1728 at Naples, died 1800. Composed above 130 Operas, several Oratorios, psalms, etc.

GLUCK (CHRISTOPH WILLIBALD VON), born 1714 at Weidenwang, Germany, died 1787. Composed 21 Operas, 8 of which are to Italian words, and 13 are to French words. A De Profundis, a Ballet entitled 'Don Juan,' some secular songs, a few instrumental pieces, etc.

Sarti (Giuseppe), born 1730 at Faenza, died 1802. Composed 44 Operas, and several sacred pieces.

Necker, Minister of Finance in France (1777).

The Sandwich Islands are discovered by Captain Cook (1778).

Death of William Pitt, first Earl of Chatham (1778).

Captain Cook is killed by the natives of Owyhee (1779).

J. Priestley, chemical philosopher (1733-1804).

Hunter, surgeon (1728-1793).

Sir W. Jones, orientalist (1746-1794).

Horace Walpole (1717-1797).

Boswell, biographer of Dr. Johnson.

Cowper, poet.

Bacon, sculptor.

Josiah Wedgewood, improver of pottery manufacture (1730-1795).

Alfieri publishes his first tragedy 'Cleopatra' (1773).

Benjamin Franklin, American philosopher and statesman (1706-1790).

A. D. 1770

Lolli (Antonio), born about 1730 at Bergamo, died 1802. Violinist. Many compositions for his instrument.

Majo (Francesco de), born 1745 at Naples, died 1774. Composed 13 Operas, many Masses, Vespers, etc.

Arteaga (Steffano), born about 1730 at Madrid, died 1799. Author of a History of the Italian Opera.

Philidor (François André), born 1727 at Dreux, died 1795. Composed 22 Operas, of which 11 are to Italian words, and 11 to French words. Philidor is also celebrated as a chess-player.

Monsigny (Piérre Alexandre), born 1729 at St. Omer, died 1817. Composed 17 Operas, ballets, etc.

Gossec (François Joseph), born 1733 at Hainault, died 1829. Composed 28 Operas, and many sacred compositions.

Hawkins (John), born 1720 in England, died 1791. Author of a History of Music.

Burney (Charles), born 1726 at Shrewsbury, died 1814. Author of a History of Music, and some other works.

Abel (Carl Friedrich), born 1725 at Köthen, in Germany, died 1787 in London. Viola-da-Gambist and composer.

Hiller (Johann Adam), born 1728 in Lusatia, Germany, died 1804. Composed 18 Operettas, many psalms, sacred and secular songs, symphonies, sonatas, and musical treatises.

HAYDN (JOSEPH), born 1732 at Rohrau, in Austria, died 1809. Composed 24 Operas (10 with German words, and 14 with Italian words), 4 Oratorios, 19 Masses, several Te Deums, a Stabat Mater, Salve Regina, many motetts and other sacred music,

A. D.

Pope Clement XIV. suppresses the Order of the Jesuits, founded in the year 1540 (1773).

1770 118 symphonies, 83 quartetts, 44 sonatas, and many other instrumental and vocal compositions.

J. Haydn wrote in 1783 the Oratorio The Seven Words, for Cadix; in 1800, The Creation; in 1803, The Seasons; in 1791 and 1793, the twelve so-called English symphonies, in London.

The Jesuits were expelled from England in 1604; from France, in 1764; from Spain, in 1767. The Order was restored by Pope Pius VII. in 1814.

Kittel (Johann Christian), born 1732 at Erfurt in Germany, died 1809. Many organ compositions.

Death of Lord Clive (1774).

1774 GLUCK in Paris, from 1774 to 1779. Representations of his Operas. Reform of the French dramatic music. Rivalry between Gluck and Piccini in Paris. First performance of Orpheus and Euridice, Vienna 1762: of Alceste, Vienna, 1767; of Iphigenia in Aulis, Paris, 1774; of Armida, Paris, 1777; of Iphigenia in Tauris, Paris, 1779.

The American Colonies deny the right of the British Parliament to tax them (1774).

The first battle of the American war at Lexington (1775).

The Operas by Gluck are the noblest musical dramas in existence. They have served as models for the most eminent operatic composers whose works have been written subsequently to those of Gluck.

Voltaire (1694-1778).

W. Herschel, astronomer (1738-1822).

1780 Sacchini (Antonio Maria Giuseppe), born 1735 at Naples, died 1786. Composed 50 Operas, several Oratorios, Masses with double choruses, a Miserere, several other sacred compositions, sonatas, violin-trios, etc.

W. Herschel discovers the planet Uranus, or Georgium Sidus (1781).

Anfossi (Pasquale), born about 1736 at Naples, died 1797. Many Operas and sacred compositions.

Mail Coaches are first set up at Bristol by Mr. Palmer, and are soon in use all through England (1784).

Traetta (Tomaso), born 1738 at Naples, died 1786. Operas and Church music.

The Crimea is given up by Turkey to Russia (1784).

Sabbatini (Luigi Antonio), born 1739 at Albano, died 1809. Church music and several theoretical works.

The power-loom for weaving is invented by E. Cartwright (1785).

Watt greatly improves the Steam Engine (1736-1819).

Watt's double Steam Engine (about 1780).

The Steam Engine is applied to cotton spinning (1785).

Lessing (1729-1781).

The United States of America declare their independence (1776).

Alliance between France and the United States (1778).

Spain and Holland in favour of the United States (1779).

United States of North America independent.

Washington their President (1783).

Washington (1732-1799).

Frederick-William II., King of Prussia, nephew of Frederick the Great (1786).

A. D. 1780

Boccherini (Luigi), born 1740 at Lucca, died 1806. Many symphonies, quintetts, quartetts, sonatas, and other instrumental compositions.

Paesiello (Giovanni), born 1741 at Taranto, died 1816. Composed 94 Operas, an Oratorio, a Requiem, many Masses, a Te Deum, and other sacred music.

Great popularity of the Operas by Paesiello, Cimaroso, Sacchini, Piccini, etc.

Langlé (Onorio Francesco), born 1741 at Monaco, died 1807. Composed 8 Operas (with French words), and wrote several theoretical works on music in French.

Grétry (André-Ernest-Modeste), born 1741 at Liége, died 1813. Composed 59 Operas, several Masses, motetts, symphonies, quartetts, pianoforte-sonatas, etc. Also Essays on Music.

Battishill (Jonathan), born 1738 in London, died 1801. Many sacred vocal compositions, and some Operas.

Arnold (Samuel), born 1740 in London, died 1802. Composed 40 Operas and Operettas (with English words), 7 Oratorios, etc.

Bach (Johann Christian), son of J. S. Bach, born 1735 at Leipzig, died 1782 in London. Composed 15 Operas (with Italian words), 18 concertos for the harpsichord, sonatas, trios, and other instrumental pieces.

Albrechtsberger (Johann Georg), born 1736 in the neighbourhood of Vienna, died 1809. Composed 26 Masses, 43 graduales, 34 offertories, and other sacred compositions, many organ-fugues, etc. Author of a work on the Theory of Music.

	A. D.	
The Quakers at Philadelphia emancipate their slaves (1788).	1780	Haydn (Michael), brother of Joseph Haydn, born 1737 in Rohrau, died 1806. Many Masses, Offertories, Te Deums, etc.
First English settlement in Australia, at Botany Bay (1788).		Dittersdorf (Carl Ditters von), born 1739 at Vienna, died 1799. Composed 37 Operas, 41 symphonies, many concertos and other instrumental pieces.
Invention of the balloon, and ascent by Montgolfier, in Paris (1783).		André (Johann), born 1741 at Offenbach, in Germany, died 1799. Composed about 30 German Operettas.
Blanchard and Jefferies cross the English Channel in a balloon (1785).		Naumann (Johann Gottlieb), born 1741 in Saxony, died 1801. Composed 26 Operas, 13 Oratorios, many Masses, psalms, cantatas, and other vocal music, many symphonies, concertos, and other instrumental pieces.
Diderot (1713—1784)	1784	Martini (Johann Paul Egydius), properly Schwarzendorf, born 1741 in Germany, died 1816. Composed 12 Operas (with French words), a Requiem, Masses, a Te Deum. Wrote several theoretical works on music.
Buffon (1707—1788).		
Herschel completes his great forty-foot telescope, discovers volcanic mountains in the moon, etc. (1787).		Festival in commemoration of Handel, in London. Mara (Gertrude Elizabeth), the celebrated German singer (born 1749 at Cassel, died 1833), visits London, and sings at the Festival.
The French Revolution (1789).		Origin of the English Musical Festivals, in which the principal performers are mostly foreigners.
Death of Mirabeau (1791).	1790	Salieri (Antonio), born 1750 at Legnano, died 1825. Composed 41 Operas, a Requiem, many vocal-canons, and other vocal pieces.
Royalty abolished in France (1792).		Zingarelli (Nicolo), born 1752 at Rome, died 1837. Composed 22 Operas, 38 Masses with organ, 45 other Masses, 4 Requiems, and many other sacred compositions.
Louis XVI. beheaded (1793).		

Marat stabbed by Charlotte Corday (1793).

Robespierre guillotined (1794).

Netherlandish Painters:—

Van Os, Vanloo, Van Spaendonk, Scheffer, Pienemann, Hodges, Kuipers, Ommegang, Wonder, etc.

French Painters: Joseph Vernet (1714 — 1789), Greuze, Vien, David, Isabey, Drouais, Gerard, Gros, Ingres, Regnauld, Guerin, Horace Vernet (born 1789), etc.

Denmark sets the example of abolishing the slave trade (1791).

France abolishes slavery in her colonies (1794).

Abolition of the slave trade by the English Parliament (1807).

Vaccination is introduced by Dr. Jenner (1796).

Lithography is invented by Alois Sennefelder (1796).

A. D.

1790 CLEMENTI (MUZIO), born 1752 at Rome, died 1832. Pianist and founder of pianoforte-playing. Composed above 60 sonatas for pianoforte alone, many others with accompaniments, fugues, studies (Gradus ad Parnassum), symphonies. Also an instruction book for the pianoforte.

Clementi and Beethoven, by their compositions for the pianoforte, especially promoted the perfecting and the popularity of the pianoforte.

Viotti (Giovanni Battista), born 1753 at Piedmont, died 1824. Violinist, and founder of a new school of violin-playing. Many concertos and other instrumental compositions.

Cimarosa (Domenico), born 1754 at Naples, died 1801. Composed 75 Operas, a Requiem, Masses, etc.

Dalayrac (Nicolas), born 1753 in Languedoc, France, died 1809. Composed 56 Operas.

Shield (William), born 1754 in London, died 1829. Composed Operas, canzonets, instrumental trios. Author of a Treatise on Harmony.

Storace (Stephan), born 1763 in London, of Italian origin, died 1796. Composed 14 Operas with English words.

Gerber (Ernst Ludwig), born 1746 in Saxony, died 1819. Author of two biographical Dictionaries of Musicians, and of some books of instruction on music.

Schulz (Johann Peter), born 1747 at Lüneburg, in Germany, died 1800. Several Operas, Oratorios, choruses, etc.

Neefe (Christian), born 1748 in Saxony, died 1798. Composed 10 Operas. Teacher of Beethoven, in Bonn.

Hahnemann, founder of Homœopathy (1796).

In the year 1792 the French nation adopted a new Calendar founded on philosophical principles. It remained in use until the end of the year 1805, when the Gregorian mode of calculation was restored at the instance of Napoleon. The public feasts or "Sansculottides," fixed in the Revolutionary Calendar, were dedicated to Les Vertus Sept. 17; Le Génie, Sept. 18; Le Travail, Sept. 19; L'Opinion, Sept. 20; Les Récompenses, Sept. 21.

Revolution in Poland: Kosciusko, in the beginning successful, is later defeated. Suwarrow storms Warsaw (1794).

The third division of Poland between Russia, Austria, and Prussia (1795).

La Place, mathematician and astronomer (1796).

A. D. 1790

Stadler (Maximilian), Abbé, born 1748 in Austria, died 1833. An Oratorio, Masses, psalms, and other sacred vocal music, compositions for the organ and the pianoforte.

Vogler (Georg Joseph), Abbé, born 1749 at Würzburg, in Germany, died 1814. Composed 5 Operas, several Masses, many other sacred compositions, symphonies, organ pieces, etc. Author of several theoretical works on music.

Forkel (Johann Nikolaus), born 1749 at Coburg, in Germany, died 1818. Wrote a History of Music, and several other musical treatises.

Koch (Heinrich Christoph), born 1749 at Rudolstadt, Germany, died 1816. Instruction books on harmony, and a Musical Dictionary.

Kauer (Ferdinand), born 1751 in Moravia, died 1831. Above 200 Operas of a light and popular character.

Reichardt (Johann Friedrich), born 1752 at Königsberg, in Prussia, died 1814. Composed 30 Operas, some Oratorios, hymns, secular songs. Author of several Treatises on Music, etc.

Knecht (Justin Heinrich), born 1752 at Bieberich, in Germany, died 1817. Masses, cantatas, and other sacred music, and an instruction book on harmony.

Türk (Daniel Gottlieb), born 1756 in Saxony, died 1813. An Oratorio, motetts, many pieces for the clavichord and the pianoforte, a Treatise on Thorough-bass, etc.

MOZART (WOLFGANG AMADEUS), born 1756 at Salzburg, died 1791. Composed 6 great Operas with Italian words, 2 great Operas with German

Stereotyping invented by Ambrose Didot, of Paris (1797).

Frederick William III., King of Prussia (1797).

Buonaparte in Egypt and Syria (1798).

Buonaparte, in France, is declared First Consul (1799).

The English take possession of most of the French and Dutch dominions in America (1803).

Napoleon, Emperor of France (1804).

Kant, philosopher (1724—1804).

Death of Nelson (1805).

Death of Pitt (1806).

Wieland (1733—1813).

Napoleon arrives at Elba (1814).

Napoleon defeated at Waterloo (1815).

The "Holy Alliance" concluded at Paris (1815).

The Jesuits expelled from Russia (1816).

The foreign troops evacuate France (1818).

Death of Marshal Blucher, aged 77 (1819).

A. D.

1790 words, 8 earlier Italian Operas, 2 German Operettas, several cantatas, a Requiem, many Masses, graduales, offertories, hymns, a Te Deum, and other sacred compositions, about 33 symphonies, 23 pianoforte concertos, some concertos for other instruments, 6 violin quintetts, 26 violin quartetts, 31 pianoforte sonatas with and without accompaniments, many other instrumental compositions, many songs, etc.

1800 Mozart composed, in 1780, the Opera 'Idomeneo' for Munich; in 1781, 'Die Entführung aus dem Serail' (his first Opera with German words) for Vienna; in 1785, 'Le Nozze de Figaro' for Vienna; in 1787, 'Don Giovanni' for Prague; in 1790, 'Cosi Fan Tutte' for Vienna; in 1791, 'La Clemenza di Tito' for Prague, and 'Die Zauberflöte' (his second Opera with German words) for Vienna. In the same year, 1791, he wrote also his Requiem.

Righini (Vincenzo), born 1756 at Bologna, died 1812. Composer of 20 Operas, several Masses and other sacred music.

Cherubini (Luigi), born 1760 at Florence, died 1842. Composer of 29 Operas, some ballets, 4 great Masses, 2 Requiems, many other sacred pieces, violin quartetts and other instrumental music. Author of a Treatise on Musical Composition.

Gervasoni (Carlo), born 1762 at Milan, died 1819. Instruction books and historical Treatises on Music.

Mayer (Simon), born 1763 in Bavaria, died 1845. From his early youth lived in Italy. Composer of 77 Operas, many Oratorios, Masses, psalms, and other sacred music.

	A. D.	
Captain Ross makes a voyage of Discovery in the Polar Sea (1818). Klopstock (1724-1803). Herder (1744—1803). Winsor, a German, obtains in England a patent as the inventor of gas for the purpose of illumination. He makes his first experiment at the Lyceum in the Strand (1804). Schiller (1759—1805). Schiller's 'The Robbers' appeared in 1781; Don Carlos, about 1785; Wallenstein, 1799; Maria Stuart, 1800; William Tell, 1804. Painters: David, Fuseli, G. F. Morland, Stothard, Benjamin West, Northcote, etc. Actors: J. P. Kemble, Mrs. Siddons, Talma. First meeting of the Imperial Parliament of Great Britain and Ireland (1801). Jefferson, President of the United States (1801).	1800	MEHUL (ETIENNE HENRI), born 1763 at Givet, died 1817. Composed 42 Operas, many hymns, cantatas, etc. Lesueur (Jean François), born 1764 at Abbeville, died 1837. Composed 10 Operas, 33 Oratorios, several Masses and motetts. Rouget de Lille (Claude Joseph), born 1760 at Lons-le-Saulnier, died 1836. Composer of romances, and of the Marseillaise. Attwood (Thomas), born 1767 in England. Many Operas and sacred compositions. Winter (Peter von), born 1755 at Mannheim in Germany, died 1825. Above 30 Operas, many Ballets, Oratorios, Masses, motetts, hymns, cantatas, etc. Pleyel (Jgnaz), born 1757 near Vienna, died 1831. Composed 29 symphonies, many violin-quartetts, pianoforte-sonatas, etc. Preindl (Joseph), born 1758 in Austria, died 1823. Many Masses, a Requiem, and other church music. Instruction books for thorough-bass, for singing, etc. Zelter (Carl Friedrich), born 1758 in Berlin, died 1832. Many vocal compositions, and some literary productions. Zelter founded, in 1808, the first German Liedertafel, or society of male singers. Similar societies have subsequently become popular in Germany and other countries. Zumsteeg (Johann Rudolph), born 1760 at Sachsenflur, in Germany, died 1802. Composed 8 Operas, many ballads, and other vocal music. Dussek (Johann Ludwig), born 1761 in Bohemia, died 1812. Pianist and composer for his instrument. Wrote

	A. D.	
Institution of the Legion of Honour in France (1802).	1800	13 concertos, 53 sonatas, several pianoforte-quartetts, etc. Also an Opera.
Men of Science born about this time:— Sir D. Brewster, philosopher, born 1781. G. B. Airy, astronomer, born 1801.		Kunzen (Friedrich), born 1761 at Lübeck, died 1817. Composed 9 Operas (8 of which are with Danish words, and one is with German words), 3 Oratorios, several cantatas, and other sacred music.
Baron Liebig, chemist, born 1803. R. Owen, comparative anatomist, born 1804.		Gyrowetz (Adalbert), born 1763 in Bohemia, died 1850. Above 30 Operas, many Ballets and Entr'actes, sacred vocal music, many symphonies, quartetts, pianoforte compositions, songs, etc.
Brassey, engineer, born 1805. Lesseps, French engineer, born 1806. J. Stuart Mill, philosopher, born 1807. Longfellow, American poet, born 1807.		Steibelt (Daniel), born about 1764 at Berlin, died 1823. Pianist. Composed 6 pianoforte concertos, 46 solo sonatas and many other compositions for the pianoforte, studies for the pianoforte, and an instruction book for that instrument; also 4 Operas.
Lyon Playfair, chemist, born 1819.	1810	Paer (Ferdinando), born 1771 at Parma, died 1839. Composer of 51 Operas, 11 cantatas, and other vocal music.
J. Tyndal, chemist, born 1820. Death of Sheridan (1816).		Berton (Henri Montan), born 1767 in Paris, died 1844. About 50 Operas, several Oratorios, cantatas, and Treatises on the Theory of Music.
Iffland, German actor and dramatic writer (1759—1814).		Baillot (Piérre), born 1771 at Passy, died 1842. Violinist. Concertos and other compositions for the violin, an instruction book for the violin, etc.
Thorwaldsen, Danish sculptor (1770-1844).		Choron (Alexandre Etienne), born 1772 at Caën, died 1834. Many theoretical works. A Musical Dictionary.
Beranger, French poet (1780—1857). Arago, French Savant (1786—1835).		Catel (Charles Simon), born 1773 at L'Aigle, died 1830. Composed 10 Operas, many instrumental and vocal pieces. Author of a Treatise on Harmony, etc.

C. Babbage, philosophical mechanist (1792-1871).

Sir Charles Lyell, geologist (1797-1875).

Statesmen born about this time:

Gladstone born 1809.

Baron Beust, born 1809.

Bismarck-Schönhausen, born 1813.

Count Cavour, born 1810.

Cobden, born 1804.

John Bright, born 1811.

Sculptors born about this time:—

Marochetti, born 1805.

Kiss, born 1802.

Powers, born 1805.

The Jesuits are expelled from Prussia (1817).

The Mahratta war in Hindustan.

Steam applied to printing in the *Times* office (1814).

The Marquess of Hastings renders British influence universal in India (1817).

The Island of Singapore is formed into a British settlement by Sir Stamford Raffles (1818).

A. D.
1810

Rode (Piérre), born 1774 at Bordeaux, died 1830. Violinist. Many concertos, quartetts, and other compositions.

Cramer (John Baptiste), born 1771 at Mannheim, in Germany, but living from early childhood in England, died 1858. Pianist. Pianoforte studies, 105 solo sonatas, and 7 concertos for the pianoforte. Also a pianoforte school, etc.

Weigl (Joseph), born 1766 at Eisenstadt, in Hungary, died 1846. About 30 Operas, 14 ballets, 21 Oratorios and cantatas, 10 Masses, and other sacred music.

Weber (Bernhard Anselm), born 1766 at Manheim, died 1821. Several Operas, melodramas, and Entr'actes.

Romberg (Andreas), born 1767 in Vechte, near Münster, in Germany, died 1821. Composed 7 Operas, a Te Deum, psalms and other sacred compositions, many symphonies and other instrumental music, secular songs, etc.

Romberg (Bernhard), brother of Andreas Romberg, born 1770 near Münster in Germany, died 1841. Violoncellist. Composed 3 Operas, many concertos and other pieces for the violoncello, quartetts, etc.

Müller (Wenzel), born 1767 in Moravia, died 1835. Above 200 Operas of a light popular character, pantomimes, etc.

Nägeli (Johann Georg), born 1773 near Zurich, in Switzerland, died 1836. Promoter of popular singing societies, composer of vocal music, and author of instruction books on singing, etc.

Beethoven (Ludwig van), born 1770 at Bonn, died 1827. An Opera, 2 dramas with music, a melodrama, several single dramatic choruses and

Reunion of the Lutheran and other reformed forms of worship in several parts of Germany (1818).

Voyage to the Polar Sea by Parry (1819).

Parry undertakes another voyage to reach the North Pole (1820).

George IV., King of Great Britain, son of George III. (1820).

Guizot, French statesman and historian (1787-1874).

Revolution in Spain; King Ferdinand VII. swears to the constitution of the Cortes (1820).

Mexico separates from Spain (1820).

Insurrection in Portugal (1820)

Revolution in the Brazils; King John VI. returns to Portugal, and his son, Dom Pedro, is made Regent of the Brazils (1820).

Peru declares herself independent (1820).

A. D. 1810

songs, an Oratorio, 2 Masses, 9 symphonies, 11 overtures, a septett, 7 concertos for pianoforte, a violin concerto, 2 violin quintetts, 17 violin quartetts, 5 violin trios, 35 solo sonatas for the pianoforte, 10 sonatas for pianoforte and violin, 6 sonatas for pianoforte and violoncello, 7 trios for pianoforte, violin, and violoncello, a pianoforte quintett, a great many other pianoforte compositions, cantatas, songs with pianoforte accompaniment, etc.

In 1793 Beethoven came to Vienna as Virtuoso on the pianoforte, and distinguished himself by his improvisations; in 1795 he published his first important work, the three pianoforte trios, Op. 1; in 1799 appeared his first symphony; in 1804 his Opera 'Leonore' (Fidelio); in 1809 his symphony in C Minor and his pastoral symphony; in 1814 his A Major symphony; in 1818 his ninth symphony.

Reicha (Anton), born 1770 at Prague, died 1836. Four Operas, symphonies, quartetts, sonatas, etc., and several Treatises on Harmony and Composition.

Tomaschek (Johann Wenzel), born 1774 in Bohemia, died 1850. An Opera, several cantatas, a Requiem, a Te Deum, Masses, and other sacred compositions, secular songs, symphonies, quartetts, pianoforte pieces.

Kiesewetter (Raphael Georg), born 1773 in Moravia, died 1850. Many dissertations relating to the history of music.

Weyse (Christoph Ernst Friedrich), born 1774 at Altona, in Germany, died 1842. Several Operas with Danish words, symphonies, sonatas and other instrumental pieces. He lived in Copenhagen.

	A. D.	
Napoleon dies at St. Helena (1821).	1820	Baini (Giuseppe), Abbate, born 1775 at Rome, died 1844. Many sacred compositions and historical Treatises on Music. Author of the 'Life of Palestrina.'
Union of the Greeks in one confederate state (1822).		Generali (Pietro), born 1783 in Piedmont, died 1832. About 50 Operas.
Dr. T. Young, natural philosopher, and discoverer of the hieroglyphic alphabet.		Paganini (Nicolo), born 1784 at Genoa, died 1840. Violinist. Concertos and other compositions for his instrument.
Sir Humphry Davy, chemist, inventor of the safety-lamp, etc.		Spontini (Gasparo), born 1784 at Rome, died 1851. Composer of about 26 Operas.
Macadam, improver of roads.		Isouard (Nicolo), born 1775 in Malta, died 1818. Composed 42 Operas, several Masses, cantatas, etc.
Francis Douce, antiquarian.		Boieldieu (François Adrien), born 1775 at Rouen, died 1834. Composed 23 Operas.
Cuvier, naturalist.		Lafont (Charles Philippe), born 1781 in Paris, died 1839. Violinist. Many compositions for the violin, and many romances.
Channing (Unitarian Preacher), Sir R. Phillips, W. Hazlitt, Charles Lamb, miscellaneous writers.		Onslow (Georges), born 1784 at Clermont, in France, died 1852. Composed 3 Operas, several symphonies, many violin quintetts, quartetts, trios, 2 pianoforte sextetts, and other pianoforte music.
P. B. Shelley, James Hogg (the "Ettrick Shepherd") Reginald Heber, Robert Southey, Sir Walter Scott, poets.		Auber (Daniel François Esprit), born 1782 at Caen, in France, died 1871. Above 30 Operas.
		Fétis (François Joseph), born 1784 at Mons, in Belgium, died 1872. Dictionary of Musicians, historical Treatises on Music, etc.
		Castil-Blaze (François Henri Joseph), born 1784 at Cavaillon, in France, died 1857. Several Treatises on Music, a Musical Dictionary, etc.
Charles X., King of France (1824).		Bishop (Henry Rowley), born 1782 in London, died 1855. Composed 63 Operas and other dramatic pieces, songs, etc.

A.D. 1820

Field (John), born 1782 at Dublin, died 1837 at Moscow. Pianist. Pupil of Clementi. Pianoforte concertos, notturnos, etc.

Hummel (Johann Nepomuk), born 1778 at Pressburg, died 1837. Pianist. Composed 5 Operas, several ballets, 2 cantatas, many pianoforte concertos, trios, sonatas, 2 pianoforte septetts, etc. Also a pianoforte school.

Neukomm (Sigismund), born 1778 at Salzburg, died 1858. Pupil of J. Haydn. Composed 10 Operas, many cantatas, 7 Oratorios, 15 Masses, many psalms, symphonies, quartetts, sonatas, etc.

Logier (Johann Bernhard), born 1777 at Kaiserslautern, in Germany, died 1846. A new method of teaching the pianoforte and the Theory of Music.

Diabelli (Anton), born 1781, near Salzburg, died 1858. Many Masses and other Church music, pianoforte compositions and songs.

Kreutzer (Conradin), born 1782 at Möskirch, in Germany, died 1849. Composed 24 Operas, an Oratorio, several Masses and other Church music, many instrumental pieces and songs.

Spohr (Louis), born 1784 at Brunswick, in Germany, died 1859. Violinist. Composed 8 Operas, several Oratorios, psalms, and other sacred music, symphonies, many violin quartetts, quintetts, concertos, and other compositions for the violin, etc. Also a violin school.

Ries (Ferdinand), born 1784 at Bonn, died 1838. Pupil of Beethoven. Pianist. Composed 2 Operas, some sacred and secular vocal music, pianoforte concertos, quartetts, trios, sonatas, etc.

Burmese war. Capture of Rangoon by the British (1824).

Denham and Clapperton's exploring expedition to Central Africa (1824).

Bowdich, on an expedition to explore the interior of Africa, died at the mouth of the Gambia (1824).

Death of Lord Byron (1824).

Nicholas I., Emperor of Russia (1825).

Death of John VI., King of Portugal (1826)

Don Pedro I., Emperor of Brazil, son of John VI., renounces the Portuguese crown in favour of his daughter, Maria da Gloria, aged seven years. The Infanta Isabella governs as Regent till the year 1828 (1826).

Canova, Sculptor (1757—1822).

Charles X. expelled from France, retires to England in the year 1830.

	A. D.	
Jean Paul, Friedrich Richter (1763—1825). First Steam Voyage to India, by Captain Johnston in the 'Enterprise' (1825). Athens, besieged by the Turks, is forced to surrender (1826). Russia at war with Persia (1827). Russia makes peace with Persia, and increases her possessions in the south (1828). Russia at war with Turkey (1828). The Turks are conquered by the Russian General Diebitch (1829). Turkey acknowledges the independence of Greece (1829).	1820	Kalkbrenner (Friedrich), born 1784 at Cassel, in Germany, died 1849. Pianist. Many pianoforte compositions, and a pianoforte school. Kuhlau (Friedrich), born 1786 at Uelzen, in Germany, died 1832, in Denmark. Composed 5 Operas with Danish words, and many compositions for the flute, the pianoforte, and for other instruments. WEBER (CARL MARIA VON), born 1786 at Eutin, in Germany, died 1826, in London. Composed 8 Operas, several dramatic scenes, Masses, hymns, overtures, pianoforte concertos, clarionet concertos, pianoforte sonatas, songs, etc. In 1821, first performance of 'Der Freischütz' at Berlin; in 1823, 'Euryanthe' at Vienna; in 1826, 'Oberon' in London. Fesca (Friedrich Ernst), born 1789 at Magdeburg, died 1826. Some Operas, many psalms and other sacred music, symphonies, quintetts, many quartetts, etc. Schneider (Johann Christian Friedrich), born 1786 in Saxony, died 1858. About 9 Oratorios, several Masses, hymns, cantatas, instrumental compositions, songs, etc. SCHUBERT (FRANZ), born 1797 in Vienna, died 1828. Several Operas, Masses and other Church music, symphonies, quartetts, trios, and other instrumental pieces, sonatas, fantasias, etc. for the pianoforte, a great many songs with pianoforte accompaniment.
Charles X. King of France, deposed (1830).	1830	Carafa (Michele), born 1785 at Naples, died 1872. About 30 Operas.

	A. D.	
Göthe (1749-1832) William IV., King of Great Britain, brother of George IV. (1830). Louis - Philippe, King of France (1830). Cholera Morbus, its first appearance in England (1831). Death of Sir Walter Scott (1832). Slavery abolished throughout the British Colonies (1834). Wilhelm von Humboldt, philologist (1767—1835). Alexander von Humboldt, naturalist (1769—1859). Edmund Kean, English actor (1787—1833). The first great English railway by steam engines is the Liverpool and Manchester Railway, opened in 1830. Queen Victoria born in 1819, ascends the throne (1837).	1830	ROSSINI (GIOACHINO ANTONIO), born 1792 at Pesaro, died 1868. About 40 Operas, a Stabat Mater, some other sacred vocal music, several secular cantatas, orchestral pieces, etc. Bellini (Vincenzo), born 1802 at Catania, in Sicily, died 1835. Composed 10 Operas, some sacred music, symphonies, overtures, etc. Herold (Louis), born 1791 in Paris, died 1833. Composed 16 Operas and several ballets. Lindpaintner (Peter Joseph), born 1791 at Coblenz, died 1856. About 25 Operas, 9 ballets, Oratorios, Masses, motetts, symphonies, etc. Mayseder (Joseph), born 1789 in Vienna, died 1863. Many compositions for violin, quintetts, quartetts, pianoforte trios, sonatas, etc.; also a Mass. Moscheles (Ignaz), born 1794 at Prague, died 1870. Pianist. Many pianoforte compositions; also some symphonies, etc. Klein (Bernhard), born 1794 at Cologne, died 1832. About 3 Operas, 4 Oratorios, a Stabat Mater, and other sacred music. Meyerbeer (Jacob), born 1794 in Berlin, died 1864. Composed 16 Operas, an Oratorio, a Stabat Mater, a Te Deum, a Miserere, many psalms and other sacred music, secular songs, etc. Czerny (Carl), born 1791 in Vienna, died 1857. Many Pianoforte pieces; also Masses, Te Deums, and other sacred music; theoretical works.
Marriage of Queen Victoria with Prince Albert of Saxe-Coburg (1840).	1840	Hauptmann (Moritz), born 1794 at Dresden, died 1868. Several sacred compositions, quartetts, sonatas, secular songs, and theoretical works. Pacini (Giovanni), born 1796 at Syracuse, died 1867. Composed 34 Operas.

	A. D.	
Prince of Wales born (1841). Frederick William IV., King of Prussia (1840). Pius IX., Pope (1846). G. C. Prichard, English ethnologist (1786—1848). Revolution in France (1848). The Monarchy abolished in France. Louis - Philippe, King of France, deposed (1848). He dies in exile, in England (1850). New Republic in France. Louis Napoleon Charles Buonaparte (son of Louis Buonaparte, for a short time King of Holland, and nephew of Napoleon I.) is elected President of the Republic (1848).	1840	Donizetti (Gaetano), born 1797 at Bergamo, died 1848. Above 70 Operas, a Miserere, and other sacred music, many romances and other songs. Mercadante (Saverio), born 1797 at Altamura, in Italy, died 1870. Above 30 Operas. Panseron (Auguste), born 1796 in Paris, died 1859. Some Operas, a Requiem, 3 Masses, other sacred music, many romances, an instruction book on singing, etc. Halevy (Jacques), born 1799 in Paris, died 1862. Above 20 Operas. Marschner (Heinrich), born 1795 at Zittau, in Saxony, died 1861. Many Operas, Masses, secular songs, etc. Reissiger (Carl), born 1789 near Wittemberg, in Germany, died 1859. Ten Operas, many Masses, symphonies, quartetts, pianoforte trios, songs, etc. Marx (Adolph Bernhard), born 1799 at Halle, died 1866. Two Oratorios and some other compositions; a work on musical composition, and several other treatises on music. Lvoff (Alexis), born 1799 at Reval, died 1870. Violinist. Composer of the Russian National Hymn, and of other music. Löwe (Johann Carl), born 1796 near Halle, died 1869. Many ballads and other songs, also several Operas, Oratorios, and pianoforte compositions.
Botta & Layard excavate the Assyrian mounds (about 1840—1850). Death of Wordsworth (1850). Great Exhibition in London projected by Prince Albert (1851).	1850	Beriot (Charles Auguste de), born 1802, at Louvain, died 1870. Violinist. Concertos and other compositions for the violin. A violin school. Berlioz (Hector), born 1803, at La Côte Saint-André, in France, died 1869. Requiem, symphonies, overtures, other orchestral works with and without vocal music. A Treatise on Instrumentation, and many Musical Essays.

A. D. 1850

Mendelssohn-Bartholdy (Felix), born 1809 at Hamburg, died 1847. Composed two Oratorios, other sacred compositions, 2 Operas, other dramatic music, symphonies, overtures, ottett, quintetts, quartetts, etc., organ compositions, pianoforte concertos, sonatas, etc., 'Songs without Words' for the pianoforte, secular songs for a single voice, and for several voices, etc.

Chopin (Frederic François), born 1810 near Warsaw, died 1849, in Paris. Pianist. Many pianoforte compositions, studies, etc.

Schumann (Robert), born 1810 at Zwickau, in Saxony, died 1856. Operas, symphonies, quartetts, etc. Pianoforte compositions, songs. Essays on Music.

Thalberg (Sigismund), born 1812 at Geneva, died 1871. Pianist. Compositions for the pianoforte, mostly on themes of other composers. Also two Operas, etc.

Bennett (William Sterndale), born 1816 at Sheffield, died 1875. Some sacred compositions, overtures, pianoforte music, songs, etc.

During the first half of the present century great progress in the construction of musical instruments, especially of wind instruments.

Innumerable celebrated pianists, violinists, flutists, etc.

Celebrated female singers: Catalani, Malibran, Grisi, Persiani, Pasta, Pauline Viardot, Henriette Sontag, Sophie Löwe, etc.

Celebrated male singers: Lablache, Rubini, Tamburini, Braham, Wild, etc.

Monster Concerts.

Attempt of a reform of the Opera.

Death of the Duke of Wellington (1852).

The Prince President of the French Republic is declared Emperor of the French and assumes the title of Napoleon III. (1852).

Historians:—Thos. Carlyle, Macaulay, Guizot, Thiers, Rotteck, etc.

Painters: Rosa Bonheur, Cooper, Landseer, Millais, W. von Kaulbach, etc.

Novelists: Chas. Dickens, W. M. Thackeray, Lytton Bulwer, George Eliot, (Mrs. Lewis), Victor Hugo, Alexandre Dumas, etc.

Michael Faraday, chemist.

Charles Darwin, philosopher and naturalist.

Helmholtz, German philosopher and writer on acoustics. Important discoveries.

Alfred Tennyson. Poet Laureate.

Livingstone, African traveller.

Bismarck, German statesman.

Moltke, German General.

	A. D.	
Great progress in sciences relating to natural philosophy, and in practical arts. Gradual dying out of many old superstitions and prejudices. However, in some countries attempts to return to a Mediæval state of civilization.	1850	There are among our living musicians so many celebrated ones that it would really be difficult to make a satisfactory selection of them for incorporation into a concise Chronology. Fortunately, the plan adopted in the compilation, as previously explained, renders this delicate task unnecessary. As standard works on the history of music, easily accessible, may be recommended the treatises by Forkel, Kiesewetter, Bellermann, Ambros, Burney, Hawkins, Fétis, and Coussemaker.

THE MUSICAL SCALES IN USE AT THE PRESENT DAY.

In 'An Introduction to the Study of National Music' (London, 1866) I have endeavoured to give some account of the musical scales of different nations. The subject requires, however, fuller investigation than the aim of that book would permit. The 'Introduction to the Study of National Music' is intended to acquaint the student with the facts respecting the music of foreign nations and tribes which have been transmitted to us by travellers and through other sources. It can therefore scarcely claim more than to be a collection of materials which will prove useful for the erection of an edifice called the Science of National Music, as soon as the necessary additional materials have been obtained, without which it would be premature to design in detail the plan of the edifice, and to determine precisely its dimensions and internal divisions. The acquisition of useful materials will probably be promoted by the step recently taken by the British Association for the Advancement of Science.* There can be no greater mistake in such pursuits than to form a theory before the examples which are to serve as illustrations have been most carefully examined and verified. It is by no means easy to commit to notation a popular tune of a foreign country which possesses peculiarities with which we are unfamiliar. Even musicians who have had experience in writing down national songs which they happen to hear, find this difficult. How unreliable, therefore, must be the notations of many travellers who know but little of music! Still, the student of National Music, by careful attention and comparison, is gradually

* See above, Vol. I., p. 23.

enabled to discern what is genuine, and valuable for his purpose. He knows that if there prevails a certain peculiarity in the scale on which the tunes collected are founded, the cause may be owing to want of musical experience in the person who wrote the tunes down, or to an individual whim of the performer by whom they were sung or played to the writer of the notation. But, supposing the student examines several collections of popular tunes from the same country, the collections having been formed by different persons independently of each other, and he finds all exhibiting the same peculiarity, he has no reason to doubt that it really exists in the music of that country. Nothing gives to the popular music of a country a more distinctive feature than the order of intervals on which it is founded; when the scale has been clearly ascertained, such other characteristics as the music possesses are generally soon discerned with sufficient exactness to be definable by the experienced musical inquirer.

The notations of musical scales of uncivilized nations emanating from European travellers who have heard the people sing, are certainly to be received with caution. Of this kind of communication is, for instance, the notation of the vocal effusions progressing in demi-semitones of the Marquesas Islanders at their cannibal feasts, written down by Councillor Tilesius, and published in the Allgemeine musikalische Zeitung, Leipzig, 1805; or the notation of songs of the New Zealanders containing smaller intervals than semitones, which Mr. Davies has written down, and which Sir George Grey has published in his 'Polynesian Mythology of the New Zealand Race' (London, 1855). It is, however, often possible to ascertain the musical scale of a nation with exactness by examining the musical instruments appertaining to the nation. Thus, for instance, the Chinese close some of the finger-holes of their flutes by sticking pieces of bladder over them, in order to ensure the pentatonic scale; the Javanese construct instruments of percussion with sonorous slabs of metal or wood, arranged in conformity with the pentatonic scale; the Arabs, and most Mohammedan nations who have cultivated their music after the system of the Arabs, possess wind-instruments of the oboe kind on which the finger-holes are placed in accordance with the division of seventeen intervals in the compass of an octave; and also several stringed instruments of the Arabs, which are supplied with frets made of gut wound round the neck or finger-board, exhibit the same order of intervals; again, certain stringed instruments of the Hindus contain a number of little bridges, stuck with wax beneath the strings so as to produce, on a string being pressed down on the bridges successively, twenty-two intervals in the compass of the octave. Other instruments have marks on the sound-board as a guide to the performer where he has to press down the strings in exact conformity with the established scale.

What we observe with different nations of the present day, respecting the diversity of musical scales, might evidently also have been observed in ancient time. The Greeks had several kinds of scales, the popularity of which changed at different periods. So also had our forefathers during the Middle Ages. There is no necessity to refer to the Tetrachord of the ancient Greeks and the Hexachord of Guido Aretinus for evidences of the mutability of taste in these matters, since it can be observed sufficiently by referring to the music of nations around us. However, the so-called Modes of our old ecclesiastical music require here, at any rate, a passing notice.

Some theorists maintain that our diatonic major scale is alone a true scale, and that any other regular succession of tones in which the two semitones of the diatonic scale occur upon other intervals than 3-4 and 7-8 is, properly speaking, a Mode. According to this doctrine, which was evidently suggested by the ecclesiastical Modes, our minor scale must be called a Mode, and the scales with steps exceeding a whole-tone, of which some examples will presently be given, are Imperfect Modes. It is unnecessary to refute such pedantic definitions; suffice it to remember that they exist.

Again, the diatonic major scale is regarded by many musicians as the natural order of intervals on which the compositions must be founded whenever the art of music has attained to a high degree of development, and which will therefore be universally adopted in the course of time. They form this opinion especially from the laws of Acoustics, since the intervals constituting the diatonic major scale are those which as harmonics stand in the most simple relation to the fundamental tone produced by a vibrating body. Here, however, it must be observed that the intervals of our diatonic scale are not all of them precisely the same as those harmonics, but are "tempered;" since, did we tune them pure, as nature gives them, we could not use our system of harmony as it has been developed by our classical composers.

Moreover, if the diatonic major scale is thus suggested by nature, the minor scale with its flat third must be more artificial, and less likely to be universally adopted. Howbeit, the minor scale is especially popular, not only with several uncivilized races, but also with several who have cultivated the art of music to a high degree. Some of our most eminent composers have written perhaps more beautiful music in minor than in major keys.

Besides, certain deviations from the diatonic major scale, which we meet with in the music of foreign nations, possess a particular charm, which we are sure to appreciate more and more as we gradually become familiar with them. This, for instance, is the case with the Superfluous Second introduced as an essential interval of the scale. Many of our musicians regard such intervals as whimsical deviations, which ought not to be liked because they do not well agree with the rules laid down in our treatises on the theory of music. To such learned Professors the scale of the Arabs, with its seventeen intervals in the compass of an octave, instead of twelve semi-tones, as in our own system, is of course a flagrant misconception—not to speak of the twenty-two demi-semitones of the Hindus, which ought to be twenty-four. Those nations have musical systems very different from ours, for which their order of intervals is well suited. Our rules of harmony and forms of composition are unknown to them; still, their popular legends and traditions clearly prove that they appreciate the beauty and power of music not less keenly than we do; and they demonstrate the superiority of their scales with the same confidence as any of our theorists are capable of displaying.

Could we trace our diatonic Major Scale in the songs of birds and in the euphonious cries of certain quadrupeds, we should have a more cogent reason for regarding it as the most natural scale than is afforded by a comparison of the vibrations required for the production of its several intervals. The songs of various birds have been written down in notation, from which it would appear that these feathered songsters possess an innate feeling for the diatonic major scale; but, unfortunately, unless the melodious phrases, or passages, thus noted down are distinguished by some remarkable rhythmical peculiarity, they are seldom easily recognizable when they are played on a musical instrument. There may be among the numerous birds a few which in their natural song, untaught and uninfluenced in any way by man, emit a small series of tones strictly diatonic; but no such musicians are to be found among our own birds, although we have in Europe the finest singing birds in existence. The nightingale, it is true, produces occasionally a succession of tones which nearly corresponds with the diatonic Major Scale in descending, and which might possibly be mistaken for it by a listener charmed by the exquisite purity and sweetness of the tones which he does not investigate with the ear of a pianoforte-tuner. Even the two melodious sounds of the cuckoo cannot be properly written down in notation; nor can they be rendered on the pianoforte, because they do not exactly constitute a Major Third, for which they are generally taken, and still less a Minor Third. A certain ape of the Gibbon family is said to produce exactly the chromatic scale through an entire octave in ascending and descending. Darwin, who in his work on 'The Expression of the Emotions in Man and Animals' (London, 1872; p. 87) mentions the astonishing musical skill of this ape, remarks that some quadrupeds of a much lower class than monkeys, namely Rodents, "are able to produce correct musical tones," and he refers the reader to an account of a "singing

Hesperomys" [a mouse] by the Rev. S. Lockwood, in the 'American Naturalist,' Vol. V., December, 1871; p. 761. Notwithstanding the great authority of Darwin, the musical inquirer will probably desire to ascertain for himself whether the "correct musical tones" are exactly in conformity with our diatonic and chromatic intervals. However, even if this should be the case in a few instances, it can only be regarded as quite exceptional.

During the present century, our musical composers have so frequently employed in the diatonic major scale the Minor Sixth instead of the Major Sixth, that some theorists—among them Moritz Hauptmann—notice this order of intervals as a new and characteristic scale, and desire to have it as such generally acknowledged by musicians. A. Krauss, a teacher of music in Florence, has recently published a pamphlet, entitled 'Les Quatre Gammes diatoniques de la Tonalité moderne,' in which he designates this new scale with the name 'La Gamme semimajeur' (The Half-major Scale,) which is at any rate better than that suggested by Moritz Hauptmann, in his 'Die Natur der Harmonik und der Metrik,' which is 'Die Moll-Dur-Tonart' (the Minor-Major-Key, or scale).

We possess then, according to these theorists, now four diatonic scales, namely :—

The Half-Minor Scale contains the Minor Third, while its other intervals are identical with those of the Major Scale. This is the case in descending, where the seventh and sixth are lowered, as well as in ascending.

Furthermore, we have the Chromatic Scale, a regular progression in semitones, which is much used by modern composers; and the Enharmonic Scale, which may be said to exist only in notation, since it is not executable on most of our musical instruments, but which is likely to become important in the music of a future period when our instruments have been brought to the degree of perfection which permits the most delicate modifications in pitch by the performer, and which is at present almost alone obtainable on instruments of the violin kind.

5. THE CHROMATIC SCALE.

6. THE ENHARMONIC SCALE.

Furthermore, we find at the present day the following scales in use among foreign nations:—

7. THE MINOR SCALE WITH TWO SUPERFLUOUS SECONDS.

If the lover of music is acquainted with the popular songs and dance-tunes of the Wallachians, or with the wild and plaintive airs played by the gipsy bands in Hungary, he need not be told that the Minor Scale with two Superfluous Seconds is capable of producing melodies extremely beautiful and impressive. Indeed, it would be impossible to point out more charming and stirring effects than those which characterise the music founded on this scale.

8. THE PENTATONIC SCALE.

The Pentatonic Scale was in ancient times apparently more universally in use than it is at present. It is still popular in China, in Malaysia, and in some other Eastern districts. Traces of it are found in the popular tunes of some European nations, especially in those of the Celtic races. Its charming effect is known to most of our musicians through some of the Scotch and Irish melodies. Also among the Javanese tunes, which have been brought to Europe by travellers, and which are generally strictly pentatonic, some specimens are very melodious and impressive.

9. THE DIATONIC SCALE WITH MINOR SEVENTH.

The Diatonic Scale with Minor Seventh is likewise an Eastern scale. Among European nations, the Servians especially have popular tunes which are founded on this scale. The Servian tunes frequently end with the interval of the Fifth instead of the First or the Octave. As the leading tone of our diatonic order of intervals—the Major Seventh—is wanting, our common cadence, or the usual harmonious treatment of the conclusion of a melody to which our ear has become so much accustomed that any other appears often unsatisfactory, cannot be applied to those tunes. Nevertheless, they will be found beautiful by inquirers who are able to dismiss prejudice and to enter into the spirit of the music. Although the scale with Minor Seventh bears a strong resemblance to one of our antiquated Church Modes, called Myxo-Lydian, it is in some respects of a very different stamp, since its characteristic features would become veiled if it were harmonised like that Church Mode.

In addition to the nine scales which have been enumerated, some others could be pointed out which are popular in European countries; but, as they resemble more or less those which have been given above, and as they may be regarded as modifications, it will suffice here to refer to them only briefly. There are, for instance, in the Irish tunes many of a pentatonic character in which one of the two semitones of the diatonic scale is extant, and the scale of which therefore consists of six intervals, either thus

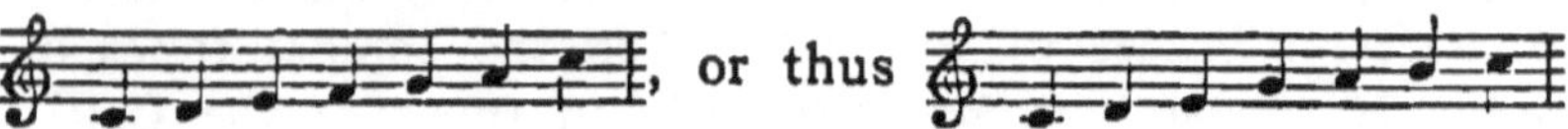

We also meet with a pentatonic order of intervals in which the Third is flat like in our diatonic minor scale.

Again, some nations which have the diatonic order of intervals deviate slightly from it by habitually intoning some particular interval in a higher or lower pitch than it occurs in our tempered system. For instance, careful observers have noticed that the Swiss peasants in singing their popular airs are naturally inclined to intone the interval of the Fourth sharper than it sounds on the pianoforte. Thus, in C-major it is raised so as to give almost the impression of *F sharp*. This peculiarity is supposed to have arisen from the Alphorn, a favourite instrument of the Swiss, on which the interval of the Fourth, like on a trumpet, is higher than it is in our Diatonic Scale. No doubt many peculiarities of this kind are traceable to the construction of certain popular instruments. This is perhaps more frequently observable among uncivilized nations than with Europeans. Professor Lichtenstein, who, during his travels in South Africa, in the beginning of the present century, investigated the music of the Hottentots, asserts that these people sing the interval of the Third slightly lower than the Major Third, but not so low as the Minor Third; and the Fifth and Minor Seventh likewise lower than in our intonation. He found that the same deviations from our intervals exist on the *Gorah*, a favourite stringed instrument of the Hottentots.

Other peculiarities of the kind are more difficult to explain. In the Italian popular songs of the peasantry, for instance, we not unfrequently meet with the Minor Second, where to an ear accustomed to our Minor Scale it appears like a whimsical substitution for the Major Second.

It occurs, however, only occasionally. When it is used, the scale is as follows; the Seventh being Major in ascending, and Minor in descending:—

In some instances such peculiarities have evidently been derived, as has already been stated, from the series of tones produced on a popular instrument. But there are many instances in which the tones yielded by the instrument have been purposely adopted in the construction of the instrument from the previously existing popular scale of the vocal music. Thus, it may possibly be that, as some inquirers maintain, the pentatonic character of certain Irish airs has its origin in the primitive scale of the ancient rural bagpipe of Celtic races, or, as others believe, in the simple construction of the ancient Irish harp;—on the other hand, the Chinese and Javanese, as we have seen, contrive in the construction of their instruments to obtain the pentatonic scale on which their vocal music is usually founded.

Those theorists who regard our diatonic major scale as the most perfect one, which ultimately must be universally accepted as the only true one, will probably not admit that under certain circumstances the sounding of one or other of its intervals a little "out of tune" may actually increase the beauty of a musical performance. Such is, however, unquestionably the case. To note a curious instance in proof of the correctness of this assertion as afforded by the clavichord, a contemporary of the harpsichord and predecessor of the pianoforte:—The strings of the clavichord are not sounded by being twanged with quills, as is the case in the harpsichord, but are vibrated by means of iron pins, called tangents, which press under the strings when the keys are struck. The pressure of the tangent lasts as long as the key to which the tangent is attached is held down. The deeper the performer presses the key down with his finger, the stronger is the pressure of the tangent against the string, and the more the string is raised by it.

The raising of the string has the effect of slightly raising the pitch of its tone. The performer, therefore, has it in his power to modify in some degree the pitch of a tone, and by this means to distinguish any tone to which he desires to give emphasis, or to render prominent in expressing a melody, or in executing a passage with delicacy. The aptness of the clavichord for yielding to these deviations from the intonation of the intervals in which it is tuned, combined with its aptness for producing with great delicacy different degrees of loudness, constitute the principal charms of the instrument, and sufficiently account for the love which our old classical composers,—Handel, Bach, etc.,—bore for the clavichord.

A musical instrument containing all conceivable perfections for performance, we do not yet possess. Such an instrument would be required to yield not only Whole-Tones and Semitones, but likewise Demi-semitones, Semidemi-semitones,—in short, every modification of an interval which the performer desires. It must have the greatest compass obtainable in tones. All its tones must be of equal power, sonorousness and beauty. The sustaining, the increasing and decreasing in loudness, must be possible with each tone separately, at the option of the performer, even in harmonious combinations. Likewise the difference in manner of expression, such as legato, staccato, etc., must be thus obtainable. The greatest possible difference in the quality of sound (*timbre*) must be at the command of the performer for any tone which he wishes to be thus affected. The instrument must permit the simultaneous sounding of as many of its tones as the performer desires, whatever their distance from each other may be, and this must be achievable by him with about the same facility as he requires for the production of a single tone. The instrument must be playable by only one performer; it must not present any extraordinary difficulty to musicians to play it well; and it must permit being easily kept in tune. Perhaps the organ approaches the nearest to this perfection, but is still far from it. The violin and the violoncello are in some respects ahead of all—at any rate, as regards delicacy of expression.

But, fascinating though it may be to depict such a nearly perfect musical instrument of the Future, the real substitutes of our present contrivances, a century or two hence, will probably be very different from our ideal, especially if we found our speculation on the impression that our Tonal System is the only right one, and that our diatonic major scale will be as everlasting as a mathematical truth, or as the axiom that two and two are four.

Indeed, the mutability of the musical taste of man appears to be unlimited, and it is certainly possible that our children's children may find decidedly objectionable some rule of musical composition which is now thought highly satisfactory. Did not our ancestors at the time of Hucbald relish consecutive Fifths and Octaves as an harmonious accompaniment to a melody? A Chinese Mandarin, on hearing a French Jesuit, at Pekin, play on a clavecin some *Suites de Pièces* of a celebrated French composer, endeavoured to convince the performer that the Chinese music was the only true music "because," he said, "it appeals to the heart, while yours makes only noise." When Villoteau, during his residence in Egypt, investigated the Arabic music, his Arab music-master at Cairo endeavoured to convince him that the division of the Octave into seventeen intervals was more natural and tasteful than the European division into twelve chromatic intervals. A Nubian musician, on hearing Mr. Lane play the pianoforte, remarked: "Your instrument is very much out of tune, and jumps very much." He evidently missed the accustomed small intervals connecting the whole-tones in his own music. Livingstone, in his 'Missionary Travels in South Africa,' relates that on a certain occasion when an English missionary sang a hymn to an assembly of Bechuana Kafirs, "the effect on the risible faculties of the audience was such that the tears actually ran down their cheeks;" and the same may have happened to the missionary when he heard the Kafirs sing.

Many more examples from nations in different stages of civilization could be cited evidencing the remarkable variety and instability of musical taste. Much of our own music, which about a century ago was greatly admired, appears now unimpressive; and great masters who introduce important innovations are sure at first not to be understood by the majority of musical people.

Instead of regarding our Tonal System as exhibiting the highest degree of perfection attainable, and of repudiating musical conceptions which reveal another foundation, as our musicians are apt to do, it would be more wise in them to study the various systems on which the music of different nations is founded, to acquaint themselves especially with the characteristics of the various scales, and, by adopting them on proper occasions, to produce new effects more refreshing than the hackneyed phrases and modulations which usually pervade their works.

NOVELLO, EWER & CO., PRINTERS, 69 & 70, DEAN STREET, SOHO.

www.ingramcontent.com/pod-product-compliance
Lightning Source LLC
Chambersburg PA
CBHW031738230426
43669CB00007B/389

* 9 7 8 3 3 3 7 0 8 4 8 5 1 *